Bullet Proof

Report Writing

A FIELD GUIDE FOR LAW ENFORCEMENT

Anthony Bandiero, JD, ALM

Blue To Gold Law Enforcement Training, LLC
SPOKANE, WASHINGTON

Blue to Gold, LLC
1818 West Francis Ave #101
Spokane, WA 99205
info@bluetogold.com
www.bluetogold.com

Ordering Information:
Quantity sales. Special discounts are available on quantity purchases by government agencies, police associations, and others. For details, contact us at the address above.

Bulletproof Report Writing —6th Edition. Updated 12-2023
ISBN 979-8623055354

ADDITIONAL RESOURCES

FREE WEEKLY WEBINARS

VISIT WWW.BLUETOGOLD.COM/CALENDAR FOR MORE DETAILS

 ### ASK THE EXPERT!
Submit your questions

bluetogold.com/show

ON-DEMAND COURSE AVAILABLE

VISIT WWW.UNIVERSITY.BLUETOGOLD.COM FOR MORE DETAILS

BlueToGold

Table of Contents

Step Three: What Crimes Need to be Proven?

We have an incredible warrior class in this country - people in law enforcement…, and I thank God every night we have them standing fast to protect us from the tremendous amount of evil that exists in the world.

—— *Brad Thor*

Step One: How to Write Police Reports

This Book's Overall Purpose

This book has one simple mission: to teach you how to master articulation. In the world of cops and courts, being able to explain yourself well can make all the difference when things get legal, whether it's at trial or when defending yourself in a lawsuit.

So, what do we mean by "expressing yourself well"? It's about sharing your side of the story so clearly that anyone reading—like a judge or someone on the jury—can see the situation through your eyes. They should get not just the facts, but also why you did what you did. That's what good report writing is all about.

When you're writing up your reports, you've got one big goal: tell the story so well that anyone, even someone who knows nothing about crime or police work, gets it. They should have no doubts that what you did was right and by the book.

Here's another pro-tip: Your audience is not just judges and prosecutors. If you write with a judge in mind, you might skip over stuff thinking everyone knows what you're talking about. Like, if you say you saw a "hand-to-hand" transaction, they likely know it's a drug buy, but will a member of the jury get that without more details?

That's where your narration skills come in. You've got to explain every little thing, especially if you want to get through to someone who's hearing about it for the first time. Why is a quick chat by a car suspicious? What's so fishy about a "handshake" at 1 am in a sketchy part of town? It's on you to make it crystal clear, breaking down the innocent-looking stuff to show the real story behind it.

Remember, jurors are just regular folks. They might want to think the best of people, like mistaking a shady midnight meet-up for a simple chat about directions. Your job is to convince them otherwise, using your street smarts and what you've seen out there. You need to lay out the evidence and connect the dots to show them why things aren't as innocent as they seem. Remember, their version of real police work comes from NCIC Hawaii.

Get good at this, and you'll stand a much better chance when you're in the hot seat in court. It's not just about the facts; it's about painting a picture so vivid that everyone in the courtroom gets it, agrees with you, and sees that you were doing a great job. So, the key to all this? Keep it clear, keep it detailed, and keep it real. In the end, articulate, articulate, articulate.

3 Golden Rules for Report Writing

The task of writing reports should be among the most straightforward responsibilities for a police officer. Contrary to common belief, report writing doesn't have to be a daunting task. It's essentially recounting an event or experience—a story where you are both the narrator and the witness. You've lived it; you've seen it. There's no room required for creative flair or dramatic embellishment. What it demands, however, is a sharp memory, attention to detail, and the ability to convey observations accurately on paper.

It's important to acknowledge that while the process can be simplified, it doesn't necessarily make it the most enjoyable part of the job. The thrill of the chase, the adrenaline of active duty—these are the aspects that officers live for. The administrative task of documenting it all? Not quite as exhilarating. But this is where this guide comes in, turning a mundane task into a manageable one, ensuring efficiency without compromising quality.

To navigate the complexities of report writing, one must adhere to three Golden Rules—principles that uphold the integrity and effectiveness of a report.

Golden Rule One: Justify All Conclusions with Facts and Evidence.

Officers often fall into the trap of drawing conclusions without providing a factual basis. Terms like "nervous," "furtive movement," or actions taken for "officer safety" are thrown around without the necessary context. These conclusions, without substantiating evidence, are empty statements.

Consider this: rather than vaguely stating, "I observed the driver to be nervous," provide specifics that paint a clear picture. A more effective articulation would be, "The driver exhibited signs of extreme nervousness, evidenced by his hands shaking uncontrollably and a constant, rapid movement of his legs."

When officers arrive at a conclusion in their reports, it is imperative that they don't leave it hanging without justification. The conclusions drawn from observations at the scene must be accompanied by a rationale. This is where "because" comes into play, transforming subjective observations into objective statements backed by evidence and fact.

Golden Rule Two: The most powerful word in a police report is "because."

The ability to articulate conclusions effectively in reporting is not just a skill but a necessity. A well-documented report serves as the foundation for legal proceedings and the pursuit of justice. The linchpin of such reports? The simple, yet powerful word: "because."

Remember, the term "because" is potent in report writing. It compels you to explain your reasoning, solidifying your observations with context. For instance:

"I initiated a stop because the vehicle matched the description of a car used in a recent armed robbery."

"I requested additional backup because the suspect was un-cooperative and appeared to be reaching for something in his pocket."

When officers arrive at a conclusion in their reports, it is imperative that they don't leave it hanging without justification. The conclusions drawn from observations at the scene must be accompanied by a rationale. This is where "because" comes into play, transforming subjective observations into objective statements backed by evidence and fact.

Consider the difference between the statements "The suspect was acting suspiciously" and "The suspect was acting suspiciously because they were pacing back and forth near the closed store, repeatedly glancing over their shoulder, which is consistent with the behavior of individuals looking to avoid detection." The latter sentence, prompted by "because," provides context and reasoning that can be scrutinized, understood, and accepted in a court of law.

The use of "because" compels the officer to delve deeper, to provide the "why" behind their assertions. It encourages a narrative that is not just descriptive but explanatory. This not only aids in painting a clearer picture for those who weren't present, such as prosecutors, judges, and jurors, but also ensures that the officer's thought process is transparent and logical.

Moreover, articulating the "why" helps in pre-empting questions that might arise during suppression hearings and trials. It shows that the officer's actions and decisions were not arbitrary but were based on a series of observations and facts that led to a logical conclusion.

In essence, the word "because" acts as a bridge between raw data and interpreted information. It's the difference between a report that reads as a series of disjointed notes and one that tells a cohesive story. For law enforcement officers, mastering the use of "because" in their reports is not just about following protocol; it's about ensuring that each conclusion is rooted in reality, defensible, and ultimately, that justice is served with convictions.

Golden Rule Three: Document Every Liberty or Property Intrusion.

Every action that affects an individual's freedom or property must be accounted for. This rule is not just about legal protocol; it's about transparency and justification for your actions. For example, if you stop a suspect or conduct a patdown that yields nothing incriminating, it's still imperative to record the incident. It's not about the results of the action, but the reasoning behind it.

Documenting these instances protects not just the community, but also law enforcement officers. It demonstrates that actions were taken based on reasonable suspicion and not arbitrary judgment. It's a practice that reinforces the trust between law enforcement and the communities they serve.

In conclusion, effective report writing is less about literary prowess and more about clear, logical communication. It's about presenting the truth, backed by facts, in a manner that is comprehensible and accessible to all. By adhering to these golden rules, you safeguard your profession's integrity and contribute to upholding justice.

Report Writing Goals

Report writing in law enforcement serves several critical functions that contribute to the efficiency and effectiveness of the judicial process. The primary objectives can be summarized as follows:

1. Preventing Suppression Motions: The initial goal of a well-crafted report is to deter defense attorneys from pursuing motions to suppress evidence. By meticulously documenting the facts and ensuring that the report is devoid of any constitutional issues, law enforcement officers can preemptively address potential challenges that might arise during suppression hearings. A comprehensive and constitutionally sound report can render such hearings redundant, saving valuable time and resources.

2. Promoting Guilty Pleas: The second objective of a robust report is to streamline the plea bargaining process. Public defenders, often burdened with heavy caseloads and limited resources, are not in a position to take every case to trial. A comprehensive and well-articulated report can be a decisive factor for a defense attorney in advising a client towards accepting a plea deal. When the evidence against a defendant is clearly and convincingly laid out in the report, it increases the likelihood of the defendant opting to plead guilty rather than face the uncertainties of a trial.

3. Aiding the Prosecution: Thirdly, a well-written report acts as a crucial guide for prosecutors. Often, prosecutors may not be intimately familiar with the nuances of a case until it is time for trial, a scenario that is particularly common with lesser offenses such as DUIs. A clear and detailed report equips prosecutors with the necessary information to understand the case quickly and proceed with confidence, essentially enabling them to "pick up the report and go."

4. Assisting in Recall During Trial: Lastly, and perhaps most significantly, a report serves as a vital tool for officers to recall the specifics of an incident. While body-worn cameras can capture the event, they may not capture the rationale behind an officer's actions. A report can fill in these critical details, providing context and justification for the decisions made during the incident.

In conclusion, the importance of a well-written report cannot be overstated. It is a key component of law enforcement that can significantly reduce the likelihood of trials. Many officers express a preference for avoiding trials when possible, and a solid report is instrumental in achieving this preference, thereby streamlining the judicial process and enhancing the administration of justice.

RS/PC Pocket Guide

There is a companion book to this one, the RS/PC Pocket Guide. That book offers hundreds or articulation example for various police practices. Here are some sample table of contents:

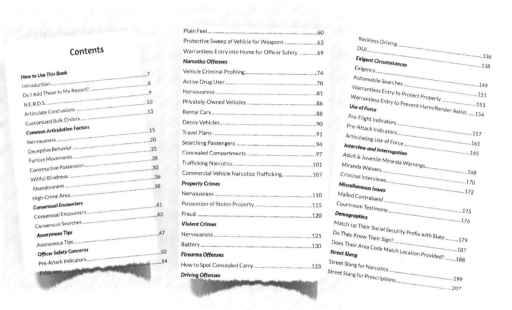

This book is an essential tool for any police officer who aims to master the art of articulating reasonable suspicion (RS) and probable cause (PC) within their reports. The reason is simple yet profound: the power to win cases and circumvent suppression hearings lies in the skill of articulation. When the stakes are high, and the details matter, knowing how to express the justification for your actions in writing can make the difference between a case won and a case lost.

This book may be obtained through store.bluetogold.com

Pre-narrative Information

Overview

In law enforcement, the articulation of events through official documentation stands as a pillar of the justice process. The initial segment of a police report, often unnoticed yet pivotal, sets the stage for the narrative that unfolds. This crucial piece of information, commonly termed the "top-sheet," serves as the reader's introductory guide to the subsequent detailed account. It typically encompasses a broad overview of the incident, delineating key individuals involved, ranging from officers, witnesses, and victims, to any other relevant parties. The essence of the top-sheet is to offer a snapshot, preparing the reader for the context they are about to dive into.

However, modern advancements in administrative tasks have seen the integration of automated report writing software within agencies. These sophisticated systems are capable of generating a standard top-sheet, filled with the requisite preliminary details. In such instances, officers are relieved of the redundancy of manually replicating this information, thereby streamlining the documentation process and ensuring uniformity and accuracy in the reports generated.

Subsequent to the top-sheet, a strategically placed "disclaimer" significantly fortifies the integrity of a police report. This standard text serves multiple fundamental purposes. Firstly, it clarifies that the report is a summarized account, not an exhaustive chronological narrative, thereby setting realistic expectations for the report's content. Secondly, it emphasizes that direct speech is indicated explicitly within quotation marks, distinguishing it from paraphrased dialogue. Such disclaimers are instrumental in safeguarding officers against unwarranted scrutiny and contentious nitpicking common in legal confrontations, particularly from defense attorneys seeking to exploit any perceived omissions or subjective language.

The inclusion of a disclaimer acts as a preemptive measure, mitigating challenges regarding the comprehensiveness of the report or the verbatim accuracy of statements recorded. It curtails attempts by skeptics to discredit the officer's account by overemphasizing inconsequential details, thereby maintaining the report's credibility and the officer's professional integrity.

In addition to these elements, a well-crafted synopsis serves as a valuable precursor to the main narrative in police reports, particularly extensive ones. This brief overview, usually confined to a short paragraph, encapsulates the crux of the incident reported. It affords readers the advantage of understanding the core scenario, themes, and initial findings before delving into the intricacies of the full narrative. Especially for administrative personnel or legal professionals who sift through numerous reports, a synopsis offers immediate insight, facilitating a quicker assimilation of the event's nature and significance.

In conclusion, the meticulous composition of a police report, beginning with an informative top-sheet, a protective disclaimer, and a concise synopsis, contributes immensely to its effectiveness and reliability. These preliminary sections, though brief, hold substantial weight in shaping the reader's understanding and perception of the incidents reported. They collectively serve to enhance the report's clarity, shield officers from unnecessary legal quibbles, and ensure that the document stands as a credible and authoritative source in the pursuit of justice.

Top-sheet Information

Top-sheet information is simply an outline of who was involved (e.g., officers, suspects, witnesses, etc.), what was involved (i.e. evidence and vehicles), evidence seized, and so forth. If this information is summarized somewhere else then there's no need to duplicate it.

Here are some examples of sections that can be included in the top-sheet:

- Officer(s) Involved:

- Witness(es):

- Victim(s):

- Defendant(s):

- Driver:

- Passenger(s):

- Evidence Seized:

- Vehicle(s) Involved:

- Weapon(s):

- Jurisdiction (e.g., what court has jurisdiction):

Here's an example:

Officers Involved:

B. Rad, P#12345 (Initiated vehicle stop, SITA, located & field test of cocaine)
D. Noir, P#12347 (located firearm/ammunition)
C. Dean, P#12346 (Sgt.)

Evidence Impounded:

Smith and Wesson, 9mm, serial #A301256 (driver's side door by Officer Noir)
Six 9mm Lugar cartridges (trunk by Officer Noir, during inventory of vehicle)
4.2 grams Cocaine (located SITA & field tested by Officer Rad)

Suspect/Arrestee/Driver:
John Doe
DOB: 1/2/89   ID: 1234567

Passenger:
Jane Doe
DOB: 1/2/90   ID: 1234568

Vehicle (Subject Vehicle):
2014 Jeep Grand Cherokee, VIN SBM11BAA7DW002889, Red, NV Plate "IMT8S" (expired)

Details of Vehicle Stop:

On January 1, 2021, I, Officer B. Rad, while operating an unmarked unit, noticed the **Subject Vehicle** fail to yield..........

Synopsis

The first paragraph of a lengthy or complex report should be a synopsis, or a quick summary of what happened during the incident and the report's status. This synopsis is designed to offer readers—often pressed for time—a clear and immediate understanding of the report's contents and the main outcomes of the incident in question. By presenting this snapshot at the outset, it allows those who may not have the opportunity to delve into the full text to grasp the essential information and context without the necessity of reading the entire document. This approach is particularly beneficial in fast-paced environments where decision-makers need to quickly assimilate the facts and make informed decisions based on the critical points and conclusions drawn within the report.

A synopsis contains seven elements, which may be written in this order:

1. First, state when you got the call or made the observation;

2. Next, describe how you got the call or whether it was self-initiated;

3. Next, describe the nature of the call (e.g. domestic, accident, etc.);

4. Now describe the location of the incident;

5. Briefly describe what you did during the incident;

6. Next, state the investigative outcome (e.g. made an arrest, allegation unfounded, and so forth);

7. Finally, describe the report's status (closed, follow-up planned, etc.).

Here's a synopsis example:

"On June 10, 2020 at approximately 1520 hours, I was dispatched to 555 Main Street to investigate a domestic battery. My investigation concluded that John Harris ("husband") unlawfully struck his wife in the right side of her head during a verbal argument. I arrested the husband and transported him to the county jail for processing. This investigation is complete and will be forwarded to the district attorney's office."

Keep in mind a synopsis should be short and sweet! Don't give details. That's what the report is for. Just make short statements and then write your full report.

How to Write Narratives

Step One: Write in the First Person

Please, I beg you, do not write any report, including search warrant affidavits, in the third person. A third person report reads like this: "Officer Johnson then walked up to the suspect and asked him if he was involved in a bar fight. The suspect told Officer Johnson, "No." Or like this: "Your affiant spoke to the C.I. and the C.I. told your affiant...." Please shoot me now. My brain ached just writing those examples.

Third person reports should be banned outright for three reasons.

First, the author, which means you, doesn't typically use the third person for communication. It's quite an unnatural way to converse. Consider this scenario: when a family member or friend inquires about your day, you wouldn't typically respond like this: "Your family member had a full day. To begin with, your family member attended to a situation involving a homeless individual behaving inappropriately outside a restaurant. The individual rudely addressed your family member with offensive language." Rather, you would start with "I" because it's more natural communication.

Second, you include more facts and evidence when you write in the first person. Let's test this out. Describe your last vacation in the third person. Try to be as detailed as possible. For example, describe your vacation by starting with: "Your affiant went to Disneyland. Your affiant rode the Matterhorn and...." How awkward was that? Are you leaving out details? Ok, now tell the same story in the first person. Which one was easier to tell? Which version had more detail? Unless you're just a weirdo the first person method was much easier to share and was filled with way more facts and details. Why? Because you're telling the story from how you experienced it.

Third, your readers will better understand what happened. That's because the reader will be walking in your shoes! When readers read a report written in the first person, they put themselves in your shoes. That's exactly what you want. You want them to agree with everything you did on-scene. Therefore, take them on your journey and explain why you did what you did. I promise that this will persuade your reader (usually prosecutors, judges, and so forth) that you were right, much more so than if the same report were written in the hard-to-read third person.

Still not convinced? Then pick up any best-selling novel and see if it's written in the first person or third person. It's usually written in the first person because it's the best way for the reader to "feel" what the character is experiencing.

Step Two: Write Chronologically

Most officers try to write their reports in chronological order. This is the best method to share what happened during the incident. Still, most police reports are not truly chronological because the report describes the incident when police arrive. Think about it. The incident likely did not start upon your arrival. It started before you arrived unless you saw the incident occur before your eyes, like reckless driving, impaired driving, and so forth.

Here's an example of a truly chronological report:

"On March 4, 2020 at approximately 1945 hours, I responded to 555 Main Street to investigate an alleged domestic battery. My investigation revealed the following information.

At approximately 1800 hours, Jane Smith ("Girlfriend") said she was at home making dinner. She told me that John Reynolds, her live-in boyfriend ("Boyfriend") is an alcoholic who sometimes gets violent when he drinks.

The Boyfriend came home around 1815 hours and the Girlfriend heard him yelling about something before he came into the home…

After approximately an hour and a half of arguing, the Girlfriend told me that her Boyfriend threw her against the bedroom wall and kicked her in the stomach with his bare foot.

[more info, up to you getting call]

…I arrived at approximately 1955 hours and observed…."

You see what happened here? The narrative quickly introduces how and when the cop got the call, the location, and then goes back in time to the beginning of the incident. In other words, it does not start with, "Upon my arrival…" because that is not when the incident started. Make sense?

Still, most cops will continue to write their reports using modified chronology and that is okay too. Here's an example:

"On March 4, 2020 at approximately 1032 hours I responded to the Walmart at 705 First Street for a shoplifting investigation.

Upon arrival, I spoke with loss prevention officer Tim Williams, who told me…"

Use whatever technique that best fits your needs.

Step Three: Use Topic Headings

A true report-writing pro uses topic headings throughout their report. There are two primary reasons why you should use topic headings. First, topic headings break up your report into nice bite-sized sections. Second, it's easier to scan for information.

For example, a drunk driving report may have the following topic headings:

Pre-contact Observations

[Articulate those facts here.]

Driver Contact Observations

[Articulate what you observed while you made contact with the driver or other occupants.]

Standardized Field Sobriety Tests Performance

[Articulate how the driver performed the SFSTs, what he said, his demeanor, and so forth.]

Breath Test Results

[Articulate how you properly followed the breath testing procedures and the results.]

Driver Booking

[Articulate when, where, and how the driver was booked.]

And so forth. Do you agree why I say that a "true pro" uses topic headings? Do you also agree that adding these topic headings helps your report?

Here are more topic heading examples:

- Details
- Call Details
- Initial Observations
- Traffic Stop
- Driver Contact
- Interviews
- Miranda/Suspect Statements
- Suspect Criminal History
- Victim/Witness Contact/Statement

- Evidence Located/Impounded
- Consent to Search
- Patdown of Suspect
- Search of Vehicle
- Search of Residence
- Preliminary investigation
- Investigation
- Investigation Continued
- P&P Contact
- Victim's Injuries
- Suspect's Injuries
- Field Tests
- Crime Scene Description
- Video Surveillance
- Photo Line-up
- Neighborhood Canvas
- Conclusion/Probable Cause Statement

Also, prosecutors should also appreciate topic headings. It makes your report easy to navigate when they argue before the court and need to reference your report.

Here are real-life examples:

PHASE 1 Vehicle in Motion / Interview with Officer:

On October 16, 2019 at approximately 1644 hours, I responded to the area of 1100 Dunson Road Davenport, Florida in reference to assisting Lt. Da████927 with a possible intoxicated person. Lt. Davis advised he observed a Segway driving east bound on Dunson Rd in the westbound lanes going head on with vehicles. Lt. Davis advised vehicles were having to go around the Segway because it was in their lane of travel.
When Lt. Davis made contact with the Segway he stated he could smell the odor of an alcoholic beverage coming from her person and breathe as well as watery eyes. Lt. Davis also stated that the operator of the Segway made multiple spontaneous statements about being drunk and that was an alcoholic.

Lt. Davis then contacted me and requested I respond to the scene and conduct a DUI evaluation. See Lt. Davis' supplement for further information

PHASE 2 Personal Contact:

I made contact with the white male operator of the Segway, who I identified by his passport card to be Andy Sigears. Upon contact with Sigears, I observed his speech to be slurred and eyes to be watery. I could also smell a strong odor of an alcoholic beverage coming from his person and his breathe.

Based on these indicators I asked Sigears to submit to a series of Standardized Field Sobriety Test (SFST's) and he consented to those test.

PHASE 3 Pre-Arrest Screening / Standardized Field Sobriety Testing (SFST's):

I conducted the following Field Sobriety test (SFST's) with the following results:

BWC

CALL DETAILS

On 4/17/21 at approximately 2003 hours, I Officer Z. Howard P#████ operating as marked patrol unit 3M34 was dispatched to a family disturbance at Mandalay Bay 3950 S Las Vegas Blvd Rm ████ Las Vegas, NV 89119. Call details stated that security had a male and female subject in custody relating to a family disturbance where a battery had occurred.

DEANNA INTERVIEW

I made contact with Green, Deanna DOB: 9/9/1990 whos identity was verified via her California drivers license and the following information was obtained. Deanna stated that while in her hotel room her husband of 5 months Yellow, Christopher DOB: 1/1/1983 started an argument with her over loosing a pair of sunglasses at Moorea day club at Mandalay Bay. Deanna stated during the argument Christopher slapped her on the left side of her face and she took off her engagement ring and threw it at him. Deanna then went to lay down on her bed and called a friend so she could make plans to leave. Christopher still angry and arguing with her then grabbed her by her legs and pulled her off the bed onto the ground resulting in her back being pulled across the floor. Christopher then grabbed her clothing and started to rip it, because of Christopher's actions Deanna ran out of her room wearing only bikini bottoms and was found crying in the hallway by a housekeeping attendant. Security was called and then Deanna was taken down to Mandalay Bay's security office to await officers.

I did not observe any injury to Christopher's person, Deanna had visible reddening to the left side of her face and a large red mark on the left mid portion of her back. Deanna's injuries corroborated with her story of how Christopher slapped her and pulled her off the bed onto the ground. Security stated that the received a call from housekeeping about a topless female crying in a hallway of the 58th floor. Upon arrival they observed Deanna crying and stating that she had been pulled off the bed and dragged and then hit by her husband. Photos were taken of Deanna's injuries and uploaded to OnBase, she was also provided with Domestic Violence information card but SafeNest representatives were not able to come speak with her due to their call volume.

| CR No: 190008████ | Written By: FEHARWOODJ████ | Date: 07/05/2019 05:17 PM |

REPORT WRITER: Ofc. Justin Harwood #602

SUMMARY: On 07/05/2019 at approximately 1101 hours, I was on routine patrol on E Chesterfield near Wanda when I heard Ofc. Jerome notify dispatch that he had just had his patrol vehicle stolen on Woodward near E Nine Mile. Ofc. Jerome notified dispatch that a black female with a white t-shirt had stolen his patrol vehicle and was headed northbound on Woodward (See Ofc. Jerome's Report).

OFFICER ACTIONS: Lt. Spellman notified officers that the vehicle was headed east on I-696 near Hilton. I headed north on Wanda to E Nine Mile and turned northbound on Bonner. I turned west on to Orchard and followed Orchard to Hilton. Lt. Spellman notified officers that the vehicle had turned onto southbound I-75 from I-696. I got to the intersection of Hilton and Ten Mile and headed east on Ten Mile near S. Chrysler Drive. I observed Ofc. Heath in fully marked P#64 pull on to the Nine Mile exit from I-75 and followed Ofc. Heath in his pursuit as we approached Nine Mile (See Ofc. Heath's report).

PURSUIT: As officers approached W Seven Mile from southbound Woodward, P#60 turned onto W Seven Mile and headed westbound in the eastbound lane. Avoiding a collision, Ofc. Heath fell

Step Four: N.E.R.D.S.

Reasonable suspicion only requires a "moderate chance"[1] that criminal activity is afoot. It's not a high standard but requires more than an unparticularized hunch. When looking to articulate reasonable suspicion, as well as probable cause, keep an eye out for the below listed circumstances. Remember, one or two suspicious factors are often not enough. Therefore, look for a combination of factors that will lead a reasonable person to believe the person is engaged in criminal activity.

Think: NERDS

1. Nervousness

2. Evasive conduct

3. Reactions

4. Deception

5. Specifics

Mere nervousness is worthless. Instead, articulate abnormal nervousness like sweating, fumbling, shaking, no eye contact, and so forth.

Evasiveness is also suspicious. It's one thing if the person wants to avoid you, but it's another if they are trying to "avoid" you or quickly get away from you.

Articulating abnormal reactions are very important. For example, if you drive next to someone and their immediate reaction is to light up a cigarette it's a little suspicious. If they then turn into the next available commercial parking lot, park, and not leave their car, it's odd. You don't have enough yet to make a stop but these reactions are at least pointing you in the right direction.

Deception is always relevant. It's one thing if people don't want to talk to you, it's another to lie and try to deceive you. Look for verbal fillers, non-answers to simple questions; (e.g. "Who owns the car?" Answer: "I borrowed it."), and so forth.

Finally, include specific suspicious circumstances involving the suspect, like his criminal history, high-crime area, being under the influence, nice rental car but not gainfully employed, and so forth.

---

[1] See Safford Unified School District v. Redding, 557 US 364 (2009)

Step Five: Don't Write in All Caps

WRITING A POLICE REPORT IN ALL CAPS MAKES IT HARDER TO READ. IT ALSO SHOWS THAT THE WRITER WAS LAZY! Why? Because lazy writers don't even want to hold down the shift button to start sentences with capitals or to identify proper nouns. Instead, this sloth-style of writing allows the writer to just hit caps-lock and blaze away.

If this method did not distract from the quality of report writing then I would not care. But ALL CAPS writing should be discarded for two reasons. First, readers hate it. Second, it prevents you from identifying proper nouns in your report since everything is capitalized. Sometimes, proper nouns are important information.

Briefly look over these two reports. Without reading them, which one do you *prefer* to read?

On October 5, 2023, at approximately 0050 hours, I, Officer A. Cadrone, P#19456, was operating as marked patrol unit, 7M92. Along with Officer S. Harris, P# 13887, who was operating as marked patrol unit, 7M91. We were dispatched to a family disturbance call involving a male and a female fighting, and one was threatened with a knife at 346 Sunset Dr., Las Vegas, NV, 89109. There were no description of the subjects at the time of the call.

Upon arrival, I observed a white male adult wearing a black jacket, and black sweat pants, who was later identified as Ortiz, Sean (DOB: 01/22/1986). Ortiz was running towards a Hispanic female adult, wearing a black crop top, and black sweat pants, who was later identified as Swartz, Karen (DOB: 10/13/1987).

Or this one?

ON OCTOBER 5, 2023, AT APPROXIMATELY 0050 HOURS, I, OFFICER A. CADRONE, P#19456, WAS OPERATING AS MARKED PATROL UNIT, 7M92. ALONG WITH OFFICER S. HARRIS, P# 13887, WHO WAS OPERATING AS MARKED PATROL UNIT, 7M91. WE WERE DISPATCHED TO A FAMILY DISTURBANCE CALL INVOLVING A MALE AND A FEMALE FIGHTING, AND ONE WAS THREATENED WITH A KNIFE AT 346 SUNSET DR., LAS VEGAS, NV, 89109. THERE WERE NO DESCRIPTION OF THE SUBJECTS AT THE TIME OF THE CALL.

UPON ARRIVAL, I OBSERVED A WHITE MALE ADULT WEARING A BLACK JACKET, AND BLACK SWEAT PANTS, WHO WAS LATER IDENTIFIED AS ORTIZ, SEAN (DOB: 01/22/1986). ORTIZ WAS RUNNING TOWARDS A HISPANIC FEMALE ADULT, WEARING A BLACK CROP TOP, AND BLACK SWEAT PANTS, WHO WAS LATER IDENTIFIED AS SWARTZ, KAREN (DOB: 10/13/1987).

Stay away from ALL CAPS writing. It does more harm than good.

Step Six: Utilize Paragraph Breaks

Another lazy writing technique is not including paragraphs in your reports. Again, just like officers who use ALL CAPS, this sloth-style of writing annoys your reader.

Additionally, paragraphs serve three very important purposes that help in comprehension. First, it give the reader's brain (and maybe writer's too) a micro break. Think about it. What if I wrote this book without any paragraphs? Wouldn't you feel mentally exhausted after a while? Jumping from one paragraph to the next gives the reader a few micro-seconds break. It's not much, but it helps.

Second, those who read your report are busy people. They get interrupted. Must answer phone calls. And sometimes have to leave the office in the middle of reading your report and when they come back they have to pick up where they left off. Paragraphs help them start near where they stopped reading. But when the page is one huge paragraph, the reader must hunt for the last spot read. Not cool. Not cool at all!

Finally, a paragraph's intended purpose is to break up big ideas. This also helps with reader comprehension. Break your report up into bite-sized paragraphs based on major ideas. For example, if you're writing a DUI report, one paragraph could be used for pre-stop intoxicated driving indicators. Another paragraph would describe what you observed while speaking with the driver, and so forth.

To help prove my point, look at the report on the next page. If you had to approve this report, or use it for trial, wouldn't you prefer it was broken down into bite-sized paragraphs?

What's interesting is that this report is well-written. It's in the first person. And the officer did not use all caps. But because it's just one massive paragraph, I simply do not want to read it. Do you?

Orange County	**ICJIS Arrest Affidavit** (continued)	
Arrested ☑ At-Large ☐ JRA ☐	Document #: 880522	Division #: CRA
Document Date: 11/02/2019		Court Case #: 48-2019-MM-008935-A-O
Defendant's Name	SHERMAN, BRIAN THOMAS	Agency Case Number: 19-98975

NARRATIVE: The undersigned has probable cause to believe the above-named defendant on the ___02___ of ___November 2019___
at 12:10 at 4601 N WORLD DR _____ (Zone: 61) in Orange County did

Probable Cause: The defendant did actually and intentionally touch the victim against her will by placing his right arm around her shoulders and reaching down with his right hand pressing and lifting the victim's right breast with his right thumb and forefinger. The defendant battered the victim while she was working as a cast member at Walt Disney World Magic Kingdom in Ariel's Grotto as the costumed character Ariel. The defendant's actions were witnessed by co-workers Stratemeyer and Owen who provided statements that were consistent with the victim's statement. On 11/02/19 I responded to Walt Disney World Magic Kingdom reference a battery. Upon arrival M/D Todd Owens had obtained written sworn statements from the victim and witnesses. Victim's Statement: The victim was performing as the costumed character Ariel in an area of the park known as Ariel's Grotto. The victim was accompanied by co-workers Stratemeyer (Photopass photographer) and Owens (character attendant) while working. At approximately 1210hrs a husband (defendant) and wife(witness Carnot) were escorted into the grotto. The defendant was very excited and immediately told Owen, "I love Ariel. Ariel is my favorite!" Witness Carnot sat down on the victim's right side. The defendant then quickly sat down on the victim's left side. The defendant sat down much more quickly than the victim expected because she expected him to join in a moment. This left the victim physically stuck in between the defendant on her left and his wife witness Carnot on her right. The defendant repeated how much he loved Ariel as he placed his right arm around the victim's shoulders. The victim has been trained by Disney that it is inappropriate to photograph a Disney princess when a guest has their arm wrapped around the princess character. The victim was immediately uncomfortable with the defendant's touch but was unable to move. Co-worker Owen was tending to the line with her back to the victim when the defendant continued to wrap his arm lower so that he could cup the victim's shell bra (right cup) with his right hand. Co-worker Stratemeyer immediately recognized the victim's body language as uncomfortable and verbally guided the guest to remove his hand from around the victim by suggesting that he pose like Prince Charming. Co-worker Owens then turned around to see what was happening. The victim looked down and saw the suspect's right hand on her right breast shell. The victim stated that the velcro on the costume is weak and as she moved to look down the plastic shell lifted and the defendant cupped the victim's right breast with his right forefinger and thumb with only the thin skin-tight fabric in between her breast the defendant's thumb and forefinger. The defendant cupped and lifted the victim's right breast for approximately three to four seconds during the battery. The victim stated that both Owens and Stratemeyer worked to verbally correct the defendant's hand placement and the defendant removed his hand from the victim's breast and slipped it back around her shoulders. The defendant took up a pose like prince Eric and the victim then took the defendant's arm while Stratemeyer took the Photopass photo to use to identify the defendant when reporting the incident. When the defendant left the room the victim began shaking and crying. Co-worker Owens closed the room immediately after. The victim stated that she does not know the defendant and did not give him permission to touch her breast. The victim provided a written sworn statement, desires prosecution, and will testify in court. The victim was provided with a victim's pamphlet including case number and contact phone number. The victim stated that she did not have any physical injuries and declined medical attention. The victim signed a victim request for confidentiality form as allowed by Marsay's Law. Witnesses Owens and Stratemeyer Statements: Witnesses Owens and Stratemeyer were interviewed by M/D Todd Owens. According to M/D Owens witnesses, Owens and Stratemeyer provided written and verbal statements that were consistent with the victim's statement. (see M/D Owens supplemental report) Defendant Interview: I read the defendant his Miranda rights using the agency issued Waivers and Affidavit form. The defendant agreed that he understood his rights and that he was willing to speak to me and M/D Owens without an attorney present. The defendant signed the Waivers and Affidavits form and the interview was recorded using my agency BWC. The defendant admitted to visiting Ariel's grotto on 11/02/19 during the time of the incident. The defendant admitted placing his arm around the victim's shoulders prior to the photo and having to be corrected by Owens and Stratemeyer. The defendant repeatedly stated that he might have touched the victim's breast and that it was accidental. The defendant offered to apologize to the victim. The defendant also told Disney manager Fernandez that he has hugged people in the past in way that has been taken as sexual. I asked the defendant if the victim and witnesses were not untruthful and he already stated that it may have happened to think very hard about his hand position. I asked the defendant if he could remember feeling his hand go inside the victim's costume. During the interview (around 1:18) the defendant stated, "I can see it in my mind that it happened." According to M/D Owen Disney security used the Magicband used by the defendant for the photo and the photo taken by Stratemeyer to locate the defendant in the park. The defendant was arrested and transported to BRC without incident. Additional details from the interviews will be included incident report for this case once the BWC video can be completely reviewed. Sexual Offender Surveillance Agent ▮▮▮▮ was notified via phone. ***BWC Video Available***

Sworn to and subscribed before me ,		I swear or affirm the above statements are correct and true	(407) 254-7000
this _2_ day of _November_ year _2019_		Officer's Signature —	Officer's Bus. Phone No.
			DOYLE, DONALD / 2328
Notary Public ☑ Law Enforcement or Corrections Officer ☐			Officer's Name/ID
Personally Known ☑ Produced Identification ☐			
Type of Identification			
	NOTARY PUBLIC STATE OF FLORIDA		
Notary Signature			GG048880 / 11/20/2020
			Notary Commission # / Exp. Date

Step Seven: Write in the Active Voice

Police reports should be written in the active voice, not passive voice. Active voice means it is clear who is doing the action or conversely who the action is being done upon. Active voice is important because there should not be confusion as to who is doing what.

Here are some examples:

"The car was searched and a S&W revolver was found in the glove box."

This sentence is passive voice because it is unclear who conducted the search and found the firearm. We can assume that the report writer was the one who conducted the search. But you know what happens when we "assume?" We make an "ass" out of "u" and "me."

For example, the officer who wrote the report is the only officer subpoenaed into court because the prosecutors "assumed" the report writer conducted the search. While on the stand the prosecutor asks the officer, "Okay, tell the court what you did after you found the gun." The officer then responds, "Wait, I didn't find the gun, my partner found the gun." Houston, we have a problem. The prosecutor is now in a very difficult position because he or she doesn't have all the necessary witnesses in the court. The result could be a mistrial or outright dismissal or charges.

The solution is simple. Start the sentence with "who" did the action and then explain what they did. For example, "Officer Bandiero searched the vehicle and found a Smith and Wesson revolver in glove box."

Here's another example: "The suspect was placed under arrest and read his Miranda rights." No, no, no. We don't know who made the arrest or who read Miranda. It could be the report writer, or one or two other officers. We just don't know and don't want to assume. Instead, write like this, "I arrested the driver and read him his Miranda rights."

Here's one last example: "Officers drove to the northwest part of the facility where the incident occurred." Okay, who are the "officers?" The report continues: "Officer took him into custody and identified him as [information omitted]." Who took the suspect into custody?

Again, the solution is simple, include the name of the person(s) doing the action and/or who the action is being done upon first, then write out the action. For example, For example, "Officer Smith and Officer Jones drove to the northwest part of the facility where the incident occurred. Officer Smith then took the suspect into custody and identified him as [information omitted]." This approach clearly indicates who is performing the action and who is affected by it, making the report more precise and understandable.

Step Eight: Identify People by Roles, not Names

Your report should include a person's name and their "role" in the incident. Are they a suspect? Employee? Victim or witness? After identifying who they are, do not refer to them by name, but by their role. Why? Because a person's name is legally irrelevant. It adds no context to the report. Who cares if the person's name is Smith versus Johnson. However, their "role" is highly relevant.

Let's assume your report mentioned a witness, Dan Jackson. After the initial identification, you should refer to Jackson as "Witness." For example, "the Witness then stated...," and so forth. If there are multiple witnesses, you should refer to them by their role and their name, for example, "Witness Jackson then called police."

This tip also handles people with the same last name. If you're writing about a domestic their roles are "husband" and "wife," "boyfriend" and "girlfriend," and so forth.   Again, referring to people by their name doesn't add any context. But their role does.

This tiny improvement will increase the comprehension of your reports.

Original:

During the fire, Walmart was open and had multiple people inside to include Mr. Lorenz and Jon Medinger and other store employees.

Rewrite:

Walmart was open to the public during the fire and multiple people were inside, including the Store Manager Medinger and cashier Lorenz.

Later in the report, state: "the Store Manager then said…" or "the Cashier told me…." Don't refer to them as "Medinger" or "Lorenz."

Step Nine: Articulate Conclusions

When you write your reports and are trying to justify legally significant actions, like patdowns and motor vehicle searches, I want you to strive to articulate at least five facts or circumstances for why you did what you did. Why? Because in my experience cops under-articulate and only put 2-3 reasons in their report. We know that the vast majority of cops are doing the right thing. But too many are not providing the court with enough reasons as to why.

I strongly believe that if you can develop at least five articulable reasons the court will likely agree that you were reasonable. On the other hand, provide only 2-3 reasons and you may have a tougher time in court. Is this rule set in stone? No way. For example, if you observe a hand-to-hand drug transaction then little else is needed to justify the stop and search. Still, most of your investigations are a tad more nuanced than that. Therefore, strive to come up with more reasons why you did what you did.

One way to improve your articulation ability is to read case law that upheld the officer's actions. As you're reading the case "reverse engineer" it and isolate why the court upheld the officer's actions. For example, in U.S. v. Herman Adair[1] an officer received a call about a "man with a gun." His initial report on the incident was apparently thin and there was a drawn-out suppression hearing. Ultimately, the court upheld the patdown for the following reasons:

- High-crime area

- Caller said man with gun was drinking: Guns and alcohol don't mix

- The caller said she did not recognize Adair as a tenant and there was a gang problem at this complex

- When the officer arrived Adair reacted by trying to evade the officer, despite the fact that Adair knew the officer and previous encounters were cordial

- The officer knew Adair was a felon

- Finally, the officer saw a bulge consistent with a firearm

Do you think if the officer articulated all of these factors in his initial report we would have had a drawn-out suppression hearing and an appeal to the Sixth Circuit? Probably not. Remember the "Rule of 5."

---

[1] U.S. v. Adair, 925 F.3d 931 (6th Cir. 2019)

After you have determined why you did something (e.g. patdown, searched car, used force, etc.) I want you to articulate these reasons with the word "because." Essentially, the word "because" is the most powerful word in a police report. In other words, cops will often state their opinion as to why they believe something, but that "opinion" is worthless without articulation.

Let's go over some examples:

Not this: "As I spoke with the suspect, I observed obvious injuries to his face and a bleeding laceration on his left thumb."

But this: "As I spoke with the suspect, I observed injuries *because* his left eye had burst blood vessels, his upper lip was inflamed, and his left thumb had a bleeding laceration."

Not this: "The suspect was about to attack my partner."

But this: "The subject was about to attack my partner *because* he said, "I'm going to kick your ass," turned his body 90° in a boxer's/fighting stance, weight shifted, clenched his fists, raised hands, sweating profusely, clenched mouth, and took off his glasses."

Not this: "The suspect was non-compliant."

But this: "The suspect was non-compliant *because* he said, "I'm not going to jail", ignored commands, acted contrary to commands, walked away, repetitive phrases, illogical responses..."

Not this: "The stop was made in a high-crime area."

But this: "The area where I stopped the suspect was dangerous *because* -Number of arrests, types of arrests, personal observations, statistics, citizen's complaints..."

Not this: "I observed a car being driven recklessly in the right travel lane."

But this: "The vehicle was being driven recklessly *because* I observed the vehicle rapidly swerve from the #1 to the #4 travel lane in one motion without using a turn signal. I estimated the vehicle to be traveling at approximately 90 miles per hour..."

Not this: "The wife appeared scared of her husband."

But this: "The wife appeared to be scared of her husband *because* she kept asking when he would be released from jail, asked if there were battered woman shelters in the area, and asked whether he would be told she accused him of spousal battery."

You get the point. Remember, the most powerful word in a police report is "because."

Step Ten: Use Bullet Points

Bullet points are an effective way to justify legally significant actions. Additionally, bullet points are a great pre-report articulation tool.

Bullet points are effective for three reasons:

1. Cops are very analytical thinkers and writing bullet points is an analytical way of conveying information.

2. Cops articulate more. For example, if an officer was writing a DUI report and wanted to articulate all of the reasons the driver was intoxicated, bullet points would be an effective way to do it.

3. Finally, some prosecutors like bullet points because they use them to help write their legal memos and it provides a list of things they can articulate during oral arguments.

Here's an example:

"Based on the following facts and circumstances, I believed the driver was under the influence because:

• He was swerving in his lane for almost a mile before I stopped him;

• I smelled the strong odor of an intoxicating beverage coming from his vehicle while I was standing on the passenger side.

• No one else was inside the vehicle;

• Both eyes were bloodshot and glassy;

• He fumbled with his paperwork and dropped it twice on the floorboard;

• (And so on)."

Here's another example:

"The witness was driven to my location for an in-field show-up. I minimized suggestive influences by doing the following:

• The suspect was not surrounded by police officers;

• No officer was holding the suspect during the in-field show-up;

• No officer made any accusatory comments about the suspect to the witness;

• The suspect was kept in mechanical restraints because the nature of the call, an armed robbery, was violent. Therefore, the restraints were not removed for both officer and suspect's safety;

- I told the witness that the person detained may or may not be the perpetrator and to base the identification on her memory, and not the present circumstances."

Here's a third example:

"At approximately 0125 hours I had reasonable suspicion that the driver was engaged in narcotics trafficking because:

- He was driving in tandem with another vehicle that did not pull over and wait;
- He was driving on I-15, a designated HIDTA area;
- He was driving a one-way rental car that was rented by a non-occupant;
- He stated he was going on vacation, but there was no luggage in the vehicle;
- He has recent drug arrests;
- He stated he is unemployed;
- Finally, there were several energy drinks and fast food trash in the vehicle, indicative of constant driving and no leisure. This is common when traffickers do not want to leave the vehicle unattended.

Therefore, I called for a k9 and..."

Also, some prosecutors like bullet points because when they argue cases they essentially argue the highlights of your case. These "highlights" are often the same things you would put in bullet point format. For example, they may argue that you had probable cause to search a vehicle because of X, Y, Z. Those factors could be your bullet points.

Finally, bullet points are an excellent pre-report brainstorming tool. For example, if you did something that is highly significant, like entering a home to prevent the destruction of evidence, then before you write your report I suggest you make a list of all of the facts and circumstances you plan to use to justify your actions. This will help immensely. When you write your narrative simply refer to the list and make sure every point makes its way into your report.

I cannot express enough how effective this technique is. Try it out and I guarantee you will articulate more facts and circumstances needed to win your case. The reason is because you're using all of your brain power on one narrow task, articulating facts and circumstances. On the other hand, when you dive right into writing a narrative, you have to divide your attention on other things like grammar, spelling, punctuation, sentence structure, and so forth.

Post-narrative Information

POST-NARRATIVE INFORMATION

Summary

Most reports should have a summary that states that you have satisfied the elements of the statutes for the offenses charged. A summary should not be another "synopsis" as discussed above. That would be repetitive and a waste of time. Most reports do not require a summary that repeats what happened. That may be helpful for college papers and so forth, but the vast majority of police reports are too short to require it.

Instead, use the summary to state that you have met the statutory requirements for the charged offenses. This serves two purposes. First, it reminds you of the criminal elements and it will confirm that you have provided sufficient evidence to prove your case. Second, it sends a strong message to the prosecutor that you feel confident you have a triable case.

Here's an example of a summary:

The defendant did commit the offense of Burglary-Battery-No Force Entry in violation of F.S.S. 810.02(2)(a) when he reached in the drive-thru window and struck the victim. The defendant did commit the offense of Battery-One Prior Conviction in violation of F.S.S. 784.03(2) when he intentionally struck the victim's face because he was dissatisfied with the service. The defendant was previously convicted of battery on August 25, 2015 (Orlando PD case #439320).

Here's another:

CONCLUSION

Due to the fact Christopher did willfully and unlawfully use force or violence against the person of another (Deanna) by slapping her with an open palm on the left side of her face and pulling her off the bed resulting in reddening to her back. Christopher was arrested for Domestic Battery, (1st)(M)-NRS 200.485.1A transported to County jail and booked without further incident.

******* End *******

And one more:

The defendant willfully left ███████████████████ at a closed police department with no one around, failing or omitting to provide the victim with the care, supervision, and services necessary to maintain physical or mental health while also failing to make a reasonable effort to protect the victim from abuse, neglect or exploitation of others. The defendant also neglected ██████████ and ██████████ by leaving them alone at their residence of ███████████████ with no adult supervision or care.

Now, some arrests are made to take care of problems for the night and evidence may not be sufficient for conviction. For example, you investigate a domestic and there is probable cause to arrest the husband, but the evidence is weak at best. You know that the DA will likely dismiss the charges. Here, you may not want to write a summary that seems to argue that your case is "trial ready." Instead, you just want to put the decision on the DA and let him or her make the decision (most likely dismiss).

For these reports, here is a sample summary:

"This report is being submitted to the DA for consideration of formal charges."

Report Writing Checklist

Straight-Forward Method to Writing Police Reports

In my opinion, most police report writing books are just condensed college English 101 books. Certainly, proper spelling and grammar are important for police reports and it must be taught. But I have NEVER seen a judge suppress evidence, or hold an officer liable, for bad spelling or grammar. Never!

Instead, I routinely see evidence suppressed and agencies collectively paying millions of dollars because police officers are not articulating the appropriate things in their reports. That's where this book comes in. I want to train you how to properly articulate. Fortunately, it's easy and straight-forward.

When writing reports you need to articulate (or prove) two things:

First, you need to prove the elements for every charged offense. That makes sense. If you arrest someone for DUI, then you need to provide evidence for every element of the offense. For example, what evidence do you have that the driver was in actual physical control? If you failed to articulate that element, the prosecutor could not win at trial.[1]

Second, how did you lawfully get your evidence? This is where search and seizure rules come into play. Remember, all warrantless searches and seizures are presumed unreasonable. Therefore, any evidence obtained without a search warrant will not come into trial unless you articulate an exception to the warrant requirement, such as consent or exigency.

That's it. Those two things are the key to winning hearings, trials, and lawsuits. Provide evidence for each element of the crime charged and articulate how you lawfully obtained your evidence. Do both and your report is bulletproof.

---

[1] Note: Idaho law has been used as a reference, which should be almost identical to your state's laws. Still, differences will exist so please adapt where required.

Completed Report Checklist

Use this checklist to confirm that you have articulated all of the elements of the crime and how you lawfully obtained your evidence. Download template at bluetogold.com/student

Step One: Offense(s) that need to be proven beyond a reasonable doubt:

☐Offense charged:_____

    ☐ Element One: The offense occurred within the officer's jurisdiction (just need to prove it happened within the state).

        ☐ Is it clear that that offense occurred inside your state?

    ☐ Element Two: When did the offense occur (prosecutor must prove that statute of limitations doesn't apply).

        ☐Is it clear when the offense occurred?

☐Element Three:_____

    ☐ Did you include evidence for this element?

    ☐ Is it clear how you lawfully obtained your evidence?

    ☐ Does your evidence include the suspect's in-custody testimony? If so, is it clear you had a Miranda waiver?

☐Element Four:_____

    ☐ Did you include evidence for this element?

    ☐ Is it clear how you lawfully obtained your evidence?

    ☐ Does your evidence include the suspect's in-custody testimony? If so, is it clear you had a Miranda waiver?

☐Element Five:_____

    ☐ Did you include evidence for this element?

    ☐ Is it clear how you lawfully obtained your evidence?

    ☐ Does your evidence include the suspect's in-custody testimony? If so, is it clear you had a Miranda waiver?

Note: Do this checklist until you know this process cold. Once you do, all you need is a piece of paper to write down the elements and evidence, along with what you need to articulate. It will become second nature and quick.

Serious Crime Pre-Report Writing Checklist

Use this checklist to remind you what needs to be articulated in your report. Use this checklist for serious or complex cases because it can be time consuming. Download template at bluetogold.com/student

Step One: Offense(s) that need to be proven beyond a reasonable doubt:

☐ Offense charged:_____

    ☐ Element One: The offense occurred within the officer's jurisdiction (just need to prove it happened within the state).

        ☐ Evidence:_____

        ☐ Evidence:_____

    ☐ Element Two: When did the offense occur (prosecutor must prove that statute of limitations doesn't apply).

        ☐Evidence:_____

        ☐Evidence:_____

    ☐Element Three:_____

        ☐Evidence:_____

        ☐Evidence:_____

        ☐Evidence:_____

    ☐Element Four:_____

        ☐Evidence:_____

        ☐Evidence:_____

        ☐Evidence:_____

Note: Step One provides an overview. Some crimes have three elements, others have seven, and so forth. Also, some elements will have one piece of evidence and others may have twenty. The point is you need to know what elements need to be proven and to isolate what evidence may be used to prove that element. Evidence can be used multiple times for different elements.

Step Two: Explain how you lawfully obtained your evidence:

☐ Evidence:_____

How did you obtain this evidence:

☐ Consent   ☐ Exigency   ☐ Abandoned Property

☐ Plain Feel   ☐ Plain View   ☐ Search Warrant

☐ Automobile Exception   ☐ Srch Incident to Arrest   ☐ Other

Identify why your search or seizure was reasonable:

☐Facts or Circumstances:_____

☐Facts or Circumstances:_____

☐Facts or Circumstances:_____

☐ Evidence:_____

How did you obtain this evidence:

☐ Consent   ☐ Exigency   ☐ Abandoned Property

☐ Plain Feel   ☐ Plain View   ☐ Search Warrant

☐ Automobile Exception   ☐ Srch Incident to Arrest   ☐ Other

Identify why your search or seizure was reasonable:

☐Facts or Circumstances:_____

☐Facts or Circumstances:_____

☐Facts or Circumstances:_____

Continue this process until you have all of your evidence identified and articulated.

Note: Do this checklist until you know this process cold. Once you do, all you need is a piece of paper to write down the elements and evidence, along with what you need to articulate. It will become second nature and quick.

Also, if you recover multiple pieces of evidence during a particular intrusion, you don't need to justify the recovery of each piece of evidence, as long as you articulate it correctly, all of the evidence found will be admissible.

Download the template from bluetogold.com/student

Definitions

Here are some common words or phrases used in this book along with their legal definition. Remember, these are general definitions and may not coincide with your state law.

Articulation: Articulation means to describe your actions in a clear and understandable manner. It means that the reader, whether judge or jury, can "feel" what happened on scene just like you experienced it. It means that they know why you did something. That's articulation.

Assault: (1) unlawfully attempts, with apparent ability, to commit a violent injury on the person of another; or

(2) intentionally and unlawfully threatens by word or act to do violence to the person of another, with an apparent ability to do so, and does some act which creates a well-founded fear in the other person that such violence is imminent.

Note, just an "apparent" ability is required, not an actual ability.

Battery: A "battery" is committed when a person:

(1) intentionally and unlawfully uses force or violence upon the person of another; or

(2) actually, intentionally and unlawfully touches or strikes another person against the will of the other; or

(3) unlawfully and intentionally causes bodily harm to an individual.

Constructive Possession: A person has constructive possession of something if the person knows of its presence and has the power and intention to control it.

Dating Relationship: "Dating relationship" is a social relationship of a romantic nature. Factors that you may consider in making this determination include:

(1) the nature of the relationship;

(2) the length of time the relationship has existed; and

(3) the frequency of interaction between the persons.

Deliver: The term "deliver" means the transfer or attempted transfer, either directly or indirectly, from one person to another.

Hazing: The word "haze" means to subject a person to bodily danger or physical harm or a likelihood of bodily danger or physical harm, or to require, encourage, authorize or permit that the person be subjected to any of the following:

(1) total or substantial nudity on the part of the person;

(2) compelling ingestion of any substance by the person;

(3) wearing or carrying of any obscene or physically burdensome article by the person;

(4) physical assaults upon or offensive physical contact with the person;

(5) participation by the person in boxing matches, excessive number of calisthenics or other physical contests;

(6) transportation and abandonment of the person;

(7) confinement of the person to unreasonably small unventilated, unsanitary or unlighted areas;

(8) sleep deprivation;

(9) assignment of pranks to be performed by the person.

Household Members: Persons are "household members" if they

(1) are married to each other;

(2) were previously married to each other;

(3) have a child in common, regardless of whether they have been married; or

(4) are cohabitating, regardless of whether they have married or hold themselves out as husband and wife.

Inhalant: A chemical substance capable of causing a condition or intoxication, inebriation, excitement, stupefaction or the dulling of the brain or nervous system as a result of the inhalation of the fumes or vapors of such chemical substances.

Lewd Conduct: To constitute lewd and lascivious conduct, it is not necessary that bare skin be touched. The touching may be through the clothing.

Mayhem: Every person who unlawfully and maliciously deprives a human being of a member of his body, or disables, disfigures or renders it useless, or cuts out or disables the tongue, puts out an eye, slits the nose, ear or lip, is guilty of mayhem.

Possession: A person has possession of something if the person knows of its presence and has physical control of it.

Premeditated: Premeditation means to consider beforehand whether to kill or not to kill, and then to decide to kill. There does not have to be any appreciable period of time during which the decision to kill was considered, as long as it was reflected upon before the decision was made. A mere unconsidered and rash impulse, even though it includes an intent to kill, is not premeditation.

Threatening: The word "threatening" means "statements where the speaker intends to communicate a serious expression of an intent to commit an act of unlawful violence to a particular individual or group of individuals."

Traumatic injury: This means a condition of the body, such as a wound or external or internal injury, whether of a minor or serious nature, caused by physical force.

Step Two: How Did You Get Your Evidence?

Consensual Encounters

Requirements

The most prevalent type of interaction between police officers and individuals is what is known as a consensual encounter. This kind of encounter is integral to community policing and investigative procedures, particularly in situations where the legal prerequisites for formal actions, such as reasonable suspicion or probable cause, are absent.

In a consensual encounter, officers engage with individuals without any specific pretext or legal justification required for more formal types of police stops. The nature of these encounters is such that individuals are approached based on voluntary compliance and are not legally obligated to respond to an officer's inquiries or remain in the conversation. The U.S. Supreme Court has recognized this practice within the bounds of the law, noting, "Police officers act in full accord with the law when they ask citizens for consent."[1]

It's crucial, however, for officers to ensure that the nature of the interaction remains clearly within the realm of a consensual encounter. This means that during the encounter, nothing should be communicated or implied by the officer's actions or words that would lead a reasonable person to conclude they are not at liberty to end the interaction and walk away.

Articulating this point is essential: officers must be able to convey, through their conduct, that the interaction is such that a reasonable person would feel they have the choice to leave or discontinue the conversation at any time. This can include, for instance, maintaining a non-threatening demeanor, avoiding the use of authoritative language that suggests compliance is compulsory, and explicitly informing the individual that they have the right to terminate the encounter at their discretion.

If an officer's actions or manner imply that the individual is not free to leave—for example, if the officer blocks the individual's path, uses an intimidating tone, or engages in actions suggestive of a formal detainment—then the nature of the interaction shifts away from a consensual encounter. This shift may necessitate the officer to then meet the more stringent legal standards associated with a detainment or arrest, such as establishing reasonable suspicion or probable cause.

In summary, the key to maintaining the integrity of a consensual police encounter lies in the officer's ability to articulate and demonstrate that any reasonable person in the individual's position would feel they are under no

---

[1] United States v. Drayton, 536 U.S. 194 (2002)

obligation to stay and engage with the officer, thereby preserving the voluntary nature of the interaction. This approach not only upholds individuals' constitutional rights but also fosters a sense of community trust and cooperation.

Here's what to articulate:

☐ Explain what you did that would cause a reasonable person to believe that he was **free to leave** or otherwise **terminate the encounter**. In other words, a reasonable person would have believed he was not being detained.

Articulation Examples

Example 1: Public Park Encounter

Narrative: On [Date], while on routine patrol at [Public Park's Name], I engaged in a consensual encounter with an individual, [Full Name], who was seated alone on a bench. Initially, the interaction was casual, with no intention of detainment. However, several behavioral cues raised my suspicion, leading to a shift in the encounter's nature.

Reasons for reasonable suspicion:

[Full Name] exhibited nervous behavior, including avoiding eye contact and providing evasive answers, which is often indicative of an individual hiding illicit activity.

They were seated in a secluded area known for recent drug transactions, increasing the likelihood of [Full Name] being involved in similar activities.

The individual's bag was excessively bulky and positioned to conceal its contents, which is a common tactic employed to hide contraband.

Upon mentioning the bag, [Full Name] displayed increased anxiety and was reluctant to discuss its contents, behavior often associated with individuals possessing illegal items.

The combination of [Full Name]'s non-coherent explanations, their location, and physical demeanor constituted a pattern consistent with drug-related offenses documented in the area.

Example 2: Community Event Scenario

Narrative: On [Date], during a community event at [Location], I initiated a friendly conversation with [Full Name], who was dressed inappropriately for the weather. The encounter, initially consensual, evolved as several factors contributed to my reasonable suspicion.

Reasons for reasonable suspicion:

[Full Name] was wearing a heavy, long coat in warm weather, which is commonly associated with concealing weapons or other illegal items.

There was a noticeable outline of a heavy object in the coat pocket, a common indicator of a concealed weapon.

[Full Name] exhibited unusual body language, such as stiffness and restricted movements, often linked with individuals carrying concealed items they wish to keep hidden.

They appeared unusually nervous during our conversation, particularly when I broached the subject of their attire, a behavior often correlated with individuals hiding contraband.

The event had heightened security due to recent threats, and [Full Name]'s attire and behavior were incongruent with typical attendees, aligning more with profiles of concern identified in recent security briefings.

Example 3: Neighborhood Patrol Incident

Narrative: On [Date], in [Neighborhood], I approached [Full Name] for a casual conversation after observing them peering into parked cars. What began as a consensual encounter changed when several aspects of [Full Name]'s behavior and circumstances led to reasonable suspicion.

Reasons for reasonable suspicion:

[Full Name] was walking along a street with a history of vehicle break-ins, pausing to look into cars, behavior often associated with casing vehicles for theft.

They provided inconsistent and nervous responses when asked simple questions about their activities, common in individuals engaged in or planning criminal activity.

[Full Name] possessed a small flashlight and was peering into cars during a time of low visibility, tools, and behavior consistent with vehicle burglary.

They had no reasonable explanation for being in the area and were unable to provide details about specific residences or individuals they were visiting.

The individual attempted to change their route and demeanor upon spotting law enforcement, a common reaction from individuals seeking to avoid police interaction due to potential criminal conduct.

Knock and Talks

Requirements

Engaging with a resident at their home without infringing on their Fourth Amendment rights requires adherence to certain protocols that respect individual privacy and societal norms. This practice, often referred to as a "knock and talk," is a permissible method for officers to gather information or make inquiries. The approach is akin to how any ordinary visitor, such as a door-to-door salesperson or a neighbor, might initiate a conversation. Below is an expanded explanation of the principles and justifications an officer might articulate when conducting a "knock and talk."

☐ **1. Utilizing Common Access Paths:** When I approached the residence, I consciously used the walkway commonly employed by the general public, such as delivery personnel, neighbors, or solicitors. This pathway, typically leading from the street or driveway directly to the front door, is universally understood to be acceptable for uninvited guests to approach without an explicit invitation. My decision to use this path was intentional, aiming to respect the resident's privacy and property, and to make my approach expected and non-threatening, consistent with societal norms.

☐ **2. Selection of the Door for Approach:** The residence featured multiple entry points. However, I opted for the [specific door] because [explain reason]. For instance, this door had a well-trodden path leading to it, was well-lit, featured a doorbell or a knocker, and had other indications of being a primary entrance for visitors. My choice was governed by a reasonable belief that this door was the customary point of contact used by other uninvited visitors, ensuring I did not intrude unexpectedly or in an uncommon manner into the resident's private space.

☐ **3. Adherence to Socially Acceptable Contact Protocols:** I initiated contact with the occupant using a standard, non-intrusive method, such as knocking or ringing the doorbell, to signal my presence. The time chosen for this interaction was deliberately within the hours generally considered appropriate for social visits, avoiding early morning or late-night disturbances. This consideration was crucial to respect the occupant's privacy and to align with typical social norms associated with uninvited guests.

☐ **4. Maintaining a Consensual Conversation:** Throughout the interaction with the occupant, I remained mindful to ensure the conversation's voluntary nature was clear. I avoided any language or behavior that could be construed as coercive or commanding. The occupant was not interrupted when speaking, and their willingness to engage was respected, emphasizing that they had the right to end the conversation at any point and retreat into their private residence without consequence.

☐ **5. Immediate Departure Post-Interaction:** Upon the conclusion of the conversation, whether initiated by me or the resident, I immediately and respectfully exited the property. I refrained from any further exploration of the premises, resisting any temptation to peer through windows, explore the property, or engage in any other actions that could be perceived as snooping. My departure was conducted promptly to respect the boundary of the private property and the occupant's personal space, ensuring no overextension of my presence beyond what was necessary for the initial, consensual interaction.

By adhering to these guidelines, law enforcement officers can conduct "knock and talk" sessions that respect citizens' rights and privacy while effectively gathering necessary information. This approach, when executed correctly, aligns with the Fourth Amendment's protections and helps foster a more trustful and cooperative relationship between law enforcement and the communities they serve.

Articulation Example

Example 1: Suspicious Activity Inquiry

Narrative: On [Date], at approximately [Time], we responded to a report of suspicious activity at [Address]. Upon arrival, my partner and I observed no immediate threat but decided to conduct a "knock and talk" for further investigation.

We approached the residence using the main pathway, identical to a route a regular visitor or delivery personnel might use.

We reached the front door, the most visible and conventional access point for guests, and knocked, adhering to the standard practice of social visitation.

The homeowner, [Homeowner's Name], answered the door. We identified ourselves, explained our presence, and asked if they had noticed any unusual activity recently. We emphasized that they didn't have to answer our questions and were free to end the conversation at any time.

[Homeowner's Name] voluntarily provided information about a suspicious vehicle they had seen in the neighborhood at night.

After gathering the information, we thanked the homeowner and immediately left the property along the same path we entered, ensuring not to linger or intrude on the homeowner's privacy.

Example 2: Noise Complaint Follow-up

Narrative: On [Date], we received a noise complaint from [Neighborhood] and proceeded to [Address] at approximately [Time] to investigate the source of the reported disturbance.

We approached the house using the clear, well-lit path leading from the sidewalk directly to the front door, avoiding any private areas of the property.

We knocked on the door in a manner consistent with a social visit, avoiding any authoritative or demanding gestures.

[Resident's Name] answered the door, and we identified ourselves and the reason for our visit. We communicated that the discussion was voluntary.

[Resident's Name] acknowledged the loud music and agreed to lower the volume. The interaction remained cordial and non-coercive throughout.

After resolving the complaint, we immediately departed without further exploration of the premises or additional inquiries.

Example 3: Drug Activity Investigation

Narrative: On [Date], following a tip-off about potential drug activity at [Address], my partner and I conducted a "knock and talk" at approximately [Time] to verify the information.

We walked up the driveway, a common route for any visitor, and proceeded to the front door, respecting the property's boundaries.

We knocked and announced ourselves, waiting for a response. When [Resident's Name] opened the door, we identified ourselves, explaining our concern about reported drug activity. We clarified that [Resident's Name] was not obligated to converse with us.

During the conversation, [Resident's Name] appeared nervous but consented to answer our questions. They denied any involvement in drug activity.

While [Resident's Name] was speaking, we observed what appeared to be drug paraphernalia in plain view behind them. This observation established probable cause for a search, leading to a shift from the "knock and talk" procedure to a lawful search under the plain view doctrine.

We secured a search warrant following the proper protocol before proceeding, respecting the resident's Fourth Amendment rights.

Requesting Identification

Requirements

Asking for ID and running a subject for warrants doesn't automatically convert the encounter into a detention. Hint, return ID as soon as possible so a reasonable person would still "feel free to leave."

Here's what to articulate:

- [ ] You **requested, (not demanded),** identification.

- [ ] You **returned** the identification as soon as practicable, otherwise a reasonable person may no longer have felt free to leave.

Articulation Example

"During the consensual encounter, I asked the subject for his identification. He said "Sure" and reached into his wallet and handed me his Nevada-issued driver's license. I provided his information to Dispatch and immediately handed his driver's license back to him."

Consent to Search

Requirements

Absent good reason, you should routinely seek consent to search a person or his property even if you have reasonable suspicion or probable cause. Why? Because this will add an extra layer of protection to your case. For example, let's imagine you have probable cause to search a vehicle for drugs but still receive consent to search, the prosecution essentially needs to prove that consent was freely and voluntarily given. If that fails, the prosecutor can fall back on your probable cause.

Here's what to articulate:

- [ ] Explain why the person's consent was **freely and voluntarily given**;

- [ ] If necessary, explain why he had **apparent authority** to give consent to search the area or item; and

- [ ] Describe how you did not exceed the **scope** provided, expressed or implied.

Articulation Examples

During a traffic stop: "While the driver was searching for his vehicle paperwork I shared with him that the area where the stop occurred was known for narcotic activity. I then asked if he had any contraband inside the vehicle and he said he did not. I then asked in a polite manner whether I could check, just to confirm. The driver immediately replied, "Sure, go ahead and opened his door to get out. Based on totality of the circumstances the driver freely and voluntarily provided me consent to search for narcotics."

During a street encounter: "During my consensual encounter with the subject, I asked in a polite manner whether I could search his backpack for weapons. The subject replied "I don't have any guns." I then repeated whether I could search, just to confirm. The subject then placed his backpack on the sidewalk and said I could search it. I then picked up the backpack and consensually searched it while the subject watched."

Consent to Search by Third-Party

Requirements

You may seek consent to search a residence from co-occupants. However, the situation changes when there is a present non-consenting co-occupant. If one occupant tells you to "Come on in and bring your friends!" and another yells "Get the hell out, I'm watching Netflix!" Well, you must stay out.

Here's what to articulate:

- [ ] The person providing consent has **apparent authority;**

- [ ] The consent provided was for **common areas,** areas under his **exclusive control,** or areas or things the person has **authorized access** to; and

- [ ] Finally, a **non-consenting** spouse or co-occupant with the same or greater authority **was not present.**

Articulation Example

"During my knock and talk with the suspect's roommate, I asked if I could come into the apartment and look around for any stolen property that I suspected was inside the apartment. The roommate said he did not have a problem if I came in and looked around.

I then entered the apartment and looked around. I walked down the common hallway and observed that the suspect's bedroom door was open. I did not open the door, nor did the roommate open the door. From this vantage point in the hallway, I saw a Sony Playstation on the suspect's bed with cords still attached. Next to the Playstation was a camouflage controller, like the one reported stolen.

I asked the roommate when he thought the Playstation was brought into the apartment. He told me he saw his roommate bring the items into the apartment last night, around 10 pm. This was approximately one hour after the reported burglary. Based on the totality of the circumstances [described in the entire report], I had probable cause that the Playstation was the one reported stolen. I did not enter the suspect's bedroom. Instead, I froze the apartment and immediately sought a search warrant."

Articulating Greater Auth. to Search a Place/Thing

Requirements

If the consenting party has greater authority over the residence or property, then police may rely on that consent. For example, if a casual visitor or babysitter objected to police entry, it may be overruled by the homeowner. Remember, you may not search personal property under the exclusive control of the visitor or babysitter.

Here's what to articulate:

- [ ] Explain why you thought the consenting party had **greater authority** over the area searched;

- [ ] If you were in doubt, tell the court you did not enter or walk through **any area** where the non-consenting occupant had **equal** or **greater authority**;

- [ ] It should be clear that you **did not search** any property under the **exclusive control** of the non-consenting occupant; and

- [ ] Finally, it should be clear that your search **did not exceed the scope** provided by the consenting occupant.

Articulation Example

"I asked the suspect's mother whether I could search her son's bedroom for narcotic evidence. The mother said yes, and began to open the son's bedroom door. The son then yelled at me and told me I could not search his room without a warrant. The mother again confirmed I could search her son's room without a warrant. Because the mother had greater authority over the room than her son, and her son was not paying rent, I searched the room based on the mother's consent."

Investigative Detentions

Involuntary Transportation

Requirements

You may voluntarily transport a person in a police vehicle. However, if the person is a suspect to a crime and you are transporting the person away from the place stopped, you need their consent or exigent circumstances.

Here's what to articulate:

☐ Make it clear to the person that he was **not under arrest**;

☐ If possible, seek his **consent** to transport him;

☐ If he denied consent, and **exigent circumstances** exist, transport the suspect and articulate why in your report.

Articulation Example

"I arrived at the location where the shooting occurred at approximately 0232 hours. I was told by Officer Bandiero that the victim was shot in the abdomen and his injuries were critical.

I spoke to a witness neighbor, self-identified as John Smith, who told me the shooter was a white male adult approximately 6' tall, skinny, and was wearing a gray jacket. After the shooting, Smith said the shooter walked southbound. Smith was unable to provide a more detailed description.

I drove around the area to search for the shooter. At approximately 0243 hours I observed a thin white male adult, approximately 5'6" walking eastbound on Adams Street. This suspect was not wearing a gray jacket.

I had reasonable suspicion to detain the suspect for the following reasons:

• I observed no other people walking in the area;

• The suspect's race and gender matched the shooter's;

• The suspect's height was similar to the shooter's;

• The suspect was walking eastbound on Adams Street, this path was going away from the scene, which is consistent with escape;

• The detention was made only 20 minutes after 911 received the call;

• The suspect was approximately seven blocks from the scene. An able person could travel seven blocks in 20 minutes;

• The suspect was not wearing a gray jacket, but it was possible he discarded it to change his appearance.

I asked the suspect if he would consent to be driven back to the scene for an in-field show-up The suspect said "No." I was informed the victim was about to be transported by ambulance to the hospital. Officer Bandiero informed me that the victim was alert and said he could identify the shooter.

Based on the totality of the circumstances, exigency existed to determine whether or not this suspect was the shooter.

I then told the suspect he was not under arrest but would be transported back to the scene for identification."

In-Field Show-Ups

Requirements

Courts are scrutinizing police identification procedures more than they have in the past. One reason is because research has shown that eyewitnesses are easily swayed by suggestive practices. For example, if police make an investigative detention on an armed robbery suspect, it would be improper to say to the victim, "We have the perpetrator, but we still need you to ID him."

You may also conduct a "show-up" between the suspect and witness under a few circumstances. Usually, these show-ups are conducted soon after the crime has occurred when police have detained a suspect (on-scene or in the vicinity).

Remember, it's vital that you stay as neutral and detached as possible when it comes to identification procedures.

Here's what to articulate:

- ☐ Explain that the procedure was not **overly suggestive** of guilt (e.g. not surrounding suspect with cops, if safe, removing handcuffs, and not telling the witness that the suspect is the perpetrator).

Articulation Example

"The witness was driven to my location for an in-field show-up. I minimized suggestive influences by doing the following:

- The suspect was not surrounded by police officers;

- No officer was holding the suspect during the in-field show-up;

- No officer made any accusatory comments about the suspect to the witness;

- The suspect was kept in mechanical restraints because the nature of the call, an armed robbery, was violent. Therefore, the restraints were not removed for both officer and suspect's safety;

- I told the witness that the person detained may or may not be the perpetrator and to base the identification on her memory, and not the present circumstances."

Unprovoked Flight

Requirements

If you are patrolling a "high crime" area and a person suddenly, and without provocation, runs upon seeing you, then these may be sufficient conditions to conduct an investigative detention in order to determine whether he is involved in criminal activity. Unprovoked flight, by itself, doesn't provide sufficient reason to conduct a patdown. You need to articulate something more, such as a known gang member, history of violence, or possible drug dealer (not just drug user).

Finally, this rule may also include wealthy areas where a rash of recent burglaries have occurred, or a business district when all the stores are closed. Articulate, articulate, articulate.

Here's what to articulate:

☐ Explain why the area was a **high-crime area**;

☐ State that upon seeing you or a readily-apparent police vehicle, the **suspect suddenly**, and **without provocation**;

☐ Engaged in a **headlong flight** commensurate with evasion; and

☐ Describe how you used a **reasonable amount of force** necessary to detain the suspect.

Articulation Example

"At approximately 0250 hours I was patrolling the Snake Pit Apartments, a complex known by me to be a high-drug activity area (explain why). I turned into the parking lot and saw a person leaning into a driver's side window of a vehicle. The vehicle appeared to be running because it had its lights on, and the brake lights were activated, likely because the transmission was in drive.

The suspect then turned around, saw my marked vehicle, and immediately ran away from my location. This flight was unprovoked. I did not have any emergency lights activated or give the suspect orders.

Based on the totality of the circumstances, I believed the suspect was engaged in illegal activity, likely a narcotic's transaction, and I pursued the suspect on foot."

Anonymous Tips

Requirements

You may make an investigative detention based on an anonymous tip if the information has some indicia of reliability and, where appropriate, the information is independently corroborated. The courts will use the totality of the circumstances test and it's vital you articulate all pertinent facts and circumstances in your report.

Here's what to articulate:

- [ ] Explain how the tip had an **indicia of reliability**; and
- [ ] If the tipster was truly anonymous (no way to contact), explain how the tip was **sufficiently corroborated** to show that the caller had information not readily available to the general public.

Articulation Example

Citizen informer who wants to remain anonymous: On March 25, 2020 at approximately 1230 hours dispatch received a call from W1, a citizen informer who wanted to remain anonymous out of fear of retribution. There was no evidence that W1 was involved in criminal activity or had a bias against the suspect.

W1 told dispatch that the suspect was currently selling narcotics in front of a house located at 555 Main Street. W1 said they knew this because three unknown suspects walked up to the suspect, reached in their pockets and pulled out money, and received a small item in return from the suspect. The unknown suspects did not stay longer than one minute during this transaction.

Based on the totality of the circumstances, W1 provided reasonable suspicion that the suspect was currently engaged in narcotics trafficking."

Tip from completely anonymous person: On March 25, 2020 at approximately 1230 hours the Anytown Police Department received an anonymous email tip from Crime Stoppers. The tipster left no contact information.

The anonymous tip stated that a suspect known as "TJ" was currently selling narcotics in front of a house located at 555 Main Street. The tipster said they knew this because three unknown suspects walked up to TJ, reached in their pockets and pulled out money, and received a small item in return from TJ. The unknown suspects did not stay longer than one minute during this transaction.

I then made a consensual encounter with a suspect matching TJ's description on the street corner. I approached the suspect and in a conversational tone asked if he was "TJ." The suspect said "Yes, what's up?" Based on this response, I now knew that the anonymous tipster had provided inside information. In particular, the general public would not know that this suspect went by the name "TJ."

Therefore, based on the totality of the circumstances, the tipster had provided information that was corroborated and I now had reasonable suspicion that the suspect was currently engaged in narcotics trafficking."

Handcuffing

Requirements

Handcuffing a suspect is a use-of-force. Therefore, it must be justified by a flight or fight risk. If not, the handcuffing could convert a detention into a de facto arrest (Latin for "arrest in fact). If so, then you would need probable cause and Miranda would apply.

Here's what to articulate:

- ☐ The suspect appears to be a **flight** risk; or
- ☐ The suspect appears to be a **danger** to himself or others.

Articulation Example

Detention of a shoplifting suspect in parking lot: "While speaking to the suspect in front of my patrol car he looked to the left and right two times. There was no obvious reason why he would be interested in anything going on around him. Based on my training and experience, the suspect was likely surveying his surroundings in order to find an escape path if he decided to flee on foot.

Based on this flight risk, I placed the suspect in mechanical restraints, checked for tightness, and double-locked them. I told the suspect he was not under arrest, but that he appeared to be considering fleeing on foot."

Detentions of Victims or Witnesses

Requirements

Generally, you cannot force a victim or witness to cooperate with your investigation. It is a "settled principle that while the police have the right to request citizens to answer voluntarily questions concerning unsolved crimes they have no right to compel them to answer."[1]

If you have located an un-cooperative witness, and they are vital for your investigation, then identify them. Give their information to the prosecutor and let him decide whether or not the witness should be subpoenaed.

Here's what to articulate:

- ☐ He is a **material witness** for your investigation;

- ☐ The detention should last no **longer than necessary** to determine his **identification** and whether he's **willing to cooperate** with your investigation;

- ☐ If the witness is **un-cooperative, identify and release**. Contact your prosecutor and get advice on how to proceed.

Articulation Example

Investigation of drive-by shooting: "While speaking with a neighbor-witness, he told me that he observed the drive-by shooting but did not want to get involved. I told him that I understood his concern for his safety and that I would include his information in my report as a confidential source, if desired. The witness still refused to provide me any information or his name because he feared retribution.

At this point in the investigation, this neighbor-witness was the only known observer to the shooting, and his information was considered vital for my investigation. Therefore, I ordered the witness to identify himself so I could provide the information to the prosecutor, who could then subpoena the witness if necessary."

---

[1] Davis v. Mississippi, 394 U.S. 721 (1969)

Pat Downs

Requirements

A patdown (or "Terry frisk") is a limited search of a suspect's outer clothing for weapons. You must articulate two things before you can conduct a patdown. First, the investigative stop itself must be lawful (based on individualized reasonable suspicion). Second, you must articulate that the person is armed and dangerous.

Additionally, if you feel an object that may be a weapon, but you're not positive, you may retrieve and inspect it.

Here's what to articulate:

- ☐ If the suspect is lawfully or unlawfully **armed with a weapon**, the weapon may be secured and a patdown of **outer clothing** conducted for additional weapons;

- ☐ If no weapon is visible, and you believe the suspect is **armed or dangerous**, a patdown of **outer clothing** may be conducted; or

- ☐ If the suspect was stopped for a violent crime or one involving weapons, an **automatic patdown** may be conducted.

Articulation Example

Detention of burglary suspect: "Based on my training and experience, those who commit burglaries typically carry tools to force entry into locked buildings. They also often carry weapons to overcome resistance while inside buildings. These tools and weapons present a danger to officers who detain suspected burglars.

Based on these considerations, I conducted a patdown of the suspect's outer clothing for weapons or tools that could be used as an improvised weapon. During my patdown I found..."

Plain Feel Doctrine

Requirements

Under the plain touch (or "feel") doctrine, you can seize any item that is immediately apparent as contraband or evidence if you are conducting a lawful patdown for weapons.

Here's what to articulate:

- ☐ Explain why you conducted a **patdown** for weapons;;

- ☐ Explain why when you felt the item, it was **immediately apparent** the item was contraband or evidence of a crime; and

- ☐ You did not build probable cause by **manipulating** the item.

Articulation Example

"During the patdown, I felt an item in the suspect's right front pant's pocket that was immediately apparent as a wrist watch. I believed this watch was evidence because:

- The suspect was detained because he was a suspect in an armed robbery;

- The victim said the suspect stole his wrist watch;

- This suspect had a wrist watch visible on his left wrist;

- In my experience, most people do not carry two wrist watches, especially where the second watch is concealed inside a pocket.

Based on the totality of the circumstances, I had probable cause to retrieve the watch as evidence of the armed robbery. After retrieving the watch, I discovered the watch was the same make and color as the one stolen from the victim."

Homes

Private Searches

Requirement

The Fourth Amendment controls government officials, not private actors. Therefore, there is generally no restriction on using information gained from a private citizen's search as long as he was not acting as a government agent. This is true even when the private search was conducted in a highly offensive, unreasonable, or illegal manner.

Remember, you may not exceed the scope of the original private search. The point here is that the suspect loses any reasonable expectation of privacy in those areas searched by the private person, so police can view the same evidence. But that doesn't mean the suspect lost his expectation of privacy in other, non-searched areas.

Here's what to articulate:

- ☐ It should be clear that you didn't **direct, encourage,** or **participate** in the original private search or seizure (if you did then all regular Fourth Amendment rules likely apply); And,

- ☐ Explain why the private person conducted the search. Was it with the **intent to help police** or **discover evidence**? Or some other personal motive?

- ☐ Finally, describe how your search, if any, didn't exceed the **scope** of the private search.

The first two factors must both be present for a private search to turn into a government search. The third factor will turn a private search into an unreasonable government search.

Articulation Example

"On March 25, 2020 at approximately 1230 hours I met with Richard Bronson in the police department lobby. Bronson told me that he was fed up with his roommate doing drugs in their shared apartment. Bronson said he went into his roommate's room this morning while the roommate was at work and searched for drug evidence. Bronson opened a red Adidas backpack and found a crystalline substance, packaged in a tiny zip-lock baggie. Bronson also observed a scale with white residue on it.

Bronson brought the backpack to the lobby to show me what he saw. I asked Bronson to show me only those things that he saw while in the apartment, and nothing else. Bronson opened the backpack and I looked inside, seeing the same evidence described above. Based on my training and experience the crystalline substance was methamphetamine because (explain why).

The search I conducted was the same as the one conducted by the suspect's roommate before he arrived at the station. Therefore, I did not expand the original private search and did not invade the suspect's reasonable expectation of privacy.

I seized the backpack as evidence and applied for a search warrant to search the entire backpack and the suspect's bedroom."

Serving Arrest Warrant

Requirement

An arrest warrant not only authorizes the suspect's arrest in public, but also authorizes you to enter the suspect's home, if he's home, to make the arrest. This is an extremely helpful option for arresting wanted suspects.

On the other hand, if the suspect is at a third-party's home, like a friend's house, you must apply for a search warrant.

Finally, the arrest warrant can be a bench warrant, misdemeanor traffic warrant, and of course, a felony warrant.

Here's what to articulate:

- [ ] Explain why you had **probable cause** that this was the **suspect's home**, and not a third-party's home (get a search warrant for third-party homes);

- [ ] Explain why you had **reason to believe** the suspect was currently home;

- [ ] Describe how you **knocked and announced** your authority and purpose (e.g., "Police, arrest warrant");

- [ ] If appropriate, explain why you conducted any **protective sweeps**; and

- [ ] It should be clear that you looked for the suspect in people-sized places, but did not search for evidence, but **plain view seizure applied**.

Articulation Example

"I confirmed that the fugitive had an active arrest warrant by [describe how you confirmed it].

I determine that 555 Main Street was the fugitive's current domicile because [describe how you confirmed it].

I had a reason to believe that the fugitive was presently home before the execution of the warrant because I observed a vehicle in the driveway belonging to the fugitive and lights were on inside the home, indicative of someone currently home.

I then executed the arrest warrant by [describe how you served it, including how you complied with knock and announce].

After approximately 30 seconds the fugitive did not answer the door. Based on the loud knocking and announcing and lack of response, it was reasonable to believe that the fugitive was denying entry into the home to effectuate the arrest.

We then forced entry into the home [explain how]. We searched for the fugitive and found him hiding under the bed in a spare bedroom."

Hot Pursuit

Requirement

There's a difference between "hot pursuit" and "fresh pursuit." Hot pursuit is when you're literally chasing a suspect who is trying to flee. You can follow him anywhere he goes. The law is not clearly established whether you can pursue a misdemeanor suspect into his home, though the answer is likely yes. Fresh pursuit, on the other hand, is where you have identified a suspect in a serious violent felony and are actively tracking him down. Once you find out where he's hiding you may make a warrantless entry and arrest him. If it's a non-violent crime, get a warrant.

Here's what to articulate:

☐ Explain that you were in **hot pursuit** (i.e. chasing) of a suspect believed to have committed an **arrestable offense** and that he ran into a home (a surround and call-out may also be done for officer safety purposes).

Articulation Example

"The driver fled the traffic stop on foot. I chased the suspect and observed him entering a home through the front door. The address was later confirmed as 555 Main Street. The driver committed an arrestable offense by fleeing a lawful traffic stop, which obstructed my duties by requiring me to capture the fleeing driver, instead of focusing on the reason for the stop.

I then entered the home under hot pursuit and searched the residence for the suspect. I found the suspect hiding in a hallway utility closet."

Fresh Pursuit

Requirement

There's a difference between "hot pursuit" and "fresh pursuit." Hot pursuit is when you're literally chasing a suspect who is trying to flee. You can follow him anywhere he goes. The law is not clearly established whether you can pursue a misdemeanor suspect into his home, though the answer is likely yes. Fresh pursuit, on the other hand, is where you have identified a suspect in a serious violent felony and are actively tracking him down. Once you find out where he's hiding you may make a warrantless entry and arrest him. If it's a non-violent crime, get a warrant.

Here's what to articulate:

☐ Explain how you were in **fresh pursuit** of the suspect after investigating a **serious violent crime** and quickly (usually no more than two hours) **traced the suspect back to his home.**

Articulation Example

"Based on my investigation, I had probable cause that the suspect fled the crime scene and retreated into his residence. Several officers and I made a forced entry into the suspect's residence to make an arrest for the following reasons:

- I had probable cause to believe that the suspect had committed a violent felony, namely a sexual assault;
- The suspect used a firearm during the felony;
- Surrounding the house while waiting for a warrant would have provided ample opportunity for the suspect to barricade, ambush, or offensively attack officers;
- Fellow officers watched security camera footage near the crime scene (describe where) and observed the suspect enter a vehicle and quickly speed away;
- The camera captured the suspect's license plate, which indicated the registered owner resided at 555 Main Street.
- Within approximately 90 minutes from the time of the sexual assault, officers arrived at 555 Main Street and observed the vehicle in the driveway;
- The residence had several interior lights on;
- Officer Johnson touched the car's hood and told me that it was hot, indicative of recent operation;

- I knocked on the door, stated that I was the police, and demanded that the suspect open the door;
- After approximately 20 seconds I heard noises coming from inside the house, but no effort was made to open the door;
- Based on the nature of the crime, the suspect probably had DNA evidence on his genital area and possibly under his fingernails. This evidence may be readily discarded with water;
- Additionally, it is probable that the suspect had trace evidence on his clothing. This evidence may be readily discarded in a washing machine.

Based on the totality of the circumstances, exigent circumstances existed to enter the residence and take the suspect into custody due to the danger presented to on-scene officers and the ready destructibility of evidence believed to be on the suspect's person and clothing."

Imminent Escape

Requirement

Under Imminent Escape, you may enter the home of a suspect who has retreated into their home after recently committing a serious crime and that they are likely to escape before the issuance of a warrant.

Here's what to articulate:

☐ Explain your **probable cause** that the suspect committed a serious violent crime, and you reasonably believe that he **would escape** before obtaining a warrant.

Articulation Example

"Based on my investigation (articulated elsewhere), I tracked the suspect back to 555 Main Street Apartment 102. I had probable cause that the suspect was presently inside his apartment because:

- Witness Smith stated that the suspect drove a late-model white Chevy Malibu bearing CA 123XYZ;

- Witness Smith stated that the suspect was a white male approximately 6' tall, weighing approximately 190 pounds;

- A records check of the vehicle revealed that the vehicle was registered to this apartment address just two months prior;

- A records check of the registered owner matched the characteristics provided by Witness Smith;

- The Malibu was in the apartment parking lot;

- I touched the Malibu's hood and perceived that it was very hot, indicating that it had been recently driven;

- Apartment #102 had lights on, despite it being just past midnight, when most people are sleeping;

I decided that the proper course would be to knock on the door and demand that the suspect come out. There was no time to obtain an arrest warrant because:

- I had probable cause that the suspect had committed an armed robbery, a serious violent crime;

- All available police resources were utilized;

- The apartment complex layout allowed the suspect to flee out the front or back patio area;

- Only two officers were available to take the suspect into custody;

- If a warrant was obtained, that would mean only one officer would be left on scene. This would be futile since it requires at least two officers to cover the back and front. This would also be dangerous because the suspect was considered armed and dangerous and a minimum of two officers should help capture this suspect if he chose to flee again.

[Now explain how you complied with knock and announce rules and how you made a forced entry if required.]

Warrantless Entry for Emergency

Requirement

Generally, you cannot make a warrantless entry into a home unless you have consent, recognized exception, or a warrant (C.R.E.W.). One of the recognized exceptions is if you have an objective reasonable basis for believing that an occupant requires emergency assistance, or an occupant is threatened with imminent injury. Remember, the scope of your entry is limited and you must leave, if demanded, once the emergency is over.

Here's what to articulate:

- ☐ Explain why you had **reason to believe** that any occupant was in immediate need of **medical assistance** or is threatened with **imminent injury**;

- ☐ Once the emergency is over, you must leave unless you receive consent or a warrant;

- ☐ Describe how you complied with **knock and announce** rules; and

- ☐ Finally, you **could not search for evidence**, but may make a plain view seizure.

Articulation Example

"On March 25, 2020 at approximately 1230 hours I was dispatched to a possible domestic battery at 555 Main Street. The nature of the call was [explain].

Upon arrival I walked up to the residence and could hear a male yelling. As I got closer I could see inside the front living room window. I observed a female adult falling back against the living room wall, as if pushed. The female hit her head on the wall and did not get back on her feet. The male was still yelling and said, 'You deserve that!'

I knocked on the front door and said, "Police, open the door." The male yelled back and told me to "Get a warrant." This reply meant the male was affirmatively refusing my lawful entry to protect occupants from further harm and to render medical aid.

I then checked the door and it was unlocked. I entered the house, still announcing my authority, and [explain the rest]."

Warrantless Entry to Prevent Destruction of Evidence

Requirement

Generally, you cannot make a warrantless entry into a home unless you have consent, recognized exception or a warrant (C.R.E.W.). One of the recognized exceptions is the warrantless entry to prevent the destruction of evidence. Remember, you cannot create the exigency. But simply knocking on the door does not count.

Here's what to articulate:

- ☐ Explain why you had **probable cause** that an occupant was or was about to **destroy evidence or contraband**;

- ☐ It should be clear you did not create the **exigency**;

- ☐ If there was no time to knock and announce, explain why;

- ☐ After you **secure** the home, you must get a warrant; and

- ☐ You **cannot search for evidence**, but may make a plain view seizure.

Articulation Example

"On March 25, 2020 at approximately 1230 hours my partner and I arrived at 555 Main Street, Apartment 102 to conduct a knock and talk with occupants. The reason for the knock and talk was because I got an anonymous tip that occupants at this apartment were in the process of packaging a large amount of heroin. The tipster stated that after the drugs were packaged, the drugs would be moved to another location. [you would go into more detail about the tip].

My partner and I were in plain clothes and knocked on the door. About ten seconds later an occupant opened the door about twenty inches and asked me what I wanted. I told him I was a narcotics detective and wanted to talk with him. The occupant immediately looked shocked, and began to stutter.

During this time I looked over the occupant's shoulder and saw a brown kitchen table with various items on it that were immediately apparent as drugs and paraphernalia [describe exactly what you saw and why].

The occupant then turned around and looked at the same table I was looking at. It appeared the occupant now knew I saw drugs and paraphernalia in plain view. The occupant then told me he had to go and immediately tried to close the door but my partner was able to prevent its closure.

Based on the totality of the circumstances, we had probable cause that narcotics trafficking was occurring inside Apartment 102 [explain everything, ideally with bullet point list].

Additionally, we also had probable cause that the suspect would be able to quickly remove heroin evidence by flushing it down the toilet. The suspect knew we were narcotics detectives, knew we saw the evidence in plain view, and would have a motive and opportunity to remove the evidence before a search warrant was received. This evidence would be the most important evidence for a trafficking charge. Therefore, we forced entry into the apartment and arrested the occupant for various drug offenses.

A protective sweep was conducted for other occupants, but none were found. While inside the apartment we did not search for any evidence.

I then secured the apartment from the outside with evidence tape, signed the tape with my initials, date, and time. I took a picture of the seal and included the picture in the search warrant affidavit."

Drug Buy: Entry with Arrest Team

Requirement

If you work undercover and enter a home to conduct a narcotic sale or purchase, you may make the arrest immediately, However, if you leave the residence and want to re-enter with an arrest team, you should articulate that the re-entry was "immediate" and necessary. Here's what to articulate:

- [ ] You are an **undercover officer** and conduct a narcotics transaction inside the home, you may leave and **immediately** re-enter with an arrest team when two conditions are met: First, there must be a **legitimate officer safety reason** why you had to leave first, instead of summoning the arrest team into the home and you must articulate that an **exigency exists**, such as destruction or loss of evidence.

Articulation Example

"After purchasing heroin from the suspect, I left the residence and met with an arrest team around the block. After coordinating our actions, we immediately approached the residence to effect the suspect's arrest. I did not arrest the suspect while initially inside the suspect's home for the following reasons:

- There were multiple suspects inside the home which meant that I was at a tactical disadvantage if I attempted to arrest the suspect without other officers;
- Drug dealers are usually considered armed and dangerous because they rely on self-help to protect their business. Therefore, drug dealers usually have weapons on their person or readily accessible,` and an immediate re-entry with an arrest team was the safest method to effectuate the arrest."

Protective Sweeps

Requirement

If you make a lawful arrest inside a home, you're allowed to conduct a protective sweep. There are three zones, or areas, you may search depending on the circumstances

Here's what to articulate:

☐ Zone 1: You may search the **immediate vicinity** where the suspect has access to weapons, evidence, or means of escape;

☐ Zone 2: You may search for **people** in people-sized places in the **same area** where the arrest occurs; and

☐ Zone 3: If you have reasonable suspicion that **dangerous confederates** are in the house, you may search for people in people-sized places and **detain the confederates** until the arrest is completed.

Articulation Example

Lunge area example: "While arresting Smith for domestic battery, I searched the area immediately within his lunge area. The arrest occurred in his bedroom, near a dresser. I opened the top drawer and saw a Glock handgun and seized it for officer safety."

Throughout house example: "While arresting Smith on a parole violation warrant I searched the entire house for dangerous confederates. I only searched people-sized places. The reason a protective sweep was conducted throughout the house was because:

• Smith was a documented active gang member;

• In my training and experience, gang members often have fellow gang members with them to help defend themselves against rival attacks;

• In my training and experience, gang members usually have weapons to attack rivals and to counterattack;

• The arrest took place in the afternoon, a common time when house guests are present;

During my protective sweep for confederates, I saw a sawed-off shotgun in plain view on top of the bed in the back bedroom. I seized the firearm as evidence against Smith."

Arrests

Collective Knowledge Doctrine

Requirement

The collective knowledge doctrine is one of the most powerful and important doctrines in law enforcement. It allows a single police officer to benefit from the collective knowledge of all officers working on a case. For example, if a detective asks another officer to search a vehicle for drugs, the search would be valid even if the officer conducting the search had no idea why he was authorized to search the vehicle, as long as the detective had probable cause.

The key with the collective knowledge doctrine is that officers communicate with each other. This doesn't mean officers have to know everything about the case, but they at least have to be working together.

Here's what to articulate:

- ☐ Describe how you and the other officer with the needed information were working on the **same investigation**, but maybe from different departments (i.e. task forces); and

- ☐ It should be clear that you both were in **communication** with each other related to the investigation.

Articulation Example

"I had probable cause to arrest Smith for narcotics trafficking for the following reasons:

- [Describe your own evidence];

- My partner spoke with the passenger and she said they were traveling to California to visit a sick relative. Yet, the driver told me they were traveling to Oregon to visit friends.

- My partner called a confidential reliable informant ("CRI") [must describe how they are reliable]. The CRI told my partner that he knew the driver because he purchased approximately two grams of heroin from the driver last week. [This information can be used later, even if you didn't know it at the time of arrest. This collective knowledge will be added to your P.C.]."

Un-arresting a Suspect

Requirement

There are two situations where you should un-arrest a suspect. The first scenario occurs when you arrest a suspect with probable cause, but later determine they are innocent. Constitutionally, you must un-arrest the suspect without unreasonable delay. The second scenario occurs when you (or supervisor) decide that continued arrest is not the best outcome for a case. This usually occurs before transportation to jail. As long as the initial arrest had P.C. and you acted reasonably (i.e. didn't arrest the person just to conduct a warrantless search or to embarrass the suspect), then it's permitted.

Either way make sure your report is rock solid and fully explain what you did and why you did it.

Here's what to articulate:

An in-custody suspect **must** be released:

- ☐ If you discover **new evidence** that clearly eliminates probable cause, the suspect must be released; or

- ☐ If you already booked the suspect, you must **notify the prosecutor** in writing.

An in-custody suspect **may** be released when:

- ☐ You made the arrest with the **intent to book** the suspect; and

- ☐ You learned of **new facts or circumstances** that warrant releasing the suspect with a citation or warning.

- ☐ Remember, you may not use an arrest-and-release as **loophole** to search the suspect without consent, exigency, or a search warrant.

Articulation Example

P.C. dissipates: "After I arrested the suspect I spoke with the apartment manager, self-identified as Steven Meyers ("Manager"). The Manager told me that the suspect I arrested was an apartment resident. I told the Manager that Jill Jones, the suspect's ex-girlfriend, told me that the suspect hasn't been to the apartment in over a month and that he unlawfully entered the apartment. The Manager said that he had complaints from other tenants that the suspect and his ex-girlfriend were arguing in the apartment last week. The Manager showed me an apartment lease which showed that the suspect was a tenant.

Based on this new information I no longer had probable cause that the suspect unlawfully entered the apartment. I explained to the suspect that he was being unarrested and he was free to leave."

Change in circumstances: After I arrested the driver for reckless driving his parents showed up on scene. The parents asked me whether they could take the driver home, instead of booking him into juvenile detention.

After speaking with Sgt. Johnson, I determined the best course of action would be to un-arrest the driver, cite him for reckless, and release him to his parents."

Committed in Your Presence

Requirement

If you have probable cause to believe that a person has committed even a very minor criminal offense in your presence, you may arrest the offender without violating the Fourth Amendment. Still, adhere to state law when making any arrest.

Additionally, most states require that misdemeanor crimes be committed "in the officer's presence." Under this requirement, you must perceive the acts or events which constitute the offense while they are taking place, and not just learn of them later or simply see evidence of the crime.

Here's what to articulate:

☐ You observed or experienced an **essential element** of the crime through **one of your senses**, namely sight, smell, hearing, or touch.

Articulation Example

"While walking around the corner I heard a male voice yell, "Fuck you." I then saw another male fall down from around the corner, and land on his back. The suspect who pushed the male victim was identified as John Smith.

I arrested Smith for a battery committed in my presence." [The officer did not need to see the suspect actually push the victim to make the arrest because the officer personally sensed (heard and saw) part of the event take place.]

Constructive Possession

Requirement

If you discover contraband inside a vehicle with multiple occupants and no one wants to claim ownership, you may charge all occupants with constructive possession. However, it's not enough that the contraband was simply in the vehicle. You also need to articulate why the arrested occupants likely knew the contraband was inside the vehicle. For example, if burglary tools were found in the trunk that would not permit you to arrest passengers without articulating that the passengers probably knew the tools were there.

Alternatively, you could choose which occupant is the most culpable (usually the driver) and only charge him. Nothing requires you to arrest everyone under constructive possession. If you could arrest all, you may arrest one.

Here's what to articulate:

- [ ] Describe why there was at least a **fair probability** that the arrested **occupant knew** contraband was inside the vehicle; and

- [ ] Explain how the occupant had the **intent** to possess the contraband in the past, present, or future.

Articulation Example

"I observed the two vehicles pull into the Chevron gas station. Both vehicles parked next to each other. None of the occupants went into the gas station or purchased fuel.

The Malibu's right front passenger exited the vehicle and walked over to the Ford F150 driver's side window. I used binoculars to see what transpired next: The passenger pulled a small item from his right front pocket, looked left and right, as if concerned about onlookers, and handed the small item to the driver. The driver then gave an unknown amount of currency to the passenger. The passenger immediately walked over to the Malibu, got in, and both vehicles began driving away, in separate directions.

Marked units then stopped both vehicles. [You would then describe any other evidence.]

Based on the totality of the circumstances, all suspects were arrested. The Malibu's right front passenger and the driver of the Ford F150 were arrested for actual possession of heroin [the evidence found post-arrest]. The driver of the Malibu was arrested for constructive possession because:

- He was within eye sight of the F150, and likely saw the same transaction I observed;

- He was with the passenger, who just sold narcotics to the other driver. In my training and experience, friends in the same vehicle usually know what another occupant is doing when he leaves the vehicle and returns shortly thereafter;

- During a search incident to arrest of the driver, heroin was found in his right front pocket;

- The driver was arrested for possessing narcotics in 2013;

- [And any other facts and circumstances help your case]."

Vehicles

Community Caretaking Stop

Requirements

You may make a traffic stop on a vehicle if you believe any of the occupants' safety or welfare is at risk. If you determine that the occupant does not need assistance, you must terminate the stop or transition the stop into a consensual encounter. Otherwise, you would need to articulate reasonable suspicion (e.g. DUI) or other criminal involvement (e.g. domestic violence).

Stranded motorists fall under this rule. It's not illegal for a vehicle to break down. So, you cannot demand ID, or otherwise involuntarily detain stranded motorists unless you can articulate that they are involved in criminal activity.

Remember, these are essentially "implied" consensual encounters unless you have a reasonable suspicion of criminal activity. In other words, if someone needs help there's a reason to believe they would have impliedly consented to police assistance. Once there's no more consent, the occupants must be left alone.

Here's what to articulate:

- ☐ Explain why you had a **reason to believe** one of the occupants needs police or medical assistance; and

- ☐ It should be clear that once you determine that no further assistance is required, the occupant was **left alone** or the encounter converted to a **consensual** one.

Articulation Example

"I stopped out with a stranded motorist on the shoulder of US95, just south of Jones eastbound exit. I observed that the hood of the vehicle was up.

I made contact with an occupant in the driver's seat. I asked the driver what the problem was with the vehicle. He told me that it just stalled and would not restart. I asked if he needed a tow service and he said that a friend of his was on the way with a tow strap.

I told the driver that if he needed anything else he could call 311. He said he had a cell phone and would do that if needed. I then walked away and turned off my forward facing emergency lights.

I walked back up to the passenger's side window and asked the driver in a conversational tone if I could ask him a few questions before I left. The driver immediately said, 'Sure.' [This is now a consensual encounter].

I asked the driver where he was heading to. He told me Reno. However, if true he would have been driving in the wrong direction. I asked what he planned to do in Reno and he said he was going to fish at Lake Tahoe. This also appeared odd because the fishing season didn't start until May, more than a month later."

I then politely asked the driver for consent to search his truck for contraband. He replied, 'Go ahead, I got nothing.'" [Describe what happened next].

Consent to Search Vehicle

Requirements

Absent good reason, you should routinely seek consent to search a person or his property even if you have reasonable suspicion or probable cause. Why? Because this will add an extra layer of protection to your case. For example, let's imagine you have probable cause to search a vehicle for drugs but still receive consent to search, the prosecution essentially needs to prove that consent was freely and voluntarily given. If that fails, the prosecutor can fall back on your probable cause.

Without consent your case depends entirely on articulating P.C. Why not have both? Plus, juries like to see officers asking for consent. Either way, do your prosecutor a solid and write a complete and articulate report.

Here's what to articulate:

- ☐ It should be clear that the driver or occupant had **authority to consent** to the search;

- ☐ Describe why consent was **freely and voluntarily given**;

- ☐ If during a traffic stop, it should be clear that seeking consent **did not unreasonably extend the stop** (the consent search itself can extend the stop, the legal question is did seeking consent unreasonably extend the stop); and

- ☐ Describe your search and how it **did not exceed the scope** of the consent provided, whether expressed or implied.

Articulation Example

Traffic stop example: "After the driver handed me his license and vehicle paperwork I asked in a conversational tone if there was any contraband inside the vehicle. The driver said no, there was nothing illegal in the vehicle. The driver immediately replied that I could search, if I wanted to. I said that would great and asked him to exit the car.

I then searched a backpack in the backseat and found the following evidence...."

Searching Vehicle for Weapons

Requirements

If you can reasonably articulate that any occupant is armed and dangerous, you may conduct a patdown for weapons. This applies even if the occupant is not suspected of any crime. Courts recognize the inherent danger of traffic stops and provide officers wide discretion when it comes to officer safety.

Here's what to articulate:

- ☐ Explain why you think any occupant is **armed or dangerous**;

- ☐ Describe how you patted down the suspect's **outer clothing**; and

- ☐ If the occupant has the ability to access the vehicle, describe how you searched inside the **passenger compartment**, including **containers**, where a weapon may be retrieved.

Articulation Example

Traffic stop of known gang member: While talking to the driver I observed a male passenger in the right passenger seat. The passenger was wearing red clothing in a manner consistent with active gang membership (describe why).

Based on the passenger's apparent affiliation with a violent street gang, I asked him to exit the vehicle. I then conducted a patdown of his person and no weapons were found. I then searched under his passenger seat, glove box, and center console. A firearm was located inside the center console, next to the passenger."

K9 Free Air Sniff

Requirements

Generally, there's no Fourth Amendment protection of the air around a vehicle. Therefore, you may run a drug detection canine around a vehicle during a traffic stop or when the vehicle is left in a place where you're lawfully allowed to be, like a parking lot. Canine alerts give you probable cause to either search it under the mobile conveyance exception or to apply for a warrant.

Keep in mind two important restrictions. First, do not intentionally command the canine to touch, climb or jump onto a vehicle as this would be a trespass in violation of U.S. v. Jones. Second, a canine sniff cannot extend the traffic stop unless you had reasonable suspicion for a drug offense.

Here's what to articulate:

If **no reasonable suspicion** exists that drug evidence is inside the vehicle, then:

- [ ] Describe how you conducted a **free air sniff** around the vehicle and there was **no break in the investigation** that led to the stop; and

- [ ] Finally, state that the free-air sniff did **not extend** the stop.

If **reasonable suspicion** exists that drug evidence is inside the vehicle, then:

- [ ] You may continue to **detain** the vehicle for a **reasonable amount of time** for a drug canine to arrive on scene; and

- [ ] You may conduct a **free air sniff around the vehicle**, but may not make a physical intrusion in or on the vehicle without probable cause.

Articulation Example

"While writing a warning to the driver for a broken windshield, and a citation to the passenger for not wearing a seatbelt, K9 handler Johnson arrived on scene. I spoke to Officer Johnson about the traffic stop and asked if he wanted to run his K9 around the vehicle. Officer Johnson stated that he would conduct a free air sniff. It should be noted that during my conversation with Officer Johnson, and while the K9 was deployed, I continued to write the citations."

Probable Cause Search

Requirements

If you have probable cause that a vehicle contains evidence or contraband, you can usually conduct a warrantless search.

Here's what to articulate:

- ☐ Describe why you had **probable cause** that contraband or evidence was inside the vehicle;

- ☐ It should be clear that the vehicle was not on **curtilage**;

- ☐ It should be clear that the vehicle appeared to be **readily mobile** (e.g. needs no more than gas, tires, or battery to become mobile); and

- ☐ Finally, it should be clear that you only searched those areas where the evidence could **fit** and would reasonably be believed to be **located** (e.g. can't search for open containers in engine compartment).

Articulation Example

Traffic stop: "While walking up to the passenger's window to make contact with the vehicle's occupants, I observed a gun magazine in the driver's door map pocket. I asked the occupants whether there was a weapon in the vehicle and they said no. I asked about the gun magazine and initially the driver stated he did not know what I was talking about. It is reasonable to believe that a driver would know that there was a gun magazine in plain view right next to him and therefore this response was likely intended to deceive. I asked the driver whether he was a convicted felon and he said he was. This response gave me probable cause to search the vehicle for additional gun parts, firearms, and ammunition.

I searched the vehicle and found a 9mm Glock handgun in the map pocket behind the front passenger's seat."

Inventory Search

Requirements

You may conduct an inventory search whenever you impound a vehicle. The main purpose of the inventory is specific—to protect your agency from false allegations about stolen or damaged property and to protect the owner from theft or damage caused by tow companies. These inventories are searches, but they are not for evidence. Of course, plain view applies.

You cannot use vehicle inventories as a pretext to search a vehicle for contraband. This behavior is unlawful and can result in the suppression of evidence and 1983 lawsuits. In other words, officers cannot use inventories as a loophole to the probable cause requirement. Additionally, some states require police to give on-scene owners the opportunity to take possession of their vehicle, if feasible, instead of towing it.

Here's what to articulate:

- [ ] Your agency has a **written inventory policy** which minimizes your discretion;

- [ ] The policy **describes** what may be searched and inventoried; and

- [ ] You should articulate a legitimate community caretaking rationale such as **blocking traffic, illegally parked, or risk of theft or vandalism**.

Articulation Example

"After the driver was arrested for DUI a tow-truck was called to impound the vehicle. Though the driver pulled into a parking stall at a checking cashing business, the area was known as a high-crime area with multiple incidents of stolen cars. Additionally, the suspect's right side window would not roll all the way up. This defect would allow anyone to readily access the car and steal any contents or the vehicle."

Container Searches

Searching Containers

Requirements

If you develop probable cause that a container (package, luggage, etc.) contains evidence or contraband, you may seize it in order to apply for a search warrant. Remember, the length of the detention must be reasonable and the more "intimate" the container, the more courts will scrutinize the detention.

Here's what to articulate:

- ☐ Explain how someone with apparent authority gave you **consent** to search; or

- ☐ Explain that he container was seized from a **vehicle** and your searched it under the Motor Vehicle Exception; or

- ☐ Explain why the container's contents were obvious under the **single purpose container** doctrine and only contraband would be in the container; or

- ☐ Explain how the container was in the suspect's possession and **searched incident to arrest**; or

- ☐ Explain why you conducted a legitimate **inventory**; or

- ☐ Explain why the container was searched under the **community caretaking** doctrine; or

- ☐ Explain why you had **exigent** circumstances.

Articulation Example

Consent: "I asked Smith if I could search his backpack for contraband. Smith immediately replied, "Sure, go ahead." I discovered the following contraband...."

Motor Vehicle Exception: While writing a warning ticket to the driver, K9 handler Johnson arrived on-scene at approximately 2340 hours. Officer Johnson then conducted a free-air sniff of the vehicle and his K9 alerted to the presence of contraband on the right passenger door area. A subsequent search of a backpack inside the vehicle revealed...."

Single Purpose Container: "During my consensual encounter with Smith I asked if he could remove his hands from his pockets for officer safety purposes. In response he voluntarily removed his hands and I then saw a tiny red balloon with a tied-off end fall to the ground. Based on my training and experience I immediately recognized that this item typically contains heroin. I then searched the container and confirmed it contained a black tar substance field-tested positive as heroin."

Search Incident to Arrest: "I saw Smith walking down Main Street with a red backpack on his shoulder. I knew Smith had an active arrest warrant for burglary out of the sheriff's department. I exited my vehicle and told Smith he was under arrest. After Smith was taken into custody (explain) I searched his backpack incident to arrest. I discovered the following contraband...."

Inventory: "Medical arrived and the injured pedestrian, later identified through a Nevada-issued driver's license as Smith, was voluntarily transported to Trinity Medical Center. Smith left a red backpack on the sidewalk. I retrieved Smith's backpack for safekeeping and conducted an inventory search per my agency's policy. I discovered the following contraband in plain view...."

Community Caretaking: "I arrived at the apartment to assist medical with rendering aide to the victim. Upon arrival I observed a white male adult, later identified as Smith through a Nevada-issued driver's license. Smith was unconscious but breathing. The cause of injury was unknown and I searched a red backpack next to Smith for medications, medical alert cards, and other causes for Smith's medical distress.

While searching the backpack I discovered a firearm and secured it. The serial number was in plain view and I ran it through dispatch. Dispatch revealed that the firearm was stolen....."

Exigency: "After Smith was arrested for outstanding warrants, he told me that he discarded a backpack under a bush before we made contact with him. Smith then volunteered that he had a pipe bomb in the backpack and was worried that an innocent person would find it and hurt themselves. The backpack was located and opened by our ordinance disposal team without a warrant. No warrant was obtained because all available resources were dedicated to road closures, notifying nearby residences, and ...."

Abandoned Property

Requirements

A person has no reasonable expectation of privacy in abandoned, lost, or stolen property. The courts have defined abandonment broadly for search and seizure purposes. Abandonment occurs whenever a person leaves an item where the general public (or police) would feel free to access it. It can also occur whenever a person disowns property.

Here's what to articulate:

- ☐ Explain why, based on the **totality of the circumstances,** a reasonable person would believe that it was **intentionally abandoned;** or

- ☐ Explain, based on the **totality of the circumstances**, that it appears the container was inadvertently abandoned, but the container's owner **would not have a reasonable expectation of privacy** that a member of the general public, including a police officer, would not search it; and

- ☐ If the container was inadvertently abandoned (e.g. accidentally left at the crime scene), your **scope of search** was similar to what a member of the public could have done (e.g. no forensic analysis).

Articulation Example

Intentional Abandonment: "During the vehicle pursuit the driver intentionally abandoned a red backpack on a public sidewalk. Based on the totality of the circumstances, the driver intentionally abandoned any privacy interest in the backpack because he intentionally left it on a public sidewalk, never came back for it, and never asked law enforcement about it. A search revealed...)

Inadvertent Abandonment During a Burglary: "During my search of the residence for evidence I found a black iPhone under the bushes, next to the window where the suspect(s) made entry into the home. I showed the homeowner the iPhone and she said it was not hers.

It appears that the phone may have been left by one of the suspect(s) during the burglary. Based on the totality of the circumstances, the iPhone was abandoned by the suspect because it was left at a crime scene, could be searched by any member of the public who found it, and the suspect made no effort to recover the iPhone.

The iPhone had no password protection and I searched it under the same conditions a member of the public could. I then observed the following (text messages, Facebook user, etc.)."

Interview and Interrogation

Ambiguous Invocations

Requirements

If a suspect intends to invoke his rights, he must do so clearly, directly, and unambiguously (You're not a mind reader for God's sake!). Suspects that merely mention abstract ideas about their rights will not be viewed as actually invoking them.

Here's what to articulate:

- [ ] Explain why the suspect made an **ambiguous statement** that did not clearly and directly invoke any Miranda rights;

- [ ] Note, if the suspect makes an ambiguous statement while seeking a Miranda, you have an obligation to clarify what they mean. However, if the ambiguous statement is made after a valid waiver is obtained, you may ignore the statement altogether. Still, best practice states that you should address it.

Articulation Example

While reading Miranda: "While reading Miranda to the suspect he said, 'Maybe I should get a lawyer.' I replied that it was totally up to him but that I would like to have his side of the story. The suspect said 'fine' and I continued reading the Miranda warnings. The suspect stated that he understood his rights. I then asked him what happened." Note: the type of waiver obtained here is called an "implied waiver" because the officer did not ask directly whether the suspect wanted to waive and speak to the officer. It's an effective technique but you must be prepared to articulate why the waiver was valid.

After obtaining a waiver: "During my questioning about the robbery the suspect mumbled that 'maybe' he should get an attorney. Since this statement was ambiguous I did not consider it an invocation, but vocalized inner thoughts."

Reinitiating After Invocation to Remain Silent

Requirements

If you begin the interrogation process, and the suspect tells you he does not want to talk, you must not question him further. The only exception would be public safety questions and routine booking questions. However, the Supreme Court said that after a "significant period of time" you may re-engage the suspect and seek a knowing and intelligent waiver as long as you "scrupulously honored" the suspect's prior invocation (left him alone).

Here's what to articulate:

- ☐ State that you **immediately ceased** the interview;

- ☐ Explain why you attempted to gain a fresh waiver after an appropriate "**cooling off**" period. In one case, the Supreme Court found a two-hour period sufficient.

Articulation Example

"On March 25, 2020, at approximately 0920 hours I attempted to obtain a Miranda waiver from Smith. However, Smith told me he did not want to talk and therefore invoked his right to silence. I immediately ceased the interrogation, sat up, handed my business card to Smith, and said if he changed his mind to call me. I then left and Smith was escorted back to his cell.

On March 25, 2020, at approximately 1530 hours I determined that sufficient time had elapsed and his invocation was scrupulously honored. I met with Smith again and asked in a conversational tone if he had changed his mind about talking about the case. Smith told me that he did change his mind and would like to talk about the case.

I then read Smith his Miranda rights from my pocket card. After each right I asked Smith if he understood, and Smith verbally responded that he did. After reading the card in its entirety I asked Smith if he was now willing to waive his rights and speak to me. Smith immediately replied that he wanted to talk to me."

Reinitiating After Invoking Right to Counsel

Requirements

If a suspect invokes his right to counsel, the interrogation must stop and there's no "cooling off" period while in custody. You're done. The only two exceptions are if he independently restarted the interrogation or you waited at least fourteen-days after he was released from custody.

Here's what to articulate:

- [ ] State that you **immediately ceased** the interview;

- [ ] State that you did not re-approach the suspect for an interview until **fourteen days** (or more) had elapsed.

Articulation Example

"After Smith invoked his right to counsel I immediately ceased the interview. I sat up, handed my business card to Smith, and said if he changed his mind to call me.

On March 25, 2020, at approximately 1230 hours I drove to Smith's house to try to interview him again about the robbery. At this point, Smith had been released from custody for twenty-one days. Therefore, his prior invocation of counsel no longer applied.

[Explain what happened next]

Suspect Reinitiates Interrogation

Requirements

If a suspect unambiguously invokes his Miranda rights, questioning must cease. However, it's possible for a suspect to change his mind after invocation if you keep the below guidelines in mind.

Here's what to articulate:

- ☐ Describe why the decision to revoke the invocation was **made freely by the suspect** and not because of undue police influence;

- ☐ Explain how the suspect wanted to **open up a general discussion** about the crime, as opposed to merely asking questions about routine matters regarding his custody; and

- ☐ State that you re-read Miranda and obtained an **express waiver**.

Articulation Example

"On March 23, 2020, at approximately 1230 hours I was told by Corrections Officer Johnson that David Smith wanted to talk to me. I arrived at the jail approximately twenty minutes later and had Smith brought over to the interview room.

When Smith arrived I asked him what he wanted to talk about. Smith replied that he wanted to talk about the case, and that he wanted to share his side of the story. I reminded Smith that he previously involved his right to an attorney (on March 21, 2020) and that I could not speak with him unless I got a valid Miranda waiver. Smith said that he would waive Miranda and talk.

I then read Smith his Miranda rights from my pocket card. After each right I asked Smith if he understood, and Smith verbally responded that he did. After reading the card in its entirety I asked Smith if he was now willing to waive his rights and speak with me. Smith immediately replied that he wanted to talk to me.

Smith independently re-initiated a general dialog about his criminal charges and provided an express waiver to Miranda. As a result, Smith lawfully revoked his prior invocation."

Public Safety Exception

Requirements

Miranda warnings are not required if you're asking legitimate public safety questions. The safety concern must be something that is pressing, and may cause substantial bodily harm or death.

Stay away from "why" type questions since that has to do with motive, not public safety. In other words, "why" questions usually violate Miranda. Also, remember that a suspect's answers to public safety questions may be used against him in court.

Here's what to articulate:

- [ ] You asked **legitimate public safety concerns** (e.g. Where did you toss the gun near the school?);

- [ ] You did not ask **"why"** type questions, but instead focused on pressing public safety concerns;

- [ ] Once the public safety questions have been handled, **Miranda** will be required for further questioning.

Articulation Example

"After Smith was taken into custody I searched him incident to arrest. I located an empty gun holster in his waistband. No firearm was found on his person and I was concerned that Smith had discarded a loaded firearm during the foot pursuit. If true, this firearm would pose a serious safety risk to the community since it could be discovered and taken by a child or a prohibited person.

Without Miranda, I asked Smith where he "ditched" the gun and he immediately told me in some bushes on Main Street. I asked for more specific information and Officer Johnson was able to locate and secure the firearm.

My questions were for Public Safety reasons. Smith was not asked any other non-booking questions without being properly advised of Miranda Warnings."

Step Three: What Crimes Need to be Proven?

Narcotics Offenses

Possession of a Controlled Substance

Criminal Elements

These elements must be proven beyond a reasonable doubt in court:[1]

☐ **State the approximate date (and time if known) when the offense occurred.**

- This confirms the offense occurred within the statute of limitations.

☐ **Specify where the offense occurred.**

- This establishes the court's jurisdiction over the offense.

☐ **Describe how the suspect actually or constructively possessed any amount of [name of substance]:**

- Actual possession is easy (e.g. was in his hand or pocket).

- For constructive possession, articulate the following:

  1. **Location**: Explain why you think the suspect knew the contraband was at the location/container found;

  2. **Ability**: Explain how the suspect had the ability to control the contraband; and

  3. **Intention**: Explain why you think the suspect had the intent to possess the contraband in the past, present, or future.

☐ **Explain why the suspect knew it was [name of substance] or believed it was a controlled substance:**

- **Suspect**: Explain why you think the suspect is involved in narcotics;
- **Environment**: Explain why the environment makes it more likely the suspect was involved in narcotics;
- **Reactions**: Finally, explain any reactions you observed that help prove the suspect knew he was committing this offense.

☐ **Finally, describe how you confirmed the evidence was a controlled substance:**

- Lab or field tested.

- Suspect admitted it was a controlled substance, etc.

---

[1] For a common statutory example, see I.C. § 37-2732

Sample Report

Note: An actual police report would typically contain additional detailed information. This sample is designed to emphasize the specific elements related to this particular crime and does not encompass other procedural aspects such as evidence collection, adherence to Miranda rights, and additional investigative measures.

On October 27, 2023, at approximately 9:15 PM, I, Patrol Officer Johnathan S. Reed, while on routine patrol, observed a male individual, later identified as John A. Doe (DOB 01/15/1990), seated in a parked vehicle outside 150 East Park Avenue. This area is known for frequent narcotics activity.

Upon approaching the vehicle, I detected a strong odor of what I recognized through my training and experience as marijuana. I observed Mr. Doe attempting to shove a small bag under the car seat, exhibiting nervous behavior, and sweating profusely, despite the cool evening temperature.

I asked Mr. Doe to step out of the vehicle and conducted a search due to probable cause based on the observed behaviors and the strong marijuana odor. A clear plastic bag containing a green leafy substance, believed to be marijuana, was recovered from under the driver's seat.

Constructive Possession Elements:

1. Location: Mr. Doe was the sole occupant of the vehicle where the marijuana was found. His immediate, nervous attempt to hide the bag when I approached serves as a behavioral indicator that he was aware of the contraband's presence.

2. Ability: As the driver and sole occupant of the vehicle, Mr. Doe had exclusive control over the vehicle's contents, including the area where the marijuana was located.

3. Intention: Mr. Doe's deliberate action to conceal the bag, coupled with his presence in an area known for drug activity, suggests the intent to maintain control over the substance. Additionally, Mr. Doe's criminal history, which I later learned includes prior narcotics offenses, reinforces this interpretation.

Knowledge of Marijuana:

1. Suspect's Background: A subsequent check into Mr. Doe's background revealed previous convictions related to narcotics, indicating familiarity with these substances, including marijuana.

2. Environment: The location is documented as a high-activity area for drug transactions. Mr. Doe's presence and subsequent behavior upon my approach are consistent with someone involved in such activities.

3. Reactions: Mr. Doe's behavior, including his attempt to hide the substance and his nervous demeanor, indicated knowledge of the illicit nature of his possession.

Confirmation of Marijuana:

I field-tested a sample of the recovered substance using a marijuana test kit I carry. The substance tested positive for the presence of THC, the active ingredient in marijuana. Mr. Doe, after being advised of his rights, admitted that the substance was indeed marijuana. He stated he had purchased it from an unknown individual at a nearby location.

Charges Filed:

Mr. Doe was placed under arrest and transported to the county jail. He was charged with possession of a controlled substance, in violation of the State Penal Code 11357(a).

The bag containing the suspected marijuana was seized as evidence and will be sent to the State Crime Lab for further analysis. A copy of the lab's report, once received, will be submitted to the prosecutor's office as part of the follow-up investigation.

End of Report

Possession of a Drug-Intent to Deliver/ Manufacture

Criminal Elements

These elements must be proven beyond a reasonable doubt in court:[1]

☐ **State the approximate date (and time if known) when the offense occurred.**

- This confirms the offense occurred within the statute of limitations.

☐ **Specify where the offense occurred.**

- This establishes the court's jurisdiction over the offense.

☐ **Describe how the suspect actually or constructively possessed any amount of a controlled substance:**

- Actual possession is easy (e.g. was in his hand or pocket).

- For constructive possession, articulate the following:

  1. **Location**: Explain why you think the suspect knew the contraband was at the location/container found;

  2. **Ability**: Explain how the suspect had the ability to control the contraband; and

  3. **Intention**: Explain why you think the suspect had the intent to possess the contraband in the past, present, or future.

☐ **Explain how the suspect intended to deliver or manufacture the controlled substance:**

- **Suspect**: Explain why you think the suspect is involved in delivering or manufacturing narcotics;

- **Environment**: Explain why the environment makes it more likely the suspect was involved in narcotics;

- **Reactions**: Finally, explain any reactions you observed that help prove the suspect knew he was committing this offense.

☐ **Finally, describe how you confirmed the evidence was a controlled substance:**

- Lab or field tested.

---

[1] For a common statutory example, see I.C. § 37-2732

Sample Report

Note: An actual police report would typically contain additional detailed information. This sample is designed to emphasize the specific elements related to this particular crime and does not encompass other procedural aspects such as evidence collection, adherence to Miranda rights, and additional investigative measures.

On November 5, 2023, at approximately 8:00 PM, I, Patrol Officer Alex K. Thompson, while on routine patrol, observed a known suspect, identified as Gary L. Martin (DOB 09/19/1987), engaging in a suspicious hand-to-hand transaction with an unidentified individual outside his residence at 735 Stonebridge Boulevard.

Delivery Elements:

Upon seeing the patrol car, Mr. Martin quickly handed a small package to the individual, hereafter referred to as Person Y, and attempted to walk back into his residence. I approached and detained Mr. Martin for investigation due to the suspicious nature of his interaction with Person Y. A patdown search for weapons led to the discovery of a bag containing approximately one pound of a green leafy substance in Mr. Martin's jacket pocket.

Constructive Possession Elements:

Location: Mr. Martin was at his known residence, and the rapid handover of the package suggests he was aware of its contents. His attempt to distance himself from the package indicates his knowledge of the contraband within.

Ability: The substance was found in Mr. Martin's direct possession, and he had immediate control over it, as evidenced by the hand-to-hand transaction observed.

Intention: Mr. Martin's swift behavioral change upon noticing law enforcement, coupled with his attempt to separate himself from the package and Person Y, indicates a clear intention to disassociate from the known illegal activity.

Delivery: Person Y, who received the package, was detained for questioning. Initial field interrogation revealed that Person Y had purchased marijuana from Mr. Martin.

Knowledge of Marijuana:

Suspect's Background: Mr. Martin has prior records for drug-related offenses, indicating a pattern of involvement in narcotics activities.

Environment: The transaction occurred at Mr. Martin's residence, located in an area known for high drug activity, making it plausible and more likely for such transactions to occur.

Reactions: Mr. Martin's immediate and furtive behavior, along with his attempt to physically distance himself from the observed transaction, indicated his awareness and acknowledgment of the illicit nature of his actions.

Confirmation of Marijuana and Quantity:

The green leafy substance found in Mr. Martin's pocket was field-tested and yielded a positive result for the presence of THC, consistent with marijuana. During the interrogation, after being advised of his rights, Mr. Martin confessed that the substance was marijuana. He admitted to possessing additional quantities and also to cultivating marijuana plants within his residence.

A warranted search of Mr. Martin's residence was conducted, leading to the discovery of a makeshift greenhouse containing 30 marijuana plants and various cultivation equipment. The seized plants and additional 5 pounds of packaged marijuana were tagged, logged, and sent to the State Crime Lab for further analysis.

Charges Filed:

Mr. Martin was arrested and charged with possession, manufacturing, and delivery of a controlled substance, specifically for possessing and delivering marijuana over the state law minimum and illegal cultivation of marijuana, in violation of the State Penal Code 11359, 11358, and 11360.

End of report.

Delivery of a Controlled Substance

Criminal Elements

These elements must be proven beyond a reasonable doubt in court:[1]

☐ **State the approximate date (and time if known) when the offense occurred.**

  ‣ This confirms the offense occurred within the statute of limitations.

☐ **Specify where the offense occurred.**

  ‣ This establishes the court's jurisdiction over the offense.

☐ **Explain how the suspect delivered any amount of a controlled substance to another person;**

☐ **Explain how the suspect either knew it was a controlled substance or believed it was a controlled substance:**

  ‣ **Suspect**: Explain why you think the suspect is involved in narcotics;

  ‣ **Environment**: Explain why the environment makes it more likely the suspect was involved in narcotics;

  ‣ **Reactions**: Finally, explain any reactions you observed that help prove the suspect knew he was committing this offense.

☐ **Finally, describe how you confirmed the evidence was a controlled substance:**

  ‣ Lab or field tested.

Sample Report

Note: An actual police report would typically contain additional detailed information. This sample is designed to emphasize the specific elements related to this particular crime and does not encompass other procedural aspects such as evidence collection, adherence to Miranda rights, and additional investigative measures.

On November 7, 2023, Officer Liam Scott and I observed a suspicious exchange between two individuals in an area known for illegal drug activities. Upon our approach, one individual fled, leaving Daniel Rodriguez on the scene. Due to certain behaviors exhibited by Mr. Rodriguez, we suspected he might be armed and potentially dangerous. These behaviors included:

• Excessive nervousness and repeated attempts to avoid eye contact.

---

[1] For a common statutory example, see I.C. § 37-2732

- Keeping his hands concealed within his jacket pockets despite instructions to make them visible.

- Visible signs of agitation upon the mention of a potential search.

- The area's reputation for drug-related and violent crimes, increasing the likelihood of individuals being armed.

- Mr. Rodriguez's known history with narcotics, often associated with carrying weapons for self-defense or criminal activities.

Investigative Actions:

Given the potential threat to public safety, we conducted a patdown for weapons. During this search, we discovered several small bags containing a white powdery substance in Mr. Rodriguez's possession. A field test identified the substance as cocaine.

Evidence Collection:

Approximately 18 grams of a substance confirmed as cocaine after laboratory testing.

Statements from witnesses at the scene who observed the exchange.

Arrest:

Mr. Rodriguez was arrested and informed of his rights. He was charged with the delivery of a controlled substance and transported to the precinct for further processing.

Conclusion and Next Steps: The arrest was based on direct and circumstantial evidence, including Mr. Rodriguez's behavior, the field test on the substance, and his known background. The case will be forwarded to the District Attorney's office for prosecution.

End of Report.

Trafficking in Controlled Substances

Criminal Elements

These elements must be proven beyond a reasonable doubt in court:

☐ **State the approximate date (and time if known) when the offense occurred.**

> ‣ This confirms the offense occurred within the statute of limitations.

☐ **Specify where the offense occurred.**

> ‣ This establishes the court's jurisdiction over the offense.

☐ **Explain how the suspect possessed, manufactured, or delivered at least [state law minimum] of heroin, cocaine, methamphetamine, etc. or any mixture or substance with a detectable amount of the controlled substance.**

> ‣ Actual possession is easy (e.g. was in his hand or pocket).
>
> ‣ For constructive possession, articulate the following:
>
> > 1. **Location**: Explain why you think the suspect knew the contraband was at the location/container found;
> >
> > 2. **Ability**: Explain how the suspect had the ability to control the contraband; and
> >
> > 3. **Intention**: Explain why you think the suspect had the intent to possess the contraband in the past, present, or future.

☐ **Finally, describe how you confirmed the evidence was a controlled substance:**

> ‣ Lab or field tested.

Sample Report

Note: An actual police report would typically contain additional detailed information. This sample is designed to emphasize the specific elements related to this particular crime and does not encompass other procedural aspects such as evidence collection, adherence to Miranda rights, and additional investigative measures.

On November 14, 2023, our patrol unit responded to an anonymous tip concerning suspicious activity on East Harbor Road, potentially related to drug trafficking. Upon arrival, we observed the suspect, Michael Thompson, engaging in behavior consistent with drug trafficking, including the transfer of large, suspicious packages from a vehicle into Warehouse 18.

Reason for Detention: Several factors led to the initial detention of Mr. Thompson:

- Known area for high drug activity.
- Transfer of large packages between vehicles, a common sign of drug trafficking.
- Nervous behavior and attempted evasion upon noticing law enforcement.

Detention and Preliminary Findings:

Given the suspicious nature of Mr. Thompson's activities, he was temporarily detained for questioning on the spot. During this brief detention, the following observations added to our suspicions:

Visible traces of a white powdery substance on Mr. Thompson's clothing, commonly associated with narcotics.

The suspect was unable to provide a reasonable explanation for his activities at the warehouse.

A police K-9 unit on the scene reacted positively to the scent of controlled substances emanating from Mr. Thompson's vehicle.

Obtaining the Warrant:

Based on the preliminary findings during Mr. Thompson's detention, we sought and obtained a search warrant for his vehicle and the warehouse.

Execution of Search Warrant and Evidence Collection:

Upon executing the search warrant, we uncovered:

Multiple packages containing approximately 5 kilograms of a substance, later confirmed as cocaine through laboratory testing.

Paraphernalia commonly used in the packaging and distribution of narcotics

Additional substances pending further lab analysis.

Surveillance footage from the warehouse, showing the suspect handling the contraband.

Arrest:

Mr. Thompson was formally arrested at the scene following the findings from the search. He was informed of his rights and the charges, including trafficking in controlled substances. He was then transported to the county jail for booking procedures.

Conclusion and Next Steps:

The evidence gathered at the scene, Mr. Thompson's behavior, and the substantial quantity of narcotics in his possession led to his arrest for drug trafficking activities. The case has been handed over to the narcotics unit for further investigation and will subsequently be forwarded to the District Attorney's office for prosecution.

End of Report.

Possession of Drug Paraphernalia

Criminal Elements

These elements must be proven beyond a reasonable doubt in court:[1]

- ☐ **State the approximate date (and time if known) when the offense occurred.**

  ‣ This confirms the offense occurred within the statute of limitations.

- ☐ **Specify where the offense occurred.**

  ‣ This establishes the court's jurisdiction over the offense.

- ☐ **Describe how the suspect actually or constructively possessed or used paraphernalia:**

  ‣ Actual possession is easy (e.g. was in his hand or pocket).

  ‣ For constructive possession, articulate the following:

    1. **Location**: Explain why you think the suspect knew the contraband was at the location/container found;

    2. **Ability**: Explain how the suspect had the ability to control the contraband; and

    3. **Intention**: Explain why you think the suspect had the intent to possess the contraband in the past, present, or future.

  ‣ If the charge was based on using paraphernalia, articulate what item was used and why it was not booked into evidence if applicable.

- ☐ **Finally, describe how the item was used for the purpose of cultivating, manufacturing, or ingesting an unlawful controlled substance:**

  ‣ Paraphernalia includes items that accomplish the following narcotic purposes:

    - Inhaling
    - Ingesting
    - Storing
    - Concealing
    - Analyzing

---

[1] For a common statutory example, see I.C. § 37–2734A

- Testing

- Growing

- Planting

- Manufacturing

- Processing

- Harvesting

- And so forth.

Sample Report

Note: An actual police report would typically contain additional detailed information. This sample is designed to emphasize the specific elements related to this particular crime and does not encompass other procedural aspects such as evidence collection, adherence to Miranda rights, and additional investigative measures.

On the evening of November 17, 2023, during a routine patrol, I observed an individual, later identified as Daniel Smith, seated in a parked vehicle on Westpark Avenue. Mr. Smith was engaged in suspicious behavior, prompting a welfare check.

Reason for Approach and Initial Observations:

Upon approach, I noticed:

- The suspect making sudden, furtive movements as I approached, common in individuals attempting to hide illegal substances or related items.

- The vehicle was filled with a cloud of smoke with a distinct chemical odor, commonly associated with the smoking of methamphetamine.

Interaction and Discovery:

During my interaction with Mr. Smith, I observed in plain view:

- A glass pipe commonly used for smoking methamphetamine on the passenger seat. The pipe contained residue consistent with burnt methamphetamine.

- The suspect displayed physical symptoms consistent with recent drug use, including dilated pupils, excessive sweating, and erratic behavior.

Given these observations, I believed Mr. Smith was in violation of drug paraphernalia possession laws.

Detainment and Search:

Mr. Smith was asked to step out of the vehicle and was temporarily detained for a search due to probable cause. During the search, no additional contraband was found. However, the glass pipe was seized as evidence, and

Charges and Evidence:

Mr. Smith was charged with possession of drug paraphernalia, specifically the glass pipe used for ingesting methamphetamine. The pipe was booked into evidence, and a residue swab was sent for laboratory testing to confirm the presence of illegal substances, supporting the charges filed.

Suspect's Constructive Possession:

Based on the circumstances, Mr. Smith had constructive possession of the drug paraphernalia as:

- The pipe was located within his immediate control and reach.

- He displayed knowledge of the pipe's presence, evidenced by his attempt to conceal it upon my approach.

- His physical symptoms and the environment indicated intent and actual use of the paraphernalia for illegal drug ingestion.

Conclusion:

The suspect was transported to the local precinct for booking procedures. The case will be forwarded to the District Attorney's office for prosecution, supported by the evidence collected and observations documented at the scene.

End of Report.

Obtaining Controlled Substance by Fraud

Criminal Elements

These elements must be proven beyond a reasonable doubt in court:[1]

☐ **State the approximate date (and time if known) when the offense occurred.**

  ‣ This confirms the offense occurred within the statute of limitations.

☐ **Specify where the offense occurred.**

  ‣ This establishes the court's jurisdiction over the offense.

☐ **The suspect knowingly and intentionally obtained possession of a controlled substance; and**

☐ **Used misrepresentation, fraud, forgery, or deception:**

  ‣ **Suspect**: Explain why you think the suspect had a motive to obtain narcotics ;

  ‣ **Environment**: Explain why the environment makes it more likely the suspect was involved in narcotics;

  ‣ **Reactions**: Finally, explain any reactions you observed that help prove the suspect knew he was committing this offense.

Sample Report

Note: An actual police report would typically contain additional detailed information. This sample is designed to emphasize the specific elements related to this particular crime and does not encompass other procedural aspects such as evidence collection, adherence to Miranda rights, and additional investigative measures.

While on duty, I was dispatched to Springfield Pharmacy regarding a potential fraudulent prescription. Upon arrival, I spoke with the pharmacist, Dr. Emily Clark, who presented a prescription form that she believed to be forged.

Obtaining Possession of Controlled Substance:

Dr. Clark informed me that a female individual, later identified as Ms. Sarah White, presented a prescription for Oxycodone, a Schedule II controlled substance. The prescription appeared to have an altered date and a suspicious signature that did not match the known signature of the listed prescribing physician, Dr. Alan Brown.

Use of Misrepresentation, Fraud, Forgery, or Deception:

---

[1] For a common statutory example, see I.C. § 37-2734(a)(3).

Suspect: Ms. White was questioned about the prescription. She claimed that she had recently undergone surgery and needed the medication for pain management. However, upon contacting Dr. Brown's office, his receptionist confirmed that Dr. Brown had not seen Ms. White for over a year and had not issued any recent prescriptions in her name. This suggests a motive for Ms. White to fraudulently obtain narcotics.

Environment: Springfield Pharmacy has recently reported an uptick in fraudulent prescriptions, particularly for narcotics. The pharmacy's location near a known drug trafficking area makes it a target for such fraudulent activities.

Reactions: When confronted about the discrepancies in the prescription, Ms. White became visibly agitated and attempted to retrieve the prescription form from Dr. Clark. She repeatedly insisted that the prescription was legitimate and became defensive when questioned further. Her reactions indicated a consciousness of guilt.

Action Taken:

Ms. Sarah White was placed under arrest for obtaining a controlled substance by fraud. The fraudulent prescription was seized as evidence and will be submitted for further forensic analysis. Dr. Emily Clark and Dr. Alan Brown will be contacted for official statements regarding the incident.

End of Report.

Possession of an Inhalant

Criminal Elements

These elements must be proven beyond a reasonable doubt in court:[1]

☐ **State the approximate date (and time if known) when the offense occurred.**

- ‣ This confirms the offense occurred within the statute of limitations.

☐ **Specify where the offense occurred.**

- ‣ This establishes the court's jurisdiction over the offense.

☐ **The suspect possessed an inhalant and used it in a manner that was not pursuant to the instructions or health care provider:**

- ‣ Actual possession is easy (e.g. was in his hand or pocket).

- ‣ For constructive possession, articulate the following:

  1. **Location**: Explain why you think the suspect knew the inhalant was at the location/container found;

  2. **Ability**: Explain how the suspect had the ability to control the inhalant; and

  3. **Intention**: Explain why you think the suspect had the intent to possess the inhalant in the past, present, or future.

☐ **The purpose was to be under the influence of such inhalant:**

- ‣ **Suspect**: Explain why you think the suspect had a motive to commit this offense;

- ‣ **Environment**: Explain why the environment makes it more likely the suspect was involved in this offense (e.g. back alley);

- ‣ **Reactions**: Finally, explain any reactions you observed that help prove the suspect knew the purpose of the inhalant was to be under the influence of it.

Sample Report

Note: An actual police report would typically contain additional detailed information. This sample is designed to emphasize the specific elements related to this particular crime and does not encompass other procedural aspects such as evidence collection, adherence to Miranda rights, and additional investigative measures.

---

[1] For a common statutory example, see I.C. § 18–1502B

While on routine patrol in the Warehouse District, an area known for illicit drug activities, I observed a male individual, later identified as Mr. Daniel Green, in a secluded spot behind a dumpster at the dead-end of 9th Street. He was alone and appeared to be engaging in the act of inhaling a substance from a small bag.

Possession and Misuse of an Inhalant:

Actual Possession: As I approached Mr. Green, I clearly observed that he held a canister of what appeared to be a common aerosol computer duster in his left hand. He was actively using the canister to spray into a small bag, which he then held to his face to inhale the contents. The canister was not being used for its intended purpose as per the manufacturer's instructions or for any legitimate medical treatment.

Purpose of Influence:

Suspect: Upon questioning, Mr. Green exhibited signs of intoxication, such as slurred speech and disorientation, which are consistent with the effects of inhaling psychoactive substances. He admitted to using the inhalant to achieve a "quick high" due to personal stress, indicating his motive for this offense.

Environment: The secluded nature of the location, known for drug-related activities, suggests it was chosen by Mr. Green to use the inhalant privately, undisturbed, and undetected. This context makes it more probable that he was involved in the offense at this location.

Reactions: Mr. Green's behavior upon my approach, including his startled reaction and attempt to quickly discard the canister and bag, indicated his awareness of the illegality of his actions. His immediate response and subsequent admission to using the substance for an intoxicating effect confirm that he understood the purpose of the inhalant was to be under its influence.

Action Taken:

Mr. Daniel Green was arrested for possession and misuse of an inhalant. The aerosol canister and bag were confiscated as evidence. Due to the health risks associated with inhalant abuse, Mr. Green was transported to the police station for booking and a mandatory health evaluation.

End of Report.

Property Crimes

Theft

Criminal Elements

These elements must be proven beyond a reasonable doubt in court:[1]

☐ **State the approximate date (and time if known) when the offense occurred.**

  ‣ This confirms the offense occurred within the statute of limitations.

☐ **Specify where the offense occurred.**

  ‣ This establishes the court's jurisdiction over the offense.

☐ **Describe the property and explain how the suspect wrongfully, took, detained, withheld, or deliberately killed (e.g. animal) it.**

☐ **Specify who the victim was.**

☐ **Explain why you believe the suspect did it with the intent to permanently deprive the owner of the property:**

  ‣ **Suspect**: Explain why you think the suspect had a motive to commit this offense;

  ‣ **Environment**: Explain why the environment makes it more likely the suspect was involved in this offense (e.g. back alley);

  ‣ **Reactions**: Finally, explain any reactions you observed that help prove the suspect knew the property was stolen (e.g. distanced himself from it).

☐ **Optional: If the value of the property constitutes a felony, articulate how the value of the property at the time of theft was at or above the required amount:**

  ‣ Based on the officer's training and experience (might not work);

  ‣ Officer got appraisal from trained person (e.g. pawn shop owner);

  ‣ Officer found a similar item on eBay or Craigslist, and so forth.

Sample Report

Note: An actual police report would typically contain additional detailed information. This sample is designed to emphasize the specific elements related to this particular crime and does not encompass other procedural aspects such as evidence collection, adherence to Miranda rights, and additional investigative measures.

---

[1] For a common statutory example, see I.C. § 18–2407

At approximately 3:15 PM, I responded to a call regarding a theft at Springfield Park. Upon arrival, I was approached by the victim, Ms. Jane Foster, who reported that her backpack, which had been next to her on a park bench, was missing.

Description of Property and Wrongful Taking:

Ms. Foster described the property as a blue canvas backpack containing various personal items, including a wallet, house keys, and a digital tablet. She reported that the backpack was taken when she briefly left the bench to retrieve her fallen hat, approximately five feet away. A witness, Mr. Mark Evans, stated he saw an individual, later identified as Mr. Kyle Brown, sitting near Ms. Foster. Mr. Evans saw Mr. Brown grab the backpack and hastily walk away once Ms. Foster was distracted.

Victim:

The victim, Ms. Jane Foster, is a resident of Springfield and was utilizing the park's facilities at the time of the incident.

Intent to Permanently Deprive the Owner:

Suspect: Upon detaining and questioning Mr. Brown, it was discovered that he had been recently evicted from his residence and was experiencing financial difficulties. These circumstances suggest a potential motive for the theft, as the stolen items could be sold for monetary gain.

Environment: The environment of the busy park, specifically the area around the central gazebo, is known for occasional petty thefts, particularly during peak hours when individuals can easily be distracted, and belongings can quickly be taken unnoticed.

Reactions: When approached by law enforcement, Mr. Brown appeared nervous and attempted to walk in a different direction. Upon stopping him for questioning, he denied any wrongdoing, but he was unable to explain the possession of Ms. Foster's belongings satisfactorily. His behavior, including his attempt to evade police interaction, suggests consciousness of guilt.

Action Taken:

Mr. Kyle Brown was placed under arrest for theft. Ms. Foster's backpack and its contents were recovered and returned to her. Mr. Brown was transported to the local precinct for further processing. Statements were taken from both Ms. Foster and Mr. Evans regarding the incident, and they were informed of the follow-up procedures.

End of Report.

Robbery

Criminal Elements

These elements must be proven beyond a reasonable doubt in court:[1]

☐ **State the approximate date (and time if known) when the offense occurred.**

> ‣ This confirms the offense occurred within the statute of limitations.

☐ **Specify where the offense occurred.**

> ‣ This establishes the court's jurisdiction over the offense.

☐ **Specify the victim and describe how the suspect took the property within the victim's immediate presence.**

☐ **Specify that this taking was against the victim's will.**

☐ **Explain how the suspect intentionally used force or fear of force to overcome the victim's will. Fear includes:**

> ‣ Threatened or actual injury to the victim or relative;
>
> ‣ Threatened or actual injury to a person in the victim's presence;
>
> ‣ Threatened or actual damage to the victim's property.

☐ **Finally, describe why there was intent to permanently to deprive the victim of the property:**

> ‣ **Suspect**: Explain why you think the suspect had a motive to commit this offense;
>
> ‣ **Environment**: Explain why the environment makes it more likely the suspect was involved in this offense (e.g. back alley);
>
> ‣ **Reactions**: Finally, explain any reactions you observed that help prove the suspect knew the property was stolen (e.g. distanced himself from the stolen property).

Sample Report

Note: An actual police report would typically contain additional detailed information. This sample is designed to emphasize the specific elements related to this particular crime and does not encompass other procedural aspects such as evidence collection, adherence to Miranda rights, and additional investigative measures.

---

[1] For a common statutory example, see I.C. §§ 18-6501 & 18-6502

At approximately 8:15 PM, I responded to a 911 call regarding a robbery that had just occurred on the 200 block of Cedar Avenue. Upon arrival at the scene, I found the victim, Mr. David Harris, who was visibly shaken and anxious. He reported that he had been robbed at gunpoint.

Victim and Immediate Presence:

Mr. Harris informed me that he was walking home when an individual, later identified as Mr. Lucas Grey, confronted him. Mr. Grey demanded Mr. Harris's backpack, which he knew contained a laptop, wallet, and various personal documents, as Mr. Harris had just left a nearby coffee shop where he was working on his computer.

Against Victim's Will:

Mr. Harris stressed that the backpack was taken forcibly and against his will. He was in a state of fear due to the weapon brandished by the suspect during the encounter.

Use of Force or Fear:

Mr. Harris detailed that Mr. Grey had threatened him with what appeared to be a handgun, creating immediate fear for his life. He complied with the demands by handing over his backpack out of fear of being shot. This threat of violence was a clear use of force to facilitate the robbery.

Identification and Location of the Suspect:

After collecting Mr. Harris's preliminary statement, I broadcasted a detailed description of the suspect to other units in the area. Approximately 25 minutes later, a patrol unit responded about a person matching the suspect's description in a nearby convenience store's parking lot.

I arrived at the location with backup, where we found Mr. Grey attempting to wipe down and abandon a backpack that matched the description given by Mr. Harris. The suspect was also wearing clothing that matched Mr. Harris's detailed description and was identified by a distinctive tattoo on his neck that Mr. Harris remembered and described.

Intent to Permanently Deprive:

Suspect: Upon searching Mr. Grey post-arrest, we discovered several pawn shop receipts and a small amount of cash, suggesting a motive of financial gain. Further investigation revealed that Mr. Grey had a history of similar offenses.

Environment: The incident's location, a dimly lit and secluded area of Cedar Avenue, is known for criminal activities, particularly in the evening hours. It is likely that Mr. Grey chose this location, expecting fewer witnesses and a lower police presence.

Reactions: When confronted, Mr. Grey exhibited signs of nervousness and attempted to flee, indicating a consciousness of guilt. After a brief chase, he was apprehended and, during questioning, became defensive and evasive in his responses.

Action Taken:

Mr. Lucas Grey was arrested and charged with armed robbery. The backpack, positively identified by Mr. Harris, was recovered with all contents accounted for and returned to the victim. Mr. Grey was transported to the station for booking, and Mr. Harris was assisted in filing a formal statement. He was also provided with contacts for emotional support and legal assistance as needed.

End of report.

Burglary

Criminal Elements

These elements must be proven beyond a reasonable doubt in court:[1]

☐ **State the approximate date (and time if known) when the offense occurred.**

- This confirms the offense occurred within the statute of limitations.

☐ **Specify where the offense occurred.**

- This establishes the court's jurisdiction over the offense.

☐ **Describe what place the suspect entered:**

- Burglary does not require "breaking" into the structure. Burglary occurs even if the door is open;
- Burglary is committed even if nothing or stolen or if the suspect abandons the effort after entry.

☐ **Explain why, at the time entry was made, the suspect had the specific intent to commit theft or another felony:**

- **Suspect**: Explain why you think the suspect had a motive to commit this offense;
- **Environment**: Explain why the environment makes it more likely the suspect was involved in this offense (e.g. back alley);
- **Reactions**: Finally, explain any reactions you observed that help prove the suspect had a guilty mind (e.g. running, hiding, evasive).

Sample Report

Note: An actual police report would typically contain additional detailed information. This sample is designed to emphasize the specific elements related to this particular crime and does not encompass other procedural aspects such as evidence collection, adherence to Miranda rights, and additional investigative measures.

At approximately 10:15 PM, the Springfield Police Department received a frantic call from Mrs. Linda Bishop stating that she had just walked into her home to find an unknown individual inside. She quickly retreated to her neighbor's house at 3721 Oakwood Lane, where she then contacted the authorities. It is unclear whether the unknown individual realized that Mrs.

---

[1] For a common statutory example, see I.C. § 18-1401

Bishop saw him inside her home. I was dispatched and arrived at the scene within two minutes of the call.

Description of Entry:

Mrs. Bishop informed me that she had returned home from a social gathering when she noticed her back patio door was not only unlocked but also partially open, with pry marks visible on the door frame. She had been certain of locking it before her departure. Upon entering her residence, she heard shuffling noises from her living room and walked in and saw the suspect, later identified as Mr. Tom Sanders, going through her personal belongings. Mrs. Bishop immediately turned around and left, without saying anything to the suspect.

Apprehension of the Suspect:

After gathering the initial details from Mrs. Bishop at her neighbor's house, I requested backup and approached the residence with caution. Upon arrival, lights were visible in the ground floor of the house, and slight movements could be seen through the curtains. As I approached the front entrance, the front door suddenly opened, and an individual, matching Mrs. Bishop's description of the suspect, attempted to exit, almost running into me.

Mr. Sanders immediately turned around, trying to flee back into the house. He was ordered to stop, but he ignored the commands and continued to evade capture. After a brief pursuit through the house, Mr. Sanders was apprehended in the backyard trying to scale the fence. He was handcuffed and informed of his rights before being escorted to the patrol car.

Intent to Commit Theft or Felony:

Suspect: A search incident to arrest of Mr. Sanders upon apprehension revealed he had several of Mrs. Bishop's possessions, including jewelry and a digital camera. He also possessed burglary tools, which, along with his prior criminal record for similar offenses, suggest a clear motive.

Environment: The recent string of burglaries in the Oakwood Lane area and the specifics of this case suggest a pattern. The secluded nature of the backyards and the cover provided by foliage seem to have been exploited in this and possibly other incidents.

Reactions: Mr. Sanders appeared startled when discovered, immediately attempting to flee the scene, indicating awareness and guilt regarding his actions.

Action Taken:

Mr. Tom Sanders was arrested and charged with burglary. The items found in his possession were identified by Mrs. Bishop as her property and were seized as evidence, pending return. Mr. Sanders was transported to the station for processing. A detailed statement was taken from Mrs. Bishop, and she was reassured that a thorough investigation would be conducted, including exploring potential links to other area burglaries. She was also provided with information about victim support services.

End of Report.

Possession of Burglary Tools

Criminal Elements

These elements must be proven beyond a reasonable doubt in court:[1]

☐ **State the approximate date (and time if known) when the offense occurred.**

- ‣ This confirms the offense occurred within the statute of limitations.

☐ **Specify where the offense occurred.**

- ‣ This establishes the court's jurisdiction over the offense.

☐ **Describe what tool or instrument the suspect possessed.**

☐ **Explain why the suspect possessed this item with the intent to break or enter a structure with the intent to commit a theft or another felony:**

- ‣ **Suspect**: Explain why you think the suspect had a motive to commit this offense;
- ‣ **Environment**: Explain why the environment makes it more likely that the suspect was involved in this offense;
- ‣ **Reactions**: Finally, explain any reactions you observed that help prove the suspect had a guilty mind (e.g. running, hiding, evasive).

Sample Report

Note: An actual police report would typically contain additional detailed information. This sample is designed to emphasize the specific elements related to this particular crime and does not encompass other procedural aspects such as evidence collection, adherence to Miranda rights, and additional investigative measures.

At around 11:30 PM, during a routine patrol near Pine Street and Carson Avenue, I noticed an individual, later identified as Mr. Frank Gibbs, exhibiting suspicious behavior close to "Harrison's Jewelry Store," which was closed for the day. This area has been under increased surveillance due to a recent series of break-ins.

Suspicious Behavior Observed:

Mr. Gibbs was standing in a shadowed alcove, partially concealed from the street view. He was dressed in dark clothing and a hood that obscured most of his face, which is not in itself a crime but was notable due to the cold weather being several weeks away. He seemed to be intensely focused on the jewelry

---

[1] For a common statutory example, see I.C. §§ 18-1406 & 18-1401

store's main entrance and side windows, occasionally shifting his position as if trying to get a better view or avoid passing headlights from the street.

As I observed discreetly from a distance, Mr. Gibbs took several steps toward the store, then quickly retreated into the shadows whenever a vehicle approached. He repeated this behavior several times, each time glancing around in a manner that suggested he was checking for witnesses or surveillance. It was particularly suspicious that Mr. Gibbs kept his right hand inside his jacket pocket in a way that suggested he was either protecting something or ready to use an object concealed there.

Description of Tool and Intent:

Upon my approach for a casual inquiry, Mr. Gibbs became visibly startled, further raising suspicion. I asked standard questions, and his responses were hesitant and contradictory, especially when I asked why he was out so late near a closed store. Noticing the pronounced bulge in his jacket pocket, I asked him to slowly reveal what he was concealing. He complied, and a standard lock-picking set, a mini crowbar, and a flashlight fell out of his pocket — tools associated with burglary.

Suspect's Background and Environment Context:

Mr. Gibbs has a record of prior offenses related to burglary, providing context to his presence in an area known for similar crimes. His inability to explain his behavior, combined with the specific tools in his possession and his focus on the jewelry store, strongly suggests his intent to commit a burglary.

Reactions:

Throughout the interaction, Mr. Gibbs displayed classic signs of nervousness, including avoiding eye contact, fidgeting, and providing quick, incoherent answers. When the conversation turned to his concealed items, he exhibited signs of defensiveness and apprehension, further indicating his awareness of wrongdoing.

Action Taken:

Given the circumstances, Mr. Frank Gibbs was arrested for possession of burglary tools with the apparent intent to use them. He was transported to the Springfield Police Station for further questioning and processing. The tools were tagged as evidence. A sweep of the surrounding area was conducted to ensure no additional accomplices were present and to check for any recent break-in attempts. Local businesses were alerted to the incident, encouraging heightened security measures.

End of Report.

Tampering with a Vehicle

Criminal Elements

These elements must be proven beyond a reasonable doubt in court:[1]

☐ **State the approximate date (and time if known) when the offense occurred.**

  ‣ This confirms the offense occurred within the statute of limitations.

☐ **Specify where the offense occurred.**

  ‣ This establishes the court's jurisdiction over the offense.

☐ **Describe how the suspect tampered with a motor vehicle.**

☐ **State that the suspect did not have consent from the owner or person in charge of the vehicle.**

☐ **Explain what crime the suspect intended to commit.**

Sample Report

Note: An actual police report would typically contain additional detailed information. This sample is designed to emphasize the specific elements related to this particular crime and does not encompass other procedural aspects such as evidence collection, adherence to Miranda rights, and additional investigative measures.

At approximately 2:10 AM, I responded to a disturbance reported by a local resident in the 1400 block of Hillcrest Avenue. The caller, Mr. Jonathan Rowe, reported seeing an individual meddling with a parked vehicle across the street from his residence.

Description of the Incident:

Upon arrival at the scene, I observed an individual, later identified as Mr. Dylan Murphy, situated in the driver's seat of a 2018 Blue Ford Explorer. The interior light of the vehicle was on, and the individual appeared to be attempting to manipulate the vehicle's ignition system using a screwdriver. The vehicle's window on the driver's side was partially shattered, suggesting how Mr. Murphy might have gained access.

I approached the vehicle and asked Mr. Murphy to step out. I inquired if he owned the vehicle, to which he responded negatively and became visibly nervous.

Lack of Consent:

---

[1] For a common statutory example, see I.C. § 49-230

Contact was made with the vehicle's registered owner, Mrs. Angela Thompson, who resides at 1432 Hillcrest Avenue. Mrs. Thompson confirmed that she had not given Mr. Murphy or any other individual permission to enter or tamper with her vehicle. She was unaware of the ongoing incident until I informed her.

Suspect's Intended Crime:

Given the circumstances — specifically, Mr. Murphy's attempt to manipulate the ignition system with a tool not designed for a vehicle — it is reasonable to deduce that he intended to commit motor vehicle theft. This assumption is based on the evidence at the scene and Mr. Murphy's lack of a reasonable explanation for his actions.

Action Taken:

Mr. Dylan Murphy was placed under arrest for tampering with a vehicle with the likely intent to commit theft. He was read his Miranda rights and transported to the Springfield Police Station for further processing. Mrs. Thompson was requested to inspect her vehicle for potential theft of items or additional damage and to provide a formal statement. The screwdriver was seized as evidence, and a local service was contacted to clean up the glass debris. Additional patrol units were notified to be vigilant of similar activities in the area.

End of Report.

Disposing of Property with Defaced Serial Number

Criminal Elements

These elements must be proven beyond a reasonable doubt in court:[1]

☐ **State the approximate date (and time if known) when the offense occurred.**

- ‣ This confirms the offense occurred within the statute of limitations.

☐ **Specify where the offense occurred.**

- ‣ This establishes the court's jurisdiction over the offense.

☐ **State how the serial number was defaced:**

- ‣ Defaced;
- ‣ Altered;
- ‣ Removed;
- ‣ Covered;
- ‣ Destroyed; or
- ‣ Obliterated.

☐ **Explain what the suspect knowingly did with the item with a defaced serial number:**

- ‣ Offered to trade, barter, or sell the item;
- ‣ Actually traded, bartered, or sold the item

☐ **Finally, explain why the disposition was done with the intent to deceive or defraud another person.**

Sample Report

Note: An actual police report would typically contain additional detailed information. This sample is designed to emphasize the specific elements related to this particular crime and does not encompass other procedural aspects such as evidence collection, adherence to Miranda rights, and additional investigative measures.

I responded to a call at approximately 4:45 PM from Mr. Greg Harwood, the proprietor of Quick Cash Pawn Shop at 4772 South Plaza. Mr. Harwood

---

[1] For a common statutory example, see I.C. § 18-2410

reported a suspicious incident involving a potentially defaced serial number on a Sony PlayStation console brought in by a customer.

Description of the Defacement:

Upon my arrival, Mr. Harwood presented the Sony PlayStation in question. I observed that the area where the serial number should typically be located was heavily marred and scratched to the point of illegibility. It appeared the serial number had been deliberately destroyed to obscure the console's origin or true ownership.

Circumstances of the Incident:

Mr. Harwood recounted that a man, later identified as Mr. Terry Bolton, had entered the shop with the intent to pawn the Sony PlayStation. As part of routine verification, Mr. Harwood inspected the console for its serial number. Upon discovering the defacement, he confronted Mr. Bolton about the irregularity. Mr. Bolton, seemingly caught off guard, became extremely agitated and fled the store, leaving the PlayStation behind.

Discovery of the Actual Serial Number:

Suspecting the console might be stolen, I initiated a more thorough investigation. In collaboration with Mr. Harwood, we powered on the PlayStation and navigated its system settings. We discovered that the console's digital system information still contained its original serial number, which hadn't been erased or altered. This digital serial number was noted for further investigation.

Intent to Deceive or Defraud:

The intentional defacement of the physical serial number, combined with Mr. Bolton's abrupt and suspicious departure from the scene, strongly suggests an attempt to deceive or defraud. It is common for individuals in possession of stolen goods to alter or destroy serial numbers to prevent the items from being traced back to their owners. The discovery of the intact digital serial number provides a critical lead in tracing the console's legal ownership and determining whether it was involved in any thefts or burglaries.

Action Taken:

Given Mr. Bolton's flight from the pawn shop, an arrest warrant was issued for his arrest on suspicion of defacing property identifiers with the intent to deceive or defraud. The Sony PlayStation has been seized as evidence, and its digital serial number will be used to investigate its recent history and legal ownership.

Mr. Harwood provided a formal statement and has cooperated fully by providing surveillance footage of the incident, potentially aiding in Mr. Bolton's identification and subsequent apprehension. Further inquiries will be conducted to ascertain the PlayStation's origin and whether Mr. Bolton can be linked to any recent criminal activities involving burglary or theft.

End of Report.

Theft by Deception

Criminal Elements

These elements must be proven beyond a reasonable doubt in court:[1]

☐ **State the approximate date (and time if known) when the offense occurred.**

> ‣ This confirms the offense occurred within the statute of limitations.

☐ **Specify where the offense occurred.**

> ‣ This establishes the court's jurisdiction over the offense.

☐ **Explain how the suspect obtained or exerted control over the property that was owned by another person.**

☐ **Explain why the suspect knew one or more of the following:**

> ‣ The suspect created or confirmed another's false impression, knowing the impression was untrue;
>
> ‣ The suspect failed to correct the false impression that was created previously by the suspect;
>
> ‣ The suspect prevented another person from accessing information about the property;
>
> ‣ The suspect sold property without disclosing that another person or company had a lien or security interest in the same property;

☐ **Finally, explain why the deception was done with the intent to deprive another person of property.**

Sample Report

Note: An actual police report would typically contain additional detailed information. This sample is designed to emphasize the specific elements related to this particular crime and does not encompass other procedural aspects such as evidence collection, adherence to Miranda rights, and additional investigative measures.

At approximately 3:15 PM, I received a distress call from the Department of Motor Vehicles (DMV) located at 3050 Westridge Boulevard. The caller, an employee of the DMV, reported a distraught customer, later identified as Ms. Brenda Walsh, who had discovered she was potentially the victim of theft by deception involving a vehicle purchase.

---

[1] For a common statutory example, see I.C. § 18-2403(2)(a)

Upon my arrival at the DMV, Ms. Walsh was highly agitated and explained that she had recently purchased a 2010 Kia Sorento car from a private seller, Mr. Jason Hartley. The transaction occurred an hour earlier that day in the DMV parking lot, where Mr. Hartley presented documents that appeared to confirm his ownership of the vehicle. Ms. Walsh paid $5,000, believing the transaction was legitimate.

Deceptive Practices:

Ms. Walsh's predicament came to light when DMV officials, during the registration process, discovered discrepancies in the vehicle's paperwork. A quick check revealed that the car had been reported stolen.

When Ms. Walsh contacted Mr. Hartley from the DMV, putting him on speakerphone so I could listen in, he maintained his innocence and quickly ended the call, and would not answer again, failing to correct the false impression he had created. Additionally, the address on the paperwork was found to have no association with Mr. Hartley which further proves his intent to deceive.

Mr. Hartley's actions and use of falsified documents prevented Ms. Walsh from accessing accurate information regarding the vehicle's legal status. This helps prove that Mr. Hartley knowingly sold the stolen vehicle using falsified documents, thus creating and confirming a false impression of legitimate ownership.

Intent to Deprive:

Mr. Hartley's actions—providing falsified ownership documents and selling a stolen vehicle—clearly indicate his intent to deceive Ms. Walsh and unlawfully profit from the sale, fully aware of the vehicle's true status.

Action Taken:

After confirming the vehicle's status with the DMV and central police databases, I informed Ms. Walsh that the car she had purchased was indeed stolen and that she had been a victim of fraud. The vehicle was legally seized at the DMV parking lot and towed for impoundment and further forensic analysis.

Mr. Jason Hartley is now a suspect in a theft by deception case. An arrest warrant has been issued, and efforts to locate him are ongoing. Ms. Walsh provided a detailed statement and was reassured that the department would conduct a thorough investigation. She was also advised to maintain all records of communication with Mr. Hartley and any additional documentation related to the purchase as they are integral to the case.

The DMV was instructed to provide any CCTV footage available from the time Ms. Walsh was on the premises, potentially capturing any part of her interaction with Mr. Hartley in the parking lot. The lawful owner of the vehicle is being contacted to inform them of the recovery of their property.

End of Report.

Theft by False Promise

Criminal Elements

These elements must be proven beyond a reasonable doubt in court:[1]

- ☐ **State the approximate date (and time if known) when the offense occurred.**
  - ‣ This confirms the offense occurred within the statute of limitations.
- ☐ **Specify where the offense occurred.**
  - ‣ This establishes the court's jurisdiction over the offense.
- ☐ **Describe how the suspect obtained or exerted control over the property that was owned by another person.**
- ☐ **Explain how the suspect did so pursuant to a scheme to defraud by representing that the suspect or another person would in the future engage in particular conduct.**
- ☐ **Next, explain why the suspect knew this representation was untrue.**
- ☐ **Finally, explain why the false representation was done with the intent to deprive another person of property.**

Sample Report

Note: An actual police report would typically contain additional detailed information. This sample is designed to emphasize the specific elements related to this particular crime and does not encompass other procedural aspects such as evidence collection, adherence to Miranda rights, and additional investigative measures.

At approximately 1:30 PM, I responded to a call from a Ms. Linda Ferguson, who claimed to be the victim of theft by false promise. The incident reportedly took place at Main Street Coffee, where Ms. Ferguson met with the suspect, identified as Mr. Carl Jenkins, regarding a business proposal.

Obtaining Control Over Property:

Ms. Ferguson explained that two weeks ago, she was contacted by Mr. Jenkins, who proposed investing in a series of local real estate ventures with the promise of significant returns. On December 12, 2023, they met at the coffee shop, where Mr. Jenkins presented a portfolio of properties he claimed to be involved with, along with testimonials from previous 'satisfied investors.' Convinced by the proposal and the evidence presented, Ms. Ferguson wrote a

---

[1] For a common statutory example, see I.C. § 18–2403(2)(d)

check for $20,000 as an initial investment, which Mr. Jenkins deposited into his account.

Scheme to Defraud:

According to Ms. Ferguson, Mr. Jenkins promised to use the funds to secure a new property and begin development, assuring her of a 50% return on investment within three months. He stressed the urgency, claiming the opportunity was time-sensitive and would not be available for long.

Untrue Representation:

Ms. Ferguson became suspicious when, upon further personal investigation, she found that the properties in Mr. Jenkins's portfolio were not under his name, nor were they up for sale. Additionally, the individuals listed as 'previous investors' were unreachable or reported no knowledge of Mr. Jenkins's ventures. When she confronted Mr. Jenkins for explanations, he became defensive, refused to provide any verifiable evidence of his investments, and stopped all further communications with Ms. Ferguson.

Intent to Deprive:

It became evident that Mr. Jenkins's representations were false and that he had no ongoing real estate ventures as claimed. His actions, including the presentation of false information and cutting off communication when confronted, indicate a clear intent to defraud Ms. Ferguson. He deceived her into handing over her money, fully knowing that his promises of investment and returns were fictitious.

Action Taken:

Mr. Carl Jenkins was arrested on charges of theft by false promise. He was read his Miranda rights upon arrest and refused to talk. Ms. Ferguson was advised to compile all communications, documents, and any other evidence related to her interactions with Mr. Jenkins, as they will be crucial in the legal proceedings. The bank was contacted to place a hold on the check, though it was found that the amount had already been withdrawn by Mr. Jenkins.

The investigation is ongoing, with efforts to uncover any additional fraudulent activities involving other citizens and to determine the extent of Mr. Jenkins's deceptive practices.

End of report.

Theft by Extortion

Criminal Elements

These elements must be proven beyond a reasonable doubt in court:[1]

☐ **State the approximate date (and time if known) when the offense occurred.**

 ‣ This confirms the offense occurred within the statute of limitations.

☐ **Specify where the offense occurred.**

 ‣ This establishes the court's jurisdiction over the offense.

☐ **Describe how the suspect caused the victim to deliver property to the suspect or another person.**

☐ **Explain how the suspect did so by creating a fear that if the property were not delivered then the suspect or some other person would do one or more of the following:**

 ‣ Physically injure some person in the future;

 ‣ Damage property;

 ‣ Engage in criminal conduct;

 ‣ Accuse a person of a crime or cause criminal charges to be filed against such person;

 ‣ Expose a secret or publicize an asserted fact, whether true or false, which would tend to subject a person to hatred, contempt, or ridicule;

 ‣ Testify or provide information or withhold testimony or information about another person's legal claim or defense;

 ‣ Abuse a public position of trust in order to adversely affect another person;

 ‣ And so forth.

☐ **Finally, explain why the extortion was done with the intent to deprive another person of property.**

Sample Report

Note: An actual police report would typically contain additional detailed information. This sample is designed to emphasize the specific elements related to this particular crime and does not encompass other

---

[1] For a common statutory example, see I.C. § 18-2403(2)(e)

procedural aspects such as evidence collection, adherence to Miranda rights, and additional investigative measures.

At approximately 11:15 AM, I responded to a distress call from a Mr. Daniel Richmond, residing at 5500 Willow Lane. Upon my arrival, Mr. Richmond, visibly shaken, reported that he had been the victim of an extortion scheme executed by an individual known to him as Mr. Victor Sullivan.

Delivery of Money Under Duress:

Mr. Richmond recounted that Mr. Sullivan had approached him approximately two weeks prior with detailed knowledge about a past incident in Mr. Richmond's life. Specifically, Mr. Sullivan revealed that he knew about a prior, undisclosed bankruptcy due to gambling debts that Mr. Richmond had hidden from his employer, family, and the public. This bankruptcy occurred five years ago and was settled privately without alerting Mr. Richmond's current employer, a financial institution where such information would undoubtedly lead to his dismissal.

Creation of Fear:

Mr. Sullivan, exploiting the situation, threatened to:

Expose a Secret: He planned to reveal Mr. Richmond's concealed bankruptcy and gambling issues by sending the documented proof to his employer, family, and local media outlets. This exposure would not only tarnish Mr. Richmond's professional reputation but also cause severe personal and familial distress.

Accuse of a Crime: Mr. Sullivan also threatened to accuse Mr. Richmond of embezzlement, asserting that he had fabricated evidence suggesting Mr. Richmond funded his gambling habit with embezzled money from his workplace.

Abuse of Trust: Given Mr. Richmond's role as a financial advisor, such revelations would be career-ending, and the breach of trust with both his employer and clients would be irreparable.

Under substantial stress and fear of the repercussions, Mr. Richmond agreed to Mr. Sullivan's demand for $50,000 in exchange for Sullivan's silence. The exchange occurred at Mr. Richmond's residence, where he handed over the money. Mr. Richmond then secretly called the police and we arrived minutes later.

Intent to Deprive:

The explicit threats made by Mr. Sullivan and his demand for money under such conditions clearly indicate his intent to exploit Mr. Richmond's vulnerability for financial gain. Mr. Sullivan's knowledge of the secret, his fabrication of additional accusations, and his calculated approach in demanding hush money confirm his objective was to unlawfully profit from Mr. Richmond's dire situation.

Action Taken:

Upon gathering this information, I spoke with Mr. Victor Sullivan. Mr. Sullivan denied making threats and said that Mr. Richmond owed him $50,000 but could not explain why such a large amount of money was owed. I place Mr. Sullivan under arrest on charges of theft by extortion, informing him of his Miranda rights and he demanded a lawyer. The cash amounting to $50,000 was recovered from Mr. Sullivan's possession and taken as evidence. Mr. Richmond was advised to consolidate all related communications, such as text messages or emails, that could substantiate the extortion threats.

The investigation is proceeding, with an inquiry into Mr. Sullivan's background for prior similar offenses. Mr. Richmond was recommended to initiate legal procedures for a restraining order against Mr. Sullivan and ongoing support during the upcoming legal processes.

End of Report.

Possession of Stolen Property

Criminal Elements

These elements must be proven beyond a reasonable doubt in court:[1]

- [ ] **State the approximate date (and time if known) when the offense occurred.**
  - ‣ This confirms the offense occurred within the statute of limitations.

- [ ] **Specify where the offense occurred.**
  - ‣ This establishes the court's jurisdiction over the offense.

- [ ] **Describe how the suspect knowingly received, retained, concealed, or disposed of the property.**

- [ ] **Explain why the suspect knew the property was stolen by another or under such circumstances as would reasonably induce the suspect to believe the property was stolen.**

- [ ] **Describe how you confirmed the property was stolen.**

- [ ] **Finally, explain why this was done with the intent to permanently deprive another person of property.**

Sample Report

Note: An actual police report would typically contain additional detailed information. This sample is designed to emphasize the specific elements related to this particular crime and does not encompass other procedural aspects such as evidence collection, adherence to Miranda rights, and additional investigative measures.

At around 2:45 PM, while on routine patrol, I observed a suspicious exchange between two individuals at the corner of 5th Street and Elm Avenue. The individuals, one of whom was later identified as Mr. Thomas Barker, appeared to be engaged in a rapid, covert transaction characterized by a noticeable level of nervousness and urgency, not typical of a standard legal sale. The second individual handed over what appeared to be a high-value item, later confirmed as a Rolex watch, in a manner that suggested an attempt to avoid drawing attention.

Several factors heightened my suspicion:

Behavior and Demeanor: Both individuals frequently looked around, a common sign of nervousness or fear of being observed. Their body language

---

[1] For a common statutory example, see I.C. § 18-2403(4)

was tense, and they engaged in minimal conversation, which is unusual for a legitimate transaction of high-value goods.

Location and Setting: The transaction occurred in an open, public space where such exchanges are uncommon. Typically, legitimate sales of expensive items like watches are conducted in secure environments, not on a street corner. This setting, coupled with their behavior, was a strong indicator of a potentially illicit activity.

Nature of the Exchange: The quick handover of the item, with no formalities such as inspection or exchange of documentation, was atypical of a lawful sale. The seller's haste to depart the scene post-transaction was also concerning.

Given these observations, I found sufficient cause for an investigatory stop to assess the legality of the transaction and the origin of the item in question.

Receiving and Retaining Stolen Property:

Upon approaching Mr. Barker for questioning, I noticed he was attempting to conceal the watch in his pocket hastily. When asked about the item, Mr. Barker claimed he had just purchased the Rolex for $100. Given the known value of such items, this claim immediately seemed implausible and prompted further investigation.

Knowledge of Stolen Property:

When questioned about the low price and the hurried nature of the transaction, Mr. Barker became notably evasive and contradictory in his responses. He initially claimed ignorance about the origin of the watch but then admitted that the price and behavior of the seller led him to believe the item might be stolen.

Confirmation of Stolen Property:

A quick serial number check via our precinct database confirmed the watch was indeed reported stolen during a recent burglary. The victim, Mrs. Sarah Jennings, had described the item in detail, and the serial number matched her report.

Intent to Deprive:

Mr. Barker's willingness to purchase an expensive item under such dubious circumstances, along with his attempts to conceal the watch and his awareness of the likelihood of it being stolen, demonstrate his intent to knowingly possess stolen property. His actions deprived the rightful owner, Mrs. Jennings, of her property, and he showed no intention of attempting to return the item or report his suspicions to the authorities.

Action Taken:

Mr. Thomas Barker was placed under arrest for possession of stolen property. He was informed of his Miranda rights upon arrest. The Rolex watch was seized as evidence and will be returned to Mrs. Jennings after the necessary procedures are completed. Mr. Barker was transported to the precinct for further questioning.

Mrs. Jennings was contacted about the recovery of her property and was relieved to hear of its impending return. She will be asked to provide additional information to confirm the watch's ownership officially.

End of Report.

Theft of Lost Property

Criminal Elements

These elements must be proven beyond a reasonable doubt in court:[1]

- ☐ **State the approximate date (and time if known) when the offense occurred.**

  ‣ This confirms the offense occurred within the statute of limitations.

- ☐ **Specify where the offense occurred.**

  ‣ This establishes the court's jurisdiction over the offense.

- ☐ **Describe how the suspect exercised control over the property.**

- ☐ **Specify who actually owned the property.**

- ☐ **Explain one of these:**

  ‣ Why the suspect knew the property was lost or mislaid;

  ‣ How it was delivered to the suspect by mistake;

  ‣ Why the suspect would know that the property delivered was not actually intended (e.g. erroneous one million bank dollar deposit).

- ☐ **Explain why you think the suspect did not take reasonable steps to return the property to the owner.**

- ☐ **Finally, explain why this was done with the intent to permanently deprive another person of property.**

Sample Report

Note: An actual police report would typically contain additional detailed information. This sample is designed to emphasize the specific elements related to this particular crime and does not encompass other procedural aspects such as evidence collection, adherence to Miranda rights, and additional investigative measures.

At approximately 3:15 PM, I responded to a report received from one Ms. Diane Reynolds, who claimed that her property, a diamond bracelet, had been stolen. Ms. Reynolds reported losing the bracelet earlier that day while at Monroe Park. She noticed the loss only after leaving the park and promptly returned to search for it, with no success.

Exercising Control Over Property:

---

[1] For a common statutory example, see I.C. § 18-2403(2)(c)

Security footage from the park confirmed Ms. Reynolds' account, showing her visibly distressed, searching around the area where she was sitting. The same footage revealed an individual, later identified as Mr. Gregory Thompson, watching Ms. Reynolds from a distance. After Ms. Reynolds momentarily left the area, presumably to seek help, Mr. Thompson approached the spot where Ms. Reynolds had been searching and was seen on camera picking up the bracelet, examining it, and then pocketing it before quickly leaving the park.

Ownership of Property:

The bracelet, described in detail and substantiated with photographs by Ms. Reynolds, has been confirmed as a family heirloom. The images provided matched the item Mr. Thompson was seen finding in the security footage.

Knowledge of Lost Property:

Mr. Thompson's actions, as captured on the footage, indicated he was aware of Ms. Reynolds' distress and her active search for the lost item. His decision to retrieve and pocket the bracelet after Ms. Reynolds left, coupled with his prior observation of her, suggests he knew the item was lost and of significant value.

Failure to Take Reasonable Steps:

Despite clear evidence of understanding the situation, Mr. Thompson made no effort to alert Ms. Reynolds of his find, nor did he attempt to turn the bracelet over to park authorities or local law enforcement. Instead, his swift exit from the park following the retrieval of the bracelet suggests a deliberate avoidance of responsibility and an intention not to return the item.

Intent to Deprive:

The sequence of events, particularly Mr. Thompson's decision to take the bracelet after witnessing its owner's active search, demonstrates an intention to permanently deprive Ms. Reynolds of her property. There was a conspicuous absence of any attempt to use reasonable means to return the bracelet to its rightful owner.

Action Taken:

Based on the evidence, Mr. Gregory Thompson was located and apprehended at later that day. Upon arrest, he was read his Miranda rights and he said he found it and didn't know anyone was looking for it. He handed the diamond bracelet to me and it was positively identified by Ms. Reynolds as her property through text messages. Mr. Thompson has been charged with theft of lost property and was transported to the local precinct.

Ms. Reynolds was asked to visit the station to formally identify her property and to provide further details for the legal proceedings against Mr. Thompson.

End of Report.

Theft of Services

Criminal Elements

These elements must be proven beyond a reasonable doubt in court:[1]

☐ **State the approximate date (and time if known) when the offense occurred.**

> ‣ This confirms the offense occurred within the statute of limitations.

☐ **Specify where the offense occurred.**

> ‣ This establishes the court's jurisdiction over the offense.

☐ **Describe what labor or services the suspect obtained and identify the victim.**

☐ **Explain why the suspect should have known the labor or services were only available for hire.**

☐ **Finally, describe what method the suspect used utilized:**

> ‣ Suspect threatened victim;

> ‣ Suspect deceived the victim; or

> ‣ The suspect knew the victim didn't consent to non-payment.

Sample Report

Note: An actual police report would typically contain additional detailed information. This sample is designed to emphasize the specific elements related to this particular crime and does not encompass other procedural aspects such as evidence collection, adherence to Miranda rights, and additional investigative measures.

At approximately 1:30 PM, I responded to a call from a local mechanic, Mr. Alan Smith, who operates "Alan's Auto Repairs," a well-known service shop in our community. Mr. Smith reported a theft of services incident that occurred earlier on Westfield Road.

Labor or Services Obtained:

Mr. Smith stated that at around 1:00 PM, he received a roadside assistance request via his business's emergency line. The caller, later identified as Mr. Daniel Harris, reported a broken-down vehicle on Westfield Road. Mr. Smith promptly arrived at the scene and performed a complex emergency repair on

---

[1] For a common statutory example, see I.C. § 18-2403(5)(a)

Mr. Harris's vehicle, which included fixing a radiator hose and refilling the coolant, among other adjustments necessary to make the vehicle operational.

Knowledge of Services for Hire:

Mr. Smith explained that before commencing work, he informed Mr. Harris about the cost of the emergency services, to which Mr. Harris verbally agreed. This detail was critical as it established that Mr. Harris was aware that these specialized services were professional and not free of charge. Mr. Smith also has a decal on his service vehicle clearly stating, "All services rendered are subject to charges," further indicating the professional nature of his business.

Method Used:

Upon completion of the repairs, Mr. Harris expressed gratitude and hastily stated he needed to retrieve his payment method from the car's glove compartment. However, instead of returning to settle the payment, Mr. Harris suddenly drove off, deliberately evading the agreed charges. Mr. Smith attempted to follow him, asking for payment, but Mr. Harris sped away, clearly demonstrating he had no intention of compensating Mr. Smith for the rendered services.

Action Taken:

Mr. Harris's deliberate avoidance of payment, especially after receiving the services knowing they were subject to charges, constitutes theft of services. After gathering the report from Mr. Smith, including the description of Mr. Harris and his vehicle, efforts were initiated to locate the suspect.

At approximately 4:00 PM, Mr. Harris was located at his residence through the vehicle's registration details provided by Mr. Smith. He was placed under arrest after being informed of his Miranda rights and transported to the precinct for processing. Mr. Harris is being charged with theft of services, and a detailed invoice from Mr. Smith has been obtained to establish the value of the services stolen.

Mr. Smith has been informed about the arrest and the ongoing process. He expressed relief and agreed to provide additional documentation and testimony as required for the case.

End of Report.

Theft of Rental Vehicle

Criminal Elements

These elements must be proven beyond a reasonable doubt in court:[1]

☐ **State the approximate date (and time if known) when the offense occurred.**

‣ This confirms the offense occurred within the statute of limitations.

☐ **Specify where the offense occurred.**

‣ This establishes the court's jurisdiction over the offense.

☐ **The suspect rented or leased a motor vehicle under an agreement in writing which provided for the return of the vehicle to a particular place at a particular time.**

☐ **Explain why you believe the suspect had the intent to not return to rental vehicle.**

Sample Report

Note: An actual police report would typically contain additional detailed information. This sample is designed to emphasize the specific elements related to this particular crime and does not encompass other procedural aspects such as evidence collection, adherence to Miranda rights, and additional investigative measures.

At approximately 9:00 AM on June 15, 2024, I responded to a report from EasyRide Rentals, a car rental service located at 4777 Greenview Lane. The manager, Mr. Paul Franklin, reported an incident of a vehicle that had not been returned per the rental agreement's stipulations.

Rental Agreement Details:

Mr. Franklin provided a copy of the rental agreement, which showed that a 2024 Blue Sedona LX, license plate XYZ123, was rented to a Mr. Timothy Dalton on June 1, 2024. The agreement explicitly stated that the vehicle was to be returned on June 8, 2024, by 6:00 PM. The contract outlined late fees, procedures for reporting car issues, and legal obligations if the car was not returned as agreed.

Non-Compliance with Agreement:

According to Mr. Franklin, the vehicle was not returned on the due date, and there was no communication from Mr. Dalton regarding any delay. The rental

---

[1] For a common statutory example, see I.C. § 18-2403(5)(b)

company made several attempts to contact Mr. Dalton via the phone number provided on the rental agreement, leaving voicemails and sending text reminders regarding the vehicle's return and potential legal consequences. They received no response.

Intent Not to Return the Vehicle:

The lack of communication from Mr. Dalton, combined with his failure to return the vehicle, suggests a willful breach of the rental agreement. The company's policy is to wait for 48 hours post the return date before reporting the vehicle as stolen, considering potential reasonable delays or issues the renter might face. However, Mr. Dalton neither adhered to the agreement nor responded to any communications, indicating a possible intent not to return the rented vehicle.

Action Taken:

Given the circumstances and the clear violation of the agreement, a BOLO (Be-On-the-Lookout) was issued for the 2024 Blue Sedona LX with the license plate XYZ123. The vehicle was entered into the National Crime Information Center (NCIC) database as stolen.

At approximately 2:00 PM on June 17, 2024, the vehicle was spotted parked at a local shopping center. Mr. Dalton was found shopping inside, and upon exiting the center and approaching the vehicle, he was apprehended without incident. He was informed of his Miranda rights upon arrest.

Mr. Dalton was transported to the precinct for further questioning. During the interrogation, he admitted to intentionally keeping the vehicle beyond the rental period, citing personal financial problems and needing the car for longer than he initially anticipated. He was charged with unauthorized use of a vehicle and breach of a rental agreement.

EasyRide Rentals was informed about the recovery of the vehicle and the arrest of Mr. Dalton. They were instructed on the procedure to retrieve their vehicle and provide any additional documentation necessary for the case.

End of Report.

PROPERTY CRIMES

Driving Vehicle Without Consent

Criminal Elements

These elements must be proven beyond a reasonable doubt in court:[1]

- ☐ **State the approximate date (and time if known) when the offense occurred.**
    - ‣ This confirms the offense occurred within the statute of limitations.
- ☐ **Specify where the offense occurred.**
    - ‣ This establishes the court's jurisdiction over the offense.
- ☐ **Describe what vehicle the suspect operated.**
    - ‣ Vehicles include boats, snowmobiles, ATV, planes, etc.
- ☐ **Explain why the suspect did so without the consent of the owner.**
- ☐ **Finally, explain why this was done with the intent to temporarily deprive the owner of the vehicle.**

Sample Report

Note: An actual police report would typically contain additional detailed information. This sample is designed to emphasize the specific elements related to this particular crime and does not encompass other procedural aspects such as evidence collection, adherence to Miranda rights, and additional investigative measures.

At approximately 7:30 PM, I arrived at Lakeview Marina in response to a distress call. The complainant, Mr. Jason McCarthy, reported unauthorized use of his boat. He described the vessel as a 2024 model, 20-foot white SeaRay, registration SR20244X, with blue trim and a 150 HP outboard motor.

Vehicle Description:

Mr. McCarthy provided a detailed account of his boat, corroborated by ownership documents and recent photographs. The boat was notably equipped with several personalized items, including custom seat covers and a unique steering wheel, indicating Mr. McCarthy's familiarity with its contents and condition.

Lack of Consent:

According to Mr. McCarthy, he had taken all standard security precautions, including securing his boat at the marina using a lock and chain. He explicitly

---

[1] For a common statutory example, see I.C. § 49–227

stated that he had not granted permission for any other individual to use or operate his boat. He became aware of the incident when he saw his boat, distinctly recognizable by its custom features, being maneuvered away from the dock at a time when no other individuals had been granted access.

Circumstantial Evidence of Joyriding:

The boat was not just driven away but was seen being operated in a manner consistent with joyriding. Witnesses, including other boat owners at the marina, described the boat's operation as reckless and purposeless, with excessive speeding and sharp, unnecessary turns, none of which are consistent with the behavior of a thief intending to conceal the act of theft.

Furthermore, personal items of value within the boat were left untouched, and there was no attempt to dismantle or alter the boat's appearance, which would be consistent with an intention of resale or long-term unauthorized use. The behavior exhibited aligns more with opportunistic unauthorized use, commonly referred to as "joyriding," rather than theft with intent for personal gain through resale or other means.

Action Taken:

The local authorities, including the coast guard, were promptly notified. The boat was located abandoned at a nearby public beach, further suggesting the temporary nature of the unauthorized use. The suspect, Mr. Dylan Rodgers, was apprehended in the vicinity, attempting to depart the area on foot.

Upon questioning at the scene, Mr. Rodgers admitted to impulsively taking the boat after noticing it was unattended. He stated his intention was a brief thrill and that he planned to abandon the boat safely ashore afterward. He expressed remorse, acknowledging his lack of consideration for the potential consequences of his actions.

Mr. Rodgers has been charged with unauthorized use of a vehicle (boat). Mr. McCarthy was reunited with his boat and confirmed that, aside from the broken security chain, the vessel was undamaged. He provided a written statement and expressed his intention to press charges.

End of Report.

Shoplifting

Criminal Elements

These elements must be proven beyond a reasonable doubt in court:[1]

☐ **State the approximate date (and time if known) when the offense occurred.**

  ‣ This confirms the offense occurred within the statute of limitations.

☐ **Specify where the offense occurred.**

  ‣ This establishes the court's jurisdiction over the offense.

☐ **Explain how the suspect intentionally concealed the goods, wares, or merchandise of any store or merchant.**

☐ **State that the suspect was still on the premises during the concealment.**

☐ **Finally, explain that the suspect did so without authority.**

Sample Report

Note: An actual police report would typically contain additional detailed information. This sample is designed to emphasize the specific elements related to this particular crime and does not encompass other procedural aspects such as evidence collection, adherence to Miranda rights, and additional investigative measures.

At approximately 3:45 PM, I responded to a shoplifting report at the QuickBuy Supermarket on Jefferson Avenue. Upon arrival, I was met by the store manager, Ms. Brenda Wilson, who had detained an individual, later identified as Ms. Rachel Green, for suspected shoplifting.

Concealment of Goods:

Ms. Wilson reported that at around 3:30 PM, one of the store employees noticed suspicious behavior from Ms. Green in the cosmetics aisle. According to the employee, Ms. Green was observed selecting various items, including lipsticks, a bottle of perfume, and a compact mirror, and subtly placing them into her large shoulder bag rather than a shopping basket. She made deliberate attempts to ensure these actions were concealed, using her body to shield the view from the store's surveillance cameras and other shoppers.

Suspect's Presence on Premises:

---

[1] For a common statutory example, see I.C. § 18-4626

Ms. Green did not attempt to leave the store immediately after concealing the items. Instead, she continued to navigate through the store aisles, presumably to create the impression of being a regular shopper. However, she was closely monitored by store security personnel throughout this period.

Unauthorized Concealment:

Ms. Wilson, with the assistance of store security, approached Ms. Green before she could exit the premises. They conducted a polite inquiry, asking if she forgot to pay for the items in her bag. Ms. Green appeared nervous and hesitated to open her bag. Upon insistence and in the presence of store security, Ms. Green's bag was searched, revealing the concealed items, which she had no receipt for, confirming she had not purchased them.

Action Taken:

Ms. Green was detained by store security until my arrival. I informed Ms. Green of her Miranda rights and questioned her about the incident. Initially, she was reluctant to speak but eventually admitted to concealing the items with no intention of paying for them. She apologized and offered to compensate by paying for the items.

Despite her offer, due to the store's strict policy against shoplifting, Ms. Wilson insisted on pressing charges. Ms. Green was placed under arrest for shoplifting and transported to the local precinct for further processing.

The stolen items, totaling approximately $85, were recovered and handed back to Ms. Wilson, who provided a detailed inventory for evidence. Surveillance footage capturing the incident was also secured for further investigation.

End of Report.

Malicious Damage to Property

Criminal Elements

These elements must be proven beyond a reasonable doubt in court:[1]

- [ ] **State the approximate date (and time if known) when the offense occurred.**
    - ‣ This confirms the offense occurred within the statute of limitations.

- [ ] **Specify where the offense occurred.**
    - ‣ This establishes the court's jurisdiction over the offense.

- [ ] **Describe how the suspect maliciously damaged or destroyed property that was owned by another person.**

- [ ] **Explain how the property's owner did not give the suspect permission to injure or destroy such property.**

Sample Report

Note: An actual police report would typically contain additional detailed information. This sample is designed to emphasize the specific elements related to this particular crime and does not encompass other procedural aspects such as evidence collection, adherence to Miranda rights, and additional investigative measures.

At approximately 7:00 AM on September 5, 2024, I responded to a call from Mr. Alan Peterson, the owner of a property located at 1820 High Ridge Park. Mr. Peterson reported that his property had been significantly damaged overnight.

Description of Damage:

Upon arrival at the scene, I observed that several windows of the property were shattered. The front door appeared to have been kicked in, compromising the lock and the frame. Inside the property, various items were overturned, and graffiti was present on the walls, including explicit language and symbols. Mr. Peterson estimated the damage to be over $3,000, encompassing the broken windows, damaged door, defaced walls, and various broken furnishings.

Malicious Intent:

The nature of the destruction indicates a malicious intent rather than an attempt at burglary. No items were reported missing, and the damage appears

---

[1] For a common statutory example, see I.C. §§ 18–7001 & 18–101(4)

to have been inflicted deliberately with the intent to deface and destroy rather than for gain. The graffiti, the unnecessary overturning of furniture, and the extent of damage to the property's structural elements suggest an act of vandalism.

Lack of Consent:

Mr. Peterson confirmed that no one had been given permission to enter or alter his property and that the property was secured the previous night when he last checked at approximately 10:00 PM. He provided a list of individuals who have access to the property, all of whom were ruled out as they were accounted for during the hours of the incident.

Action Taken:

I photographed the scene and collected evidence, including a spray paint can left behind by the perpetrator(s), pieces of broken glass with potential fingerprints, and shoe prints from the door. The graffiti on the walls was also documented, which may indicate gang involvement or could serve as a form of identification.

Mr. Peterson was advised to contact his insurance company and was informed that a follow-up investigation would likely occur, including interviews with potential witnesses and a canvassing of the neighborhood for security camera footage.

A local gang unit has been informed of the incident due to the nature of the symbols used in the graffiti, and they will be conducting a parallel investigation to determine if this incident was gang-related.

Mr. Peterson was very cooperative and provided a written statement describing the incident from his perspective, the estimated value of the damaged property, and any potential individuals who might bear ill intent towards him.

The collected evidence will be forwarded to the forensics department for further analysis. The investigation is ongoing, and updates will be provided to Mr. Peterson as they become available.

End of Report.

Arson

Criminal Elements

These elements must be proven beyond a reasonable doubt in court:[1]

☐ **State the approximate date (and time if known) when the offense occurred.**

- ‣ This confirms the offense occurred within the statute of limitations.

☐ **Specify where the offense occurred.**

- ‣ This establishes the court's jurisdiction over the offense.

☐ **Describe how the suspect intentionally, by fire or explosion, damaged a structure:**

- ‣ A dwelling does not have to be occupied;

- ‣ A structure does not have to be occupied, as long as people are normally present (e.g. business at night);

- ‣ Property owned by the suspect with the intent for financial gain.

Sample Report

Note: An actual police report would typically contain additional detailed information. This sample is designed to emphasize the specific elements related to this particular crime and does not encompass other procedural aspects such as evidence collection, adherence to Miranda rights, and additional investigative measures.

At approximately 1:45 AM on October 30, 2024, the Springfield Fire Department responded to reports of visible flames emanating from the "Happy Trails Animal Clinic" on Oakwood Avenue. I arrived on the scene at approximately 2:00 AM, following notification of the fire department's involvement.

Description of the Scene:

The fire caused substantial damage to the building's front, particularly around the entrance and windows. The structure's interior was visibly charred, and remnants of what appeared to be an incendiary device were found near the building's foundation. The clinic was closed at the time of the incident, and no human injuries were reported. However, several animals that were kept overnight for observation suffered from smoke inhalation and were transferred to a nearby veterinary hospital.

---

[1] For a common statutory example, see I.C. §§ 18–80218–801(1)-(5)

Evidence of Intentional Act:

The preliminary investigation by the fire department's arson task force suggested the fire was not accidental. The remnants of a homemade incendiary device, including a partially burned cloth wick and a molotov cocktail, were discovered at the scene. The placement of the device at the building's weakest structural point near the entrance indicates a deliberate attempt to ignite and cause substantial damage.

Context of the Incident:

The "Happy Trails Animal Clinic" is unoccupied at night, with animals occasionally kept for overnight observation. The building is not a dwelling but is a structure where people are normally present during operating hours. Dr. Linda Freeman, the owner of the clinic, was contacted at the scene. Visibly distressed, she confirmed that there were no electrical or other issues that could have accidentally started the fire. She also mentioned recent anonymous threats she received in response to her clinic's support for local animal rights initiatives, suggesting a potential motive related to her business practices.

Financial Gain:

While Dr. Freeman owns the property, initial inquiries into her financial background revealed she was struggling with business debts. However, she vehemently denied any involvement, and there was no immediate evidence suggesting the arson was committed for insurance or other financial gains.

Action Taken:

The scene was secured, and a more thorough investigation was initiated. Samples from the incendiary device and surrounding areas were collected for forensic analysis. The clinic's financial records and the anonymous threats are currently under review. Nearby businesses and traffic cameras are being checked for any suspicious activity or individuals from the night of the incident.

Dr. Freeman and her employees have been asked to provide formal statements. The animals affected by the incident are receiving medical attention, and their conditions are being documented.

The investigation is ongoing, with collaboration between the police department, fire department, and other forensic specialists. Further actions will include interviewing potential witnesses, exploring motives related to the threats, and examining financial records to identify any signs of fraudulent intent.

End of Report.

Aggravated Arson

Criminal Elements

These elements must be proven beyond a reasonable doubt in court:[1]

☐ **State the approximate date (and time if known) when the offense occurred.**

  ‣ This confirms the offense occurred within the statute of limitations.

☐ **Specify where the offense occurred.**

  ‣ This establishes the court's jurisdiction over the offense.

☐ **Describe how the suspect intentionally, by fire or explosion, damaged a structure:**

  ‣ A dwelling does not have to be occupied;

  ‣ A structure does not have to be occupied, as long as people are normally present (e.g. business at night);

  ‣ Property owned by the suspect with the intent for financial gain.

☐ **Finally, describe how the arson caused, directly or indirectly, any of the following:**

  ‣ Great bodily harm;

  ‣ Permanent disability;

  ‣ Disfigurement;

  ‣ Death.

Sample Report

Note: An actual police report would typically contain additional detailed information. This sample is designed to emphasize the specific elements related to this particular crime and does not encompass other procedural aspects such as evidence collection, adherence to Miranda rights, and additional investigative measures.

At approximately 11:15 PM on November 15, 2024, both the Springfield Fire Department and I were dispatched following an emergency call reporting a fire at the "Main Street Diner." Upon arrival, firefighters engaged with the blaze, and I assisted with crowd control and initial assessment of the scene.

Description of the Scene:

---

[1] For a common statutory example, see I.C. §§ 18–805 & 18-801(1)-(7)

The diner was engulfed in flames, particularly concentrated at the rear of the building where the kitchen is located. Patrons and staff had evacuated, with most gathered across the street. One individual, a diner employee identified as Ms. Sarah Henley, was severely injured and treated on-site by emergency medical services before being transported to Springfield General Hospital. She suffered from burns and smoke inhalation, potentially leading to permanent respiratory complications.

Evidence of Intentional Act:

After the fire was contained, an on-scene investigation was conducted with the fire department's arson specialists. Preliminary findings indicated the presence of accelerants, commonly associated with intentional fires. A suspect, Mr. Paul Andrews, was detained at the scene. He was discovered by firefighters in the alley behind the diner, smelling strongly of gasoline and holding a lighter. Mr. Andrews appeared agitated and was observed watching the fire with a sense of urgency.

Context of the Incident:

The "Main Street Diner" is a popular local establishment and was occupied by staff and patrons until the fire forced an evacuation. The owner, Mr. Robert Hanley, was on the scene and confirmed that Mr. Andrews is a former employee who was recently terminated. Mr. Hanley speculated that the arson might be an act of retribution.

Aggravated Circumstances:

Ms. Henley's injuries, as confirmed by the attending EMTs and subsequent hospital reports, include second-degree burns and significant respiratory distress, consistent with smoke inhalation. These injuries may result in long-term, potentially permanent, health complications, qualifying as great bodily harm.

Suspect's Financial Gain:

While Mr. Andrews was a former employee, initial questioning at the scene revealed his disgruntled state over his termination and perceived injustices. He hinted at wanting to make Mr. Hanley "pay" for his loss. However, there was no immediate indication of Mr. Andrews seeking financial gain.

Action Taken:

Mr. Andrews was arrested at the scene. He was informed of his rights and taken to the precinct for further questioning. The area was cordoned off as a crime scene. Witness statements were taken from staff, patrons, and Mr. Hanley. The evidence collected at the scene, including the lighter in Mr. Andrews' possession, his clothing, and samples of the accelerant, have been sent for forensic analysis.

Ms. Henley's family has been notified, and a police liaison has been assigned to update them on the investigation and assist as needed. Hospital staff have been asked to provide updates on Ms. Henley's condition and a detailed report of her injuries.

The investigation is ongoing, with charges pending for Mr. Andrews. Further actions will include a detailed interrogation of Mr. Andrews, review of the diner's employment records, and collaboration with the District Attorney's office regarding the case's legal aspects.

End of Report.

Trespassing

Criminal Elements

These elements must be proven beyond a reasonable doubt in court:[1]

☐ **State the approximate date (and time if known) when the offense occurred.**

- This confirms the offense occurred within the statute of limitations.

☐ **Specify where the offense occurred.**

- This establishes the court's jurisdiction over the offense.

☐ **Describe how the the suspect intentionally refused to immediately depart from another's property after being notified, either in writing or verbally, to do so.**

☐ **Articulate that the person making the notification was the owner or the owner's authorized agent.**

Sample Report

Note: An actual police report would typically contain additional detailed information. This sample is designed to emphasize the specific elements related to this particular crime and does not encompass other procedural aspects such as evidence collection, adherence to Miranda rights, and additional investigative measures.

At approximately 8:45 PM on December 4, 2024, I responded to a disturbance call at the "Quick Stop Convenience Store" on Hamilton Road. The store manager, Mr. Ajay Singh, reported a homeless individual causing a disturbance and refusing to leave the premises.

Description of the Scene:

Upon arrival, I observed an individual, later identified as Mr. John Doe, shouting near the checkout counter while several customers moved away from him. Mr. Doe appeared agitated and was gesturing wildly, holding a half-empty plastic alcohol bottle. The store's staff were at a safe distance, and Mr. Singh was on the phone, likely reporting the incident.

Initial Contact:

I approached Mr. Doe, who smelled strongly of alcohol, and asked him to calm down and explain the situation. He responded with slurred speech, expressing

---

[1] For a common statutory example, see I.C. § 18-7008(8)

his right to be in the store. I then turned to Mr. Singh for his account of the events.

Verification of Trespass:

Mr. Singh explained that Mr. Doe had entered the store approximately 20 minutes earlier and was wandering the aisles, talking to himself, and occasionally picking up items but never attempting to purchase anything. When Mr. Singh approached him and asked if he needed help, Mr. Doe became belligerent and started causing a scene. Concerned for his customers' safety and the disruption to his business, Mr. Singh asked Mr. Doe to leave. However, Mr. Doe refused, insisting he wasn't doing anything wrong.

Mr. Singh identified himself as the store manager and showed me his identification. He stated he was acting on behalf of the store owner, Mr. Hardeep Patel, in maintaining the premises. He had asked Mr. Doe to leave several times due to his disruptive behavior and his refusal to make any purchases or use the store's services legitimately.

Action Taken:

Given Mr. Singh's authority and Mr. Doe's refusal to comply with the request to leave, I informed Mr. Doe that he was trespassing. I explained to him the legal repercussions of his actions, but he continued to resist cooperation. With no other recourse, I placed Mr. Doe under arrest for trespassing, ensuring his rights were stated clearly and understood.

Mr. Doe was transported to the local precinct for processing. Mr. Singh provided a written statement, and the store's surveillance footage was secured, which recorded the entire incident. The other customers present at the scene were identified, with two individuals agreeing to provide witness statements corroborating Mr. Singh's account.

A report was filed with the precinct, and Mr. Doe was held pending a sobriety check and further legal actions. Social services were notified regarding Mr. Doe's situation for potential assistance or intervention.

End of Report.

Homicide

Murder – Malice Aforethought

Criminal Elements

These elements must be proven beyond a reasonable doubt in court:[1]

- ☐ **State the approximate date (and time if known) when the offense occurred.**
  - ‣ This confirms the offense occurred within the statute of limitations.

- ☐ **Specify where the offense occurred.**
  - ‣ This establishes the court's jurisdiction over the offense.

- ☐ **Explain what conduct the suspect engaged in which caused the death of the victim.**

- ☐ **Explain why the suspect acted without legal justification:**
  - ‣ No valid claim of self-defense;
  - ‣ If government actor, not justified use of force, etc.

- ☐ **Explain why you think the conduct was done with malice:**
  - ‣ The suspect used poison;
  - ‣ The suspect was lying in wait for the victim to arrive;
  - ‣ Murder was willful, deliberate, and premeditated;
  - ‣ The suspect murdered a first responder while performing official duties;
  - ‣ The murder occurred while the suspect was escaping or attempting to escape a jail or prison.

Sample Report

Note: An actual police report would typically contain additional detailed information. This sample is designed to emphasize the specific elements related to this particular crime and does not encompass other procedural aspects such as evidence collection, adherence to Miranda rights, and additional investigative measures.

Incident Overview:

At approximately 10:30 PM on October 15, 2023, a murder occurred at "The Green Tavern", located at 789 Maple Street, Rivertown, New York. The victim,

---

[1] Idaho Code §§ 18-4001, 18-4003

identified as Thomas Clarkson, was fatally shot by the suspect, Michael Anderson, following a business transaction that soured.

Detailed Findings:

Initial reports indicated a verbal and physical confrontation between Anderson and Clarkson inside the tavern over a financial dispute. Clarkson had allegedly embezzled a significant sum of money from Anderson's business, "Anderson Electronics," leading to the confrontation.

Witness Interview 1 - Bartender, Julia Simmons:

Simmons reported observing the two men engaged in a heated argument around 10:15 PM. She overheard Anderson accusing Clarkson of stealing money. Shortly after, she saw Anderson leave the tavern and return minutes later, visibly agitated.

Witness Interview 2 - Patron, Edward Harris:

Harris, seated at a nearby table, witnessed Anderson returning to the tavern, confronting Clarkson again, and then pulling out a handgun. According to Harris, Anderson shouted, "You've ruined me!" before shooting Clarkson.

Suspect's Admission:

During the interrogation, Anderson admitted to shooting Clarkson. He expressed that he felt betrayed and financially ruined by Clarkson's actions. He stated, "I didn't plan to kill him when I walked in, but I just lost it when I saw him sitting there, smirking at me."

Conclusion and Recommendation:

The evidence suggests that the act was committed in a moment of heightened emotion but was nonetheless premeditated, given that Anderson left the tavern and returned with a firearm. The nature of the crime, the evidence gathered, and the admission by the suspect point towards a charge of Murder in the First Degree under New York State Law, Section 3334.3.

Attachments:

1. Witness statements from Julia Simmons and Edward Harris
2. Surveillance footage from "The Green Tavern"
3. Interrogation transcript of Michael Anderson
4. Financial records from "Anderson Electronics" indicating embezzlement
5. Ballistics report of the firearm used

Murder - Torture

Criminal Elements

These elements must be proven beyond a reasonable doubt in court:[1]

☐ **State the approximate date (and time if known) when the offense occurred.**

- ▸ This confirms the offense occurred within the statute of limitations.

☐ **Specify where the offense occurred.**

- ▸ This establishes the court's jurisdiction over the offense.

☐ **Explain how the suspect intentionally tortured the victim, resulting in the victim's death:**

- ▸ The torture consisted of the intentional infliction of extreme and prolonged pain with the intent to cause suffering;

- ▸ The infliction of extreme and prolonged acts of brutality, and the torture was inflicted with the intent to cause suffering;

- ▸ The torture was inflicted with the intent to execute vengeance;

- ▸ The torture was inflicted with the intent to extort something of value from the victim;

- ▸ The torture was inflicted with the intent to satisfy some sadistic inclination, and so forth.

Sample Report

Note: An actual police report would typically contain additional detailed information. This sample is designed to emphasize the specific elements related to this particular crime and does not encompass other procedural aspects such as evidence collection, adherence to Miranda rights, and additional investigative measures.

Incident Overview:

On November 12, 2023, a horrific case of murder involving torture was discovered at an abandoned warehouse on 112 Industrial Avenue in Brookville, Ohio. The time of the offense is estimated between 7:00 PM and 9:00 PM. James Walters, the victim, was found deceased, displaying clear signs of prolonged and extreme torture [explain why]. The primary suspect in this crime is identified as Henry Lawson.

---

[1] Idaho Code § 18-4001, 18-4003

Detailed Findings:

Investigations at the crime scene revealed that Walters suffered an array of brutal injuries, including burns, severe lacerations, and multiple fractures, suggesting a methodical and prolonged period of torture. Tools like ropes, knives, and blowtorches found at the scene pointed to a premeditated and sadistic intent behind the torture.

Interrogation of Lawson uncovered a deep-seated motive for revenge against Walters, who he blamed for a personal loss [the report would include more information]. This motive, combined with Lawson's history of violence and sadistic inclinations, indicates a plan to torture Walter..

Conclusion and Recommendation:

The evidence suggests a deliberate and calculated act of torture by Lawson, driven by a desire for vengeance and characterized by extreme brutality. The nature and severity of the crime, supported by forensic analysis, interrogation results, and psychological evaluations, warrant a charge of Murder - Torture under Ohio State Law, Section 2233.1.

Attachments:

The report includes attachments such as the autopsy report of James Walters, forensic analysis of the torture instruments, interrogation transcripts, Lawson's psychological evaluation, and crime scene photographs, all of which corroborate the findings and recommendations.

Felony Murder Rule

Criminal Elements

These elements must be proven beyond a reasonable doubt in court:[1]

- [ ] **State the approximate date (and time if known) when the offense occurred.**

  ‣ This confirms the offense occurred within the statute of limitations.

- [ ] **Specify where the offense occurred.**

  ‣ This establishes the court's jurisdiction over the offense.

- [ ] **Explain how the murder was committed in the perpetration of, or attempt to perpetrate:**

  ‣ Arson;

  ‣ Rape;

  ‣ Robbery;

  ‣ Burglary;

  ‣ Kidnapping;

  ‣ Mayhem;

  ‣ An act of terrorism;

  ‣ Other crimes listed in the statute.

- [ ] Note: to prove a suspect guilty of first degree murder in this way, the state does not have to prove that the suspect intended to kill the victim, but instead must prove that during the perpetration or attempt to perpetrate the crime, the suspect or another person who was acting in concert with the suspect, killed the victim. For example, an accidental discharge of a firearm during the commission of an armed robbery is felony murder.

Sample Report

Note: An actual police report would typically contain additional detailed information. This sample is designed to emphasize the specific elements related to this particular crime and does not encompass other procedural aspects such as evidence collection, adherence to Miranda rights, and additional investigative measures.

---

[1] Idaho Code §§ 18-4001, 18-4003

On November 15, 2023, at approximately 7:45 PM, our department received multiple 911 calls reporting a robbery at "Downtown Mini Mart" located at 1450 Elm Street. Upon arrival, officers found the store clerk, Mr. Timothy Green, age 54, suffering from a gunshot wound. Emergency medical services were summoned, and Mr. Green was transported to the hospital, where he was pronounced dead.

Investigation and Witness Statements:

The investigation at the scene, supported by witness statements and security camera footage, established that the suspect, identified as Michael Johnson, entered the store with the intent to commit robbery. Witnesses stated that Johnson was armed and demanded money from the cash register. During this felony act, the firearm was discharged, striking Mr. Green.

Witnesses provided a description of Johnson, and he was seen fleeing the scene on foot. The security footage confirmed the physical match and sequence of events as described by the witnesses.

Apprehension and Interrogation of Suspect:

A city-wide BOLO was issued for Johnson. On November 17, 2023, officers responded to a disturbance call where Johnson was identified and apprehended. He was found in possession of items linking him to the robbery, and a firearm was recovered.

During the interrogation, Johnson admitted to committing the robbery but claimed that the discharge of the firearm was accidental. He repeatedly stated, "I didn't mean to shoot him," asserting that the gun went off in a struggle with the clerk. This admission establishes the lack of premeditation but due to the death occurring in conjunction with a felony, the charge of murder is applicable under the Felony Murder Rule.

Charges and Application of the Felony Murder Rule:

Michael Johnson is being charged under the Felony Murder Rule. During the commission of this felony, a death occurred (that of Mr. Green).

The death was directly caused by an act performed during the execution of the felony (gunshot during the robbery).

Conclusion and Next Steps: The suspect has been arrested and the case has been referred to the District Attorney's office for prosecution. The investigation remains ongoing to ensure all evidence is collected and analyzed to support the case in court.

End of Report.

Second Degree Murder

Criminal Elements

These elements must be proven beyond a reasonable doubt in court:[1]

- [ ] **State the approximate date (and time if known) when the offense occurred.**
  - ‣ This confirms the offense occurred within the statute of limitations.

- [ ] **Specify where the offense occurred.**
  - ‣ This establishes the court's jurisdiction over the offense.

- [ ] **Explain what conduct the suspect engaged in which caused the death of the victim.**

- [ ] **Explain why the suspect acted without legal justification:**
  - ‣ No valid claim of self-defense;
  - ‣ If government actor, not justified use of force, etc.

Sample Report

Note: An actual police report would typically contain additional detailed information. This sample is designed to emphasize the specific elements related to this particular crime and does not encompass other procedural aspects such as evidence collection, adherence to Miranda rights, and additional investigative measures.

On November 3, 2023, at approximately 7:45 PM, I, Officer Jane Doe, responded to a call regarding a disturbance reported at the 1500 Block of Park Avenue, downtown. Upon arrival at approximately 7:50 PM, I encountered a chaotic scene with multiple bystanders gathered around a male individual lying motionless on the ground.

Scene Assessment:

The victim, later identified as Mr. John Smith, was found unresponsive with visible stab wounds to his chest. Paramedics were immediately called to the scene, who pronounced him deceased at 8:05 PM. I secured the scene and gathered initial statements from witnesses. Three witnesses pointed towards a male individual, Mr. David Johnson, who was attempting to blend in with the crowd, as the person they saw arguing with Mr. Smith before the physical altercation.

Suspect Apprehension:

---

[1] For a common statutory example, see I.C. § 18-4001, 18-4003

Mr. Johnson was detained for questioning. He was frisked for officer safety, during which a bloodied folding knife was discovered in his right jacket pocket. The knife was secured as evidence, and Mr. Johnson was read his Miranda rights before being transported to the station for further questioning.

Witness Statements:

Witnesses recounted that Mr. Johnson and Mr. Smith engaged in a heated verbal exchange that escalated quickly. They observed Mr. Johnson brandish a knife and lunge towards Mr. Smith, striking him in the chest area.

Suspect Interrogation:

During interrogation, Mr. Johnson initially claimed self-defense. However, upon presenting witness statements and evidence, he confessed that he had initiated the physical confrontation after the verbal argument. He admitted to pulling out his knife and stabbing Mr. Smith in a fit of rage, without any intention to kill him. He expressed remorse and acknowledged that Mr. Smith had not displayed a weapon or engaged in life-threatening actions towards him.

Legal Justification Assessment:

Based on witness testimonies, the suspect's admission, and the absence of any immediate threat to Mr. Johnson's life at the time of the incident, it was determined that there was no legal justification for his actions. There was no valid claim of self-defense, as Mr. Johnson was the aggressor in the situation.

Charges and Processing:

Mr. Johnson was arrested and charged with second-degree murder. The evidence, including the murder weapon and witness statements, were processed and documented for the forthcoming legal proceedings.

Conclusion:

The incident on Park Avenue on November 3, 2023, resulted in the untimely and tragic death of Mr. John Smith. The suspect, Mr. David Johnson, engaged in conduct that directly caused the death of the victim. His actions were found to be without legal justification, and he was charged accordingly. The case will be handed over to the District Attorney's office for prosecution, and counseling services have been offered to the witnesses and the victim's family due to the traumatic nature of the incident.

End of Report.

Voluntary Manslaughter

Criminal Elements

These elements must be proven beyond a reasonable doubt in court:[1]

☐ **State the approximate date (and time if known) when the offense occurred.**

- This confirms the offense occurred within the statute of limitations.

☐ **Specify where the offense occurred.**

- This establishes the court's jurisdiction over the offense.

☐ **Describe what conduct the suspect engaged in which caused the death of the victim.**

☐ **Explain how the suspect acted unlawfully upon a sudden quarrel or in the heat of passion and without malice aforethought in causing such death.**

Sample Report

Note: An actual police report would typically contain additional detailed information. This sample is designed to emphasize the specific elements related to this particular crime and does not encompass other procedural aspects such as evidence collection, adherence to Miranda rights, and additional investigative measures.

On November 10, 2023, at approximately 9:30 PM, dispatch directed me to 4725 Oakwood Drive following a 911 call reporting a violent altercation. Upon arrival at 9:35 PM, I encountered a highly agitated individual identified as Mr. Michael Thompson, standing on the front porch. Inside the living room, I found an unresponsive male on the floor, later identified as Mr. Daniel Walters, with multiple stab wounds.

Scene Assessment:

The scene was immediately secured, and EMS was requested. Despite rapid medical intervention, Mr. Walters was pronounced dead at the scene at 9:50 PM due to the severity of his injuries. Mrs. Laura Thompson, wife of Mr. Thompson and resident at the location, was found in a state of distress in the adjacent room.

Preliminary Investigation:

---

[1] For a common statutory example, see I.C. § 18-4006

Initial questioning revealed that Mr. Thompson had unexpectedly returned home and discovered his wife, Mrs. Thompson, in a compromising position with Mr. Walters. A heated confrontation ensued, during which Mr. Thompson retrieved a kitchen knife and, in the altercation that followed, inflicted fatal injuries on Mr. Walters.

Suspect Statement:

Mr. Thompson was taken into custody without resistance. Post-Miranda, he confessed that he had acted out of intense emotion upon finding his wife with another man. He acknowledged stabbing Mr. Walters in the heat of the moment, emphasizing there was no premeditated intent to kill.

Witness Statements:

Mrs. Thompson provided a statement that corroborated the sequence of events leading to the confrontation. She highlighted the sudden and intense emotional outbreak from her husband, confirming there was no prior indication of planned harm or malice towards Mr. Walters before the incident.

Legal Assessment:

The evidence and testimonies indicated that Mr. Thompson acted upon sudden quarrel and in the heat of passion. The act was not premeditated, and the extreme emotional state at the moment led to the tragic outcome. These factors align with the criteria for voluntary manslaughter, as there was no malice aforethought in Mr. Thompson's actions.

Charges and Processing:

Mr. Thompson was arrested and charged with voluntary manslaughter. He was transported to the county detention center for processing. The knife, identified as the murder weapon, was collected as evidence, and the scene was thoroughly documented for further investigation.

Conclusion:

The incident at 4725 Oakwood Drive on November 10, 2023, resulted in the death of Mr. Daniel Walters. The investigation determined that Mr. Michael Thompson, under intense emotional disturbance after discovering a situation involving his wife and the victim, committed the act without premeditation. He has been charged with voluntary manslaughter, and the case will proceed to the legal system for adjudication. Support services were offered to Mrs. Thompson due to the traumatic event.

End of Report.

Vehicular Manslaughter

Criminal Elements

These elements must be proven beyond a reasonable doubt in court:[1]

- [ ] **State the approximate date (and time if known) when the offense occurred.**
  - ‣ This confirms the offense occurred within the statute of limitations.

- [ ] **Specify where the offense occurred.**
  - ‣ This establishes the court's jurisdiction over the offense.

- [ ] **Describe how the suspect was operating a motor vehicle and committed a misdemeanor, infraction, or was driving while under the influence of alcohol.**

- [ ] **Explain how the suspect's operation of the motor vehicle was a significant cause contributing to the death of the victim.**

Sample Report

Note: An actual police report would typically contain additional detailed information. This sample is designed to emphasize the specific elements related to this particular crime and does not encompass other procedural aspects such as evidence collection, adherence to Miranda rights, and additional investigative measures.

On November 15, 2023, at approximately 10:50 PM, I, Officer Sarah Kendrick, responded to a reported traffic collision involving serious injury at the intersection of Main St. and 2nd Ave. Upon arrival at the scene, I observed two severely damaged vehicles: a red 2023 Mustang and a black 2022 Civic. A third vehicle, a blue 2019 Sedan, was also involved with less severe damage.

Scene Assessment:

The area was immediately secured, and EMS was on the scene attending to the victims. The driver of the blue Sedan, later identified as Mrs. Emily Clarkson, was pronounced dead at the scene. The drivers of the other vehicles, identified as Mr. Derek Wilson (Mustang) and Mr. Brandon Hayes (Civic), sustained minor injuries.

Preliminary Investigation:

Witness statements and preliminary analysis of the scene suggested that the Mustang and the Civic were engaged in a high-speed race heading

---

[1] For a common statutory example, see I.C. § 18-4006

northbound on Main St. As they crossed the intersection, the Mustang collided with the Sedan, which was making a legal turn onto 2nd Ave. The impact caused the Sedan to spin out of control, resulting in the death of Mrs. Clarkson.

Suspect Statement:

Post-Miranda, Mr. Wilson admitted to engaging in an illegal street race with Mr. Hayes. He stated he had lost control of his vehicle while trying to outpace the Civic, leading to the fatal collision. He showed remorse and acknowledged his reckless behavior.

Witness Statements:

Multiple witnesses confirmed the two vehicles were racing at high speeds, demonstrating erratic and dangerous driving behavior. Surveillance footage from nearby security cameras corroborated the witness statements.

Legal Assessment:

Based on the evidence and Mr. Wilson's statement, it was determined that his reckless operation of the vehicle, constituting a misdemeanor violation of street racing laws, was a significant factor contributing to Mrs. Clarkson's death.

Charges and Processing:

Mr. Wilson was arrested and charged with vehicular manslaughter. He was transported to the county detention center for processing. Mr. Hayes was also detained for his involvement in the illegal race. Both vehicles were impounded for further examination, and a detailed documentation of the scene was conducted.

Conclusion:

The incident on November 15, 2023, led to the tragic death of Mrs. Emily Clarkson. The investigation concluded that the cause was illegal street racing, specifically the reckless actions of Mr. Derek Wilson. The case highlights the severe consequences of vehicular misconduct and will be forwarded to the courts for further adjudication. Counseling and support were offered to the Clarkson family in light of their loss.

End of Report.

Invol. Manslaughter – Negligent Use of Deadly Weapon

Criminal Elements

These elements must be proven beyond a reasonable doubt in court:[1]

☐ **State the approximate date (and time if known) when the offense occurred.**

> ‣ This confirms the offense occurred within the statute of limitations.

☐ **Specify where the offense occurred.**

> ‣ This establishes the court's jurisdiction over the offense.

☐ **Describe how the suspect used a firearm or deadly weapon with reckless disregard of the consequences and of the rights of others.**

☐ **Explain how this conduct produced the death of the victim.**

Note: A "deadly weapon" is any object, instrument, or weapon which is used in such a manner as to be capable of producing, and likely to produce, death or great bodily injury.

Sample Report

Note: An actual police report would typically contain additional detailed information. This sample is designed to emphasize the specific elements related to this particular crime and does not encompass other procedural aspects such as evidence collection, adherence to Miranda rights, and additional investigative measures.

On November 20, 2023, at approximately 2:40 PM, the dispatch unit received a 911 call indicating the sound of gunshots and a potential casualty at Redwood State Park, Trail #3. I, Officer Alex Mercer, along with other units, responded to the emergency call.

Scene Assessment:

Upon arrival at the scene, we identified three individuals: Jonathan Rivers, Michael Thompson, and Alicia Fernandez, in a clearing, visibly shaken and surrounded by shooting paraphernalia. Roughly 20 yards from their makeshift shooting range, we found an unresponsive individual, later identified as hiker Peter Hanson, suffering from a gunshot wound. Despite immediate medical

---

[1] For a common statutory example, see I.C. § 18–4006(2)

assistance called to the scene, Mr. Hanson was pronounced dead due to his injuries.

Preliminary Investigation:

The preliminary investigation at the scene revealed a makeshift shooting gallery, where several targets were hung on trees, and a collection of empty shell casings on the ground. Mr. Rivers explained they had been practicing their shooting, aiming at the targets. He mentioned they had assumed the height and angle of their shots were safe and wouldn't travel beyond the immediate target area.

Critical Incident Detail:

Upon reconstructing the scene and the shooters' positions, it was determined that a bullet, fired by one of the individuals, had traveled over the top of the intended target. The bullet continued its trajectory into the hiking trail area, where it ultimately struck Mr. Hanson. The group admitted they heard a scream shortly after one of the rounds was fired but initially didn't realize the grave consequence of their actions.

Evidence Collection:

The firearms used in the shooting, along with ammunition boxes, spent shell casings, and the targets, were taken into evidence. Detailed photographs capturing the scene, the relative positions of the shooters to the victim, and the bullet trajectory were documented for further analysis.

Witness Statements:

Ms. Fernandez stated they had been taking turns shooting at the targets, and after hearing the scream, they panicked, realizing someone might have been hurt. They claimed they never intended any harm and acknowledged they should not have been discharging firearms in the park.

Legal Assessment:

The actions of Mr. Rivers, Mr. Thompson, and Ms. Fernandez, using firearms without precaution in an unauthorized area, constituted a reckless disregard for human life. Their failure to ensure a safe backdrop for shooting and the irresponsible handling of firearms directly resulted in the death of Mr. Hanson.

Charges and Processing:

In consultation with the District Attorney's office, all three individuals were placed under arrest and charged with involuntary manslaughter due to the negligent use of a deadly weapon. They were processed at the county jail.

Conclusion:

This tragic incident underscores the critical importance of responsible firearm handling and awareness of surroundings. The death of Mr. Peter Hanson was a preventable tragedy, directly resulting from the reckless actions of the individuals involved. A full report, along with collected evidence, is being submitted to the prosecuting authorities for further legal action.

End of Report.

Sex Offenses

Attempted Rape

Criminal Elements

These elements must be proven beyond a reasonable doubt in court:[1]

☐ **State the approximate date (and time if known) when the offense occurred.**

> ‣ This confirms the offense occurred within the statute of limitations.

☐ **Specify where the offense occurred.**

> ‣ This establishes the court's jurisdiction over the offense.

☐ **Explain how the suspect intentionally assaulted the victim.**

☐ **Explain why at the time of the assault, the suspect had the specific intent that his penis would penetrate, however slightly, the victim's oral, anal, or vaginal openings without her consent.**

☐ **Explain why the assault was not completed (e.g. someone came into the room).**

☐ **Explain why the suspect knew the victim did not provide consent:**

> ‣ The victim resisted, but her resistance was overcome by force or violence;
>
> ‣ The victim was prevented from resisting by the infliction or attempted infliction of force, or threatened infliction of bodily harm, accompanied by apparent ability to carry it out;
>
> ‣ The victim was unable to resist due to any intoxicating, narcotic, or anesthetic substance;
>
> ‣ The victim was unconscious or asleep;
>
> ‣ The victim submitted to the penetration under the belief that the suspect was her husband;
>
> ‣ The suspect coerced the victim by threatening physical harm to a family member, or threatened to expose a secret that would subject the victim to hatred, contempt, or public ridicule, and so forth.

☐ **Finally, explain why the suspect's purpose was for sexual arousement, gratification, or abuse.**

---

[1] For a common statutory example, see I.C. § 18–909

Sample Report

Note: An actual police report would typically contain additional detailed information. This sample is designed to emphasize the specific elements related to this particular crime and does not encompass other procedural aspects such as evidence collection, adherence to Miranda rights, and additional investigative measures.

At approximately 10:15 PM on January 20, 2025, I, Officer Stephanie Holt, responded to a 911 call regarding an attempted sexual assault at an apartment located on the 1300 block of Parkview Terrace, Springfield.

Description of the Scene:

Upon arrival, I found the victim, Ms. Jane Doe (name changed for privacy), 25, visibly shaken and distraught, sitting on the front steps of her apartment building. Ms. Doe had minor abrasions on her wrists and a torn blouse. She identified her attacker as Mr. John Smith, who had fled the scene.

Victim's Statement:

Ms. Doe stated that Mr. Smith, an acquaintance from her workplace, had followed her home, insisting on a conversation. Once inside the apartment, Mr. Smith became aggressive, attempting to initiate sexual activity. Ms. Doe explicitly refused multiple times, attempting to move away from Mr. Smith. She reported that Mr. Smith then physically assaulted her, pushing her onto the couch, and attempted to remove her clothing while pinning her wrists.

Ms. Doe stated that during the struggle, she screamed and fought, and in the process, her living room lamp was knocked over, causing a loud crash. The noise alerted her neighbor, who started knocking on the door, asking if everything was alright. Startled, Mr. Smith ceased his assault and fled the scene.

Evidence of Non-Consent and Intent:

Ms. Doe's physical state, torn clothing, and the disheveled condition of her living room suggested a struggle. She expressed that at no point did she consent to Mr. Smith's advances and that she felt her life was in danger during the assault. She was adamant that Mr. Smith's actions were driven by the intent to force non-consensual sexual penetration, as evidenced by his attempts to remove her clothing and restrain her.

Suspect's Purpose:

Ms. Doe stated that Mr. Smith's actions and statements during the assault explicitly indicated his intent was for sex. He made lewd comments about her body and his sexual intentions, clearly indicating his motive.

Action Taken:

Ms. Doe was transported to Springfield General Hospital for medical evaluation and care. A Sexual Assault Nurse Examiner (SANE) was requested for the collection of forensic evidence from Ms. Doe. Photographs of her injuries, torn clothing, and the disarray in the apartment were taken for evidence.

A search for Mr. Smith was initiated immediately, with a description of the suspect broadcasted to all patrol units. Statements from Ms. Doe and her neighbor, who intervened by knocking, were recorded at the scene. The neighbor confirmed hearing a struggle, Ms. Doe's screams, and seeing Mr. Smith exiting the apartment in a hurry.

The investigation is ongoing, with an arrest warrant pending for Mr. Smith. Further actions include a review of any security camera footage in the area, interviewing additional potential witnesses, and collaborating with the District Attorney's office for the prosecution of the suspect.

End of Report.

Rape

Criminal Elements

These elements must be proven beyond a reasonable doubt in court:[1]

☐ **State the approximate date (and time if known) when the offense occurred.**

- ‣ This confirms the offense occurred within the statute of limitations.

☐ **Specify where the offense occurred.**

- ‣ This establishes the court's jurisdiction over the offense.

☐ **Explain how the suspect intentionally caused his penis to penetrate, however slightly, into the vaginal, oral, anal opening of a female victim.**

☐ **If the victim was under the age of consent at the time, state that.**

☐ **If the victim was incapable of giving legal consent because of unsoundness of mind, due to any cause including, but not limited to, mental illness, mental deficiency, or developmental disability, whether temporary or permanent, explain that.**

☐ **Explain why the suspect knew the victim did not provide consent:**

- ‣ The victim resisted, but her resistance was overcome by force or violence;

- ‣ The victim was prevented from resisting by the infliction or attempted infliction of force, or threatened infliction of bodily harm, accompanied by apparent ability to carry it out;

- ‣ The victim was unable to resist due to any intoxicating, narcotic, or anesthetic substance;

- ‣ The victim was unconscious or asleep;

- ‣ The victim submitted to the penetration under the belief that the suspect was her husband;

- ‣ The suspect coerced the victim by threatening physical harm to a family member, or threatened to expose a secret that would subject the victim to hatred, contempt, or public ridicule, and so forth.

---

[1] For a common statutory example, see I.C. § 18–6101

Sample Report

Note: An actual police report would typically contain additional detailed information. This sample is designed to emphasize the specific elements related to this particular crime and does not encompass other procedural aspects such as evidence collection, adherence to Miranda rights, and additional investigative measures.

On March 15, 2025, at approximately 9:20 PM, I, Officer Jameson Reid, responded to a call regarding a sexual assault at a residence on the 2500 block of Willow Lane, Springfield. Dispatch informed of a possible rape incident.

Description of the Scene:

Upon arrival, I encountered the victim, Ms. Jane Roe (name changed for privacy), 27, in a highly distressed state. She was sitting on her living room floor, crying, with visible bruising on her arms and disheveled clothing.

Victim's Statement:

Ms. Roe reported that an acquaintance, Mr. John Doe, had arrived at her residence around 8:30 PM, under the pretense of returning items he had borrowed. Once inside, Mr. Doe became physically aggressive, ignoring Ms. Roe's verbal rejections and physical resistance.

Ms. Roe stated that Mr. Doe forcefully caused his penis to penetrate her vagina without her consent. She detailed her attempts to resist, pushing and hitting, but her actions were thwarted by Mr. Doe's physical force and restraint. She also mentioned being slapped repeatedly and threatened with more severe harm if she continued to resist.

Evidence of Non-Consent and Assault:

I observed physical signs consistent with Ms. Roe's statement, including bruising, redness, and minor lacerations. The living area was in disarray, indicating a struggle. Ms. Roe repeatedly stated she had not consented to any sexual activity with Mr. Doe, and her emotional state was consistent with the trauma described.

Victim's Mental State and Coercion:

Ms. Roe was fully coherent, showing no signs of intoxication or impairment due to any substances. She indicated that she was in fear for her safety during the assault, as Mr. Doe had threatened to return and harm her if she reported the incident. There was no indication of mental illness, deficiency, or developmental disability.

Action Taken:

I immediately called for medical support, and Ms. Roe was transported to Springfield General Hospital for a comprehensive examination and care. A Sexual Assault Nurse Examiner (SANE) conducted a rape kit to collect forensic evidence. Photographs of the scene, Ms. Roe's injuries, and her torn clothing were taken.

An APB was put out for the arrest of Mr. John Doe, and detectives were assigned to bring him in for questioning. Neighbors were interviewed to establish if anyone heard disturbances or noticed suspicious activity. The investigation also included securing any available surveillance footage in the vicinity.

Ms. Roe was informed of her rights, provided with resources for legal and psychological support, and procedures for protective orders. The case has been assigned to sexual assault detectives for a follow-up investigation.

End of report.

Penetration by Foreign Object

Criminal Elements

These elements must be proven beyond a reasonable doubt in court:[1]

☐ **State the approximate date (and time if known) when the offense occurred.**

> ‣ This confirms the offense occurred within the statute of limitations.

☐ **Specify where the offense occurred.**

> ‣ This establishes the court's jurisdiction over the offense.

☐ **Explain how the suspect intentionally caused an object, instrument, finger, or device, to penetrate the vaginal or anal opening of the victim.**

☐ **Explain why the purpose was for sexual arousal, gratification, or abuse.**

☐ **Explain why the suspect knew the victim did not provide consent:**

> ‣ The victim resisted, but her resistance was overcome by force or violence;
>
> ‣ The victim was prevented from resisting by the infliction or attempted infliction of force, or threatened infliction of bodily harm, accompanied by apparent ability to carry it out;
>
> ‣ The victim was unable to resist due to any intoxicating, narcotic, or anesthetic substance;
>
> ‣ The victim was unconscious or asleep;
>
> ‣ The victim submitted to the penetration under the belief that the suspect was her husband;
>
> ‣ The suspect coerced the victim by threatening physical harm to a family member, or threatened to expose a secret that would subject the victim to hatred, contempt, or public ridicule, and so forth.

Sample Report

Note: An actual police report would typically contain additional detailed information. This sample is designed to emphasize the specific elements related to this particular crime and does not encompass other procedural aspects such as evidence collection, adherence to Miranda rights, and additional investigative measures.

---

[1] For a common statutory example, see I.C. § 18–6608

On April 4, 2025, at approximately 9:45 PM, I, Officer Dana Klein, responded to a distress call from a residence on the 4700 block of Cedarwood Avenue, Springfield. The caller, a Ms. Emily Johnson, reported a sexual assault incident.

Description of the Scene:

Upon arrival, I found Ms. Johnson, 32, in a state of extreme emotional distress, with visible bruising around her wrists and upper arms. She was in her home, where the alleged assault occurred. The living room was in disarray, suggesting a struggle had taken place.

Victim's Statement:

Ms. Johnson identified her attacker as Mr. David L., a co-worker. She stated that earlier in the evening, Mr. L. had arrived at her home uninvited, demanding to talk about workplace issues. The conversation escalated, and Mr. L. became physically aggressive.

Ms. Johnson reported that Mr. L. overpowered her, using his physical strength to force her onto the sofa. He then used a foreign object from her coffee table to penetrate her vaginally. The object was identified as a leather cigar holder and was collected as evidence. Ms. Johnson stated she repeatedly protested and attempted to resist but was restrained forcefully. She confirmed that the assault was for Mr. L.'s sexual gratification, as he made several lewd and derogatory comments throughout the attack.

Evidence of Non-Consent and Assault:

Ms. Johnson's physical state, the condition of her home, and her torn clothing were consistent with her account of the assault. She explicitly stated that at no point did she consent to any of Mr. L.'s actions. Her emotional response corroborated the traumatic experience she described.

Victim's Mental State and Coercion:

Ms. Johnson was sober, alert, and fully aware during the incident. She indicated that her resistance was subdued by Mr. L.'s threats of further, more severe physical harm. She was in fear for her life, especially as Mr. L. had mentioned knowing where her family members lived, implying potential harm to them.

Action Taken:

Medical assistance was summoned immediately, and Ms. Johnson was transported to Springfield General Hospital. A Sexual Assault Nurse Examiner (SANE) conducted an examination, and a forensic kit was administered. Photographs of her injuries, the disarrayed living area, and the foreign object believed to be used in the assault were documented as evidence.

A BOLO alert was issued for Mr. David L., and detectives were dispatched to locate him. Neighbors were canvassed to determine if any suspicious activity was noticed. Security footage from nearby properties is being sought to track Mr. L.'s arrival and departure.

Ms. Johnson was provided with information about victim's rights, counseling resources, and legal protective measures. The case is currently under active investigation, with priority status due to the violent nature of the crime.

End of Report.

Sexual Abuse of a Child

Criminal Elements

These elements must be proven beyond a reasonable doubt in court:[1]

☐ **State the approximate date (and time if known) when the offense occurred.**

   ‣ This confirms the offense occurred within the statute of limitations.

☐ **Specify where the offense occurred.**

   ‣ This establishes the court's jurisdiction over the offense.

☐ **Explain how the suspect intentionally committed one or more of the following acts:**

   ‣ Genital or anal contact;

   ‣ Lewd acts;

   ‣ Sexual intercourse;

   ‣ Erotic fondling or nudity;

   ‣ Masturbation;

   ‣ Sexual excitement;

   ‣ Suspect solicited the victim to participate in a sexual act;

   ‣ Suspect engaged in conduct to gratify the sexual desires of some other person.

☐ **Finally, the age of the child may determine what felony category has been committed. Consult the state statute.**

Sample Report

Note: An actual police report would typically contain additional detailed information. This sample is designed to emphasize the specific elements related to this particular crime and does not encompass other procedural aspects such as evidence collection, adherence to Miranda rights, and additional investigative measures.

On April 4, 2025, at approximately 9:45 PM, I, Officer Dana Klein, responded to a distress call from a residence on the 4700 block of Cedarwood Avenue, Springfield. The caller, a Ms. Emily Johnson, reported a sexual assault incident involving her minor child, J.S.

---

[1] For a common statutory example, see I.C. § 18–1508A

Description of the Scene:

Upon arrival, I found J.S., in a state of extreme emotional distress, with visible bruising around her wrists and upper arms. She was in her home, where the alleged assault occurred. The living room was in disarray, suggesting a struggle had taken place.

Victim's Statement:

J.S.identified her attacker as David Lewis, her uncle.. She stated that earlier in the evening, Lewis had arrived at her home uninvited, demanding to talk about family issues. The conversation became uncomfortable when Lewis began asking J.S. if she had sexual intercourse yet. When J.S. said "No" Lewis. became physically aggressive.

J.S. reported that Lewis overpowered her, using his physical strength to force her onto the sofa. He then used his penis to penetrate her vaginally. J.S. stated she repeatedly protested and attempted to resist but was restrained forcefully. Lewis was apparently highly intoxicated and made several lewd and derogatory comments throughout the attack.

Evidence of Non-Consent and Assault:

J.S.'s physical state, the condition of her home, and her torn clothing were consistent with her account of the assault. Her emotional response corroborated the traumatic experience she described.

Victim's Mental State and Coercion:

J.S. was sober, alert, and fully aware during the incident. She indicated that her resistance was subdued by Lewis's threats of further, more severe physical harm. She was in fear for her life, especially as Lewis had mentioned potential harm to her family if she resisted.

Action Taken:

Medical assistance was summoned immediately, and J.S. was transported to Springfield General Hospital. A Sexual Assault Nurse Examiner (SANE) conducted an examination, and a forensic kit was administered. Photographs of her injuries, the disarrayed living area, and other items were documented as evidence.

A BOLO alert was issued for Lewis and detectives were dispatched to locate him. Neighbors were canvassed to determine if any suspicious activity was noticed. Security footage from nearby properties is being sought to trackLewis's arrival and departure.

J.S. and her mother were provided with information about victim's rights, counseling resources, and legal protective measures. The case is currently under active investigation, with priority status due to the violent nature of the crime.

End of Report.

SEX OFFENSES

Prostitution

Criminal Elements

These elements must be proven beyond a reasonable doubt in court:[1]

- ☐ **State the approximate date (and time if known) when the offense occurred.**

    ‣ This confirms the offense occurred within the statute of limitations.

- ☐ **Specify where the offense occurred.**

    ‣ This establishes the court's jurisdiction over the offense.

- ☐ **Describe how the suspect offered or engaged in sexual conduct with another person.**

- ☐ **Describe how the suspect accepted or was willing to accept a fee for engaging in the sexual conduct.**

- ☐ **Alternatively, describe how the suspect loitered in a public place for the purpose of being hired to engage in sexual conduct for a fee.**

Sample Report

Note: An actual police report would typically contain additional detailed information. This sample is designed to emphasize the specific elements related to this particular crime and does not encompass other procedural aspects such as evidence collection, adherence to Miranda rights, and additional investigative measures.

On the evening of November 3, 2025, while conducting a routine patrol at the Crystal Palace Casino, I, Officer Jane Clarkson, observed behavior that was consistent with the solicitation of prostitution.

Observation:

At around 10:15 PM, my attention was drawn to a female individual, later identified as Ms. Jessica Smith (approximately 32 years old), who was engaging in conversations with several casino patrons in a manner that appeared overly familiar and suggestive. Ms. Smith was dressed provocatively and was observed initiating physical contact, such as unsolicited touching and whispering in the ears of several male patrons, who seemed to respond with discomfort and disinterest.

---

[1] For a common statutory example, see I.C. § 18–5613

Initial Contact:

I decided to approach Ms. Smith after witnessing her receive what looked to be cash from a casino patron, Mr. Ben Jones. The exchange was done discreetly but caught my attention as it was consistent with a transactional nature. Upon my approach, Mr. Jones quickly excused himself, heading toward the gaming area, while Ms. Smith attempted to nonchalantly walk in the direction of the hotel's elevators.

Questioning and Evidence:

I called for Ms. Smith to stop for questioning, during which she appeared nervous and was evasive in her responses. She was unable to provide a straightforward explanation for her interactions or the exchange of money. When asked directly if she was engaging in soliciting prostitution, Ms. Smith avoided the question and became defensive.

A consensual search of her purse revealed several rolls of cash, primarily in small denominations, which is uncharacteristic for casino winnings but consistent with street-level prostitution transactions. Further, a small notepad in her purse contained various names, explicit descriptions of sexual services, and corresponding prices.

Arrest:

Based on the evidence, including her behavior, the suspicious cash exchange, and the contents found in her possession, Ms. Smith was arrested for suspicion of solicitation of prostitution, in violation of NRS 201.354. She was apprised of her Miranda rights and transported to the Clark County Detention Center without incident.

Further Actions:

Casino surveillance footage will be reviewed to validate the observed interactions and to identify potential witnesses or additional suspects. Efforts are underway to locate Mr. Jones for questioning regarding his interaction with Ms. Smith.

End of report.

Receiving Pay for Procuring Prostitute (i.e., Pimping)

Criminal Elements

These elements must be proven beyond a reasonable doubt in court:[1]

- ☐ **State the approximate date (and time if known) when the offense occurred.**

  ‣ This confirms the offense occurred within the statute of limitations.

- ☐ **Specify where the offense occurred.**

  ‣ This establishes the court's jurisdiction over the offense.

- ☐ **Describe how the suspect knowingly received money or any object of value.**

- ☐ **Explain why such money or object was received by the suspect to procure a prostitute.** This statement is asking for an explanation or evidence that demonstrates the reason why the suspect received the specified money or object was for the purpose of procuring (hiring or obtaining) the services of a prostitute.

Sample Report

Note: An actual police report would typically contain additional detailed information. This sample is designed to emphasize the specific elements related to this particular crime and does not encompass other procedural aspects such as evidence collection, adherence to Miranda rights, and additional investigative measures.

On November 3, 2025, during a routine patrol within the Crystal Palace Casino, I, Officer Jane Clarkson, observed activities indicative of an individual involved in the procurement of prostitution services.

Observation:

At around 10:15 PM, I observed a female individual, identified as Ms. Jessica Smith (approximately 32 years old), engaging in multiple interactions with various individuals throughout the casino. Her behavior was suggestive, marked by close physical proximity and private conversations with several patrons. Notably, Ms. Smith was seen receiving money from two individuals, after which she was observed pointing these individuals towards a third party, later identified as Ms. Jones, who appeared to be waiting nearby.

---

[1] For a common statutory example, see I.C. § 18–5603

Initial Contact:

After witnessing the exchange of money and the subtle handover of patrons to another individual, I approached Ms. Smith for questioning. Upon my approach, the individuals involved dispersed, leaving Ms. Smith attempting to blend in with the crowd near a slot machine.

Questioning and Evidence:

During the questioning, Ms. Smith appeared agitated and evasive in her responses. She could not provide a clear explanation for her behavior or the exchange of money. A consensual search of her person revealed a significant amount of cash, mostly in small denominations. Further, a quick inspection of a small notebook in her possession detailed various names alongside different monetary amounts and meeting spots within the casino.

Arrest:

Given the evidence, particularly the suspicious money exchange, her directing of patrons to another individual, and the detailed notebook, there was probable cause to believe Ms. Smith was receiving compensation for procuring clients for prostitutes. She was arrested under the suspicion of violating statutes concerning receiving pay for procurement. Ms. Smith was informed of her rights and transported to the Clark County Detention Center for processing.

Further Actions:

The casino's surveillance footage is currently under review to further validate the observed interactions and potentially identify the individuals who handed money to Ms. Smith. The third party, identified as Ms. [Name Redacted], is being sought for questioning to determine her involvement in the suspected prostitution ring.

The management of Crystal Palace Casino has been notified about the incident and has extended full cooperation for the ongoing investigation.

End of Report.

Failing to Register as Sex Offender

Criminal Elements

These elements must be proven beyond a reasonable doubt in court:[1]

☐ **State the approximate date (and time if known) when the offense occurred.**

- ‣ This confirms the offense occurred within the statute of limitations.

☐ **Specify where the offense occurred.**

- ‣ This establishes the court's jurisdiction over the offense.

☐ **State how you know the suspect was required to register under the Sex Offender Registration Act (i.e. convicted of rape in 2015).**

☐ **State that the suspect was not registered in the system at the time of arrest.**

☐ **Explain why you think the suspect lives or was a temporary resident for more than 10 days (or other time required) in your county or city.**

Sample Report

Note: An actual police report would typically contain additional detailed information. This sample is designed to emphasize the specific elements related to this particular crime and does not encompass other procedural aspects such as evidence collection, adherence to Miranda rights, and additional investigative measures.

On October 14, 2023, the Las Vegas Metropolitan Police Department was conducting routine patrols around the premises of Sunscape Hotel located at 3057 Las Vegas Blvd. At approximately 3:00 PM, while scanning vehicle license plates in the hotel parking lot, we identified a 2011 Blue Ford Focus registered to one Mr. Michael Richards. A quick background check revealed that Mr. Richards was convicted of a sexual offense in 2010 in Utah and, as per the Sex Offender Registration Act, is required to register any change of address with the local law enforcement.

Investigation:

Further inquiry with the hotel's front desk confirmed that Mr. Richards had been staying at the hotel for approximately 30 days. However, there was no corresponding registration record for Mr. Richards with the local authorities in Nevada, indicating a violation of the registration requirements.

---

[1] For a common statutory example, see I.C. §§ 18–8311, 18–8304, 18-8306 & 18-8307

Given the sensitive nature of the case and the potential risk to the local community, we decided to approach Mr. Richards for questioning. We obtained his room number with hotel staff's cooperation.

Confrontation:

Upon reaching Mr. Richards' room, located on the third floor of the hotel, we knocked and announced ourselves. Mr. Richards opened the door, appearing surprised at the presence of law enforcement. We informed Mr. Richards of the reason for our visit, specifically discussing his failure to register as a sex offender in the state of Nevada and his non-compliance with the laws governing the Sex Offender Registration Act. He said he had only been in Nevada for three days, which contradicts what we learned from hotel staff.

Arrest:

Mr. Richards initially attempted to dispute the claims, stating he was unaware of the specific registration laws in Nevada. However, when pressed about his legal obligations, known to him at the time of his initial conviction, Mr. Richards conceded that he had not followed through with the necessary procedures.

He was subsequently arrested without resistance and transported to the local precinct for processing. Fingerprints were taken to confirm his identity, and a detailed check with the National Sex Offender Registry further corroborated his status and non-compliance.

Charges:

Mr. Richards was charged under Nevada State Law for failure to register as a sex offender. He was held in custody at the Clark County Detention Center pending a court hearing. The district attorney's office was informed of the arrest, and a court date has been set.

Further Actions:

The case remains active, with ongoing efforts focused on community safety and strict adherence to the legal statutes regarding sex offender registration.

End of Report.

Driving Offenses

Driving Under the Influence

Criminal Elements

These elements must be proven beyond a reasonable doubt in court:[1]

- [ ] **State the approximate date (and time if known) when the offense occurred.**
  - ‣ This confirms the offense occurred within the statute of limitations.

- [ ] **Specify where the offense occurred.**
  - ‣ This establishes the court's jurisdiction over the offense.

- [ ] **Explain how the suspect drove or was in actual physical control of a motor vehicle:**
  - ‣ Keys in ignition or engine running;
  - ‣ Seen driving;
  - ‣ Seat belted in;
  - ‣ Seat position appropriate for the driver's size and weight;
  - ‣ Personal possessions within arm's reach.

- [ ] **Specify what highway, street or bridge or upon what public or private property open to the public the incident occurred.**

- [ ] **Explain why you believed the driver was under the influence of alcohol, drugs, or an intoxicating substance.**

- [ ] **Finally, the breath, urine, or blood test show:**
  - ‣ BAC 0.02 for under 21 drivers;[2]
  - ‣ BAC 0.04 for commercial drivers;
  - ‣ BAC 0.08 for all other drivers.

Sample Report

Note: An actual police report would typically contain additional detailed information. This sample is designed to emphasize the specific elements related to this particular crime and does not encompass other procedural aspects such as evidence collection, adherence to Miranda rights, and additional investigative measures.

---

[1] For a common statutory example, see I.C. § 18-8004

[2] Most states (e.g. New Jersey is 0.01)

On November 5, 2023, at approximately 11:15 PM, I, Trooper John H. Smith, was on routine patrol traveling eastbound on Interstate 80. At this time, I observed a red 2019 Chevrolet Camaro, license plate WYO1234, traveling at a high rate of speed. My radar unit confirmed the vehicle's speed at 87 mph in a 65 mph zone.

Traffic Stop:

I initiated a traffic stop, activating my patrol vehicle's lights and siren, and the vehicle in question pulled over to the shoulder near mile marker 33. I approached the vehicle on the driver's side and made contact with the driver, identified as Mr. Daniel Thompson, a 29-year-old male.

Initial Observations:

Upon interaction, I noticed several signs of impairment, which led me to believe Mr. Thompson was under the influence of alcohol. Mr. Thompson's speech was slurred, and his movements seemed uncoordinated as he searched for his driver's license and vehicle registration.

Field Sobriety Tests:

Given the aforementioned signs of impairment, I asked Mr. Thompson to step out of the vehicle to perform standardized field sobriety tests. The tests included the Horizontal Gaze Nystagmus (HGN), Walk-and-Turn, and One-Leg Stand tests, all of which Mr. Thompson failed to perform satisfactorily.

Breathalyzer Test:

Due to the failure of the field sobriety tests, I conducted a preliminary breath test using a department-issued breathalyzer. The result indicated a Blood Alcohol Content (BAC) of 0.10, which is above the legal limit of 0.08 for non-commercial drivers.

Arrest:

Based on these findings, I placed Mr. Thompson under arrest for Driving Under the Influence of Alcohol. He was handcuffed, informed of his Miranda rights, and safely secured in the back of my patrol vehicle. Mr. Thompson's vehicle was towed from the scene by Ken's Towing Service, and an inventory search was conducted, revealing no illegal substances or contraband.

Booking:

Mr. Thompson was transported to the Laramie County Detention Center for booking. At the facility, Mr. Thompson was given the opportunity to submit a formal breath sample for the chemical test, which he consented to. The chemical breath test was administered at 12:45 AM on November 6, 2023, showing a BAC of 0.09. He was processed and held for sobering, with a court date set.

Charges:

Mr. Thompson faces charges under Wyoming State Law for Driving Under the Influence of Alcohol. The case will be referred to the Laramie County District Attorney's office for prosecution.

Conclusion:

Based on my training and experience, the following are the key indicators that led me to conclude that Mr. Thompson was under the influence of alcohol:

- Excessive speed: Mr. Thompson was driving at 87 mph in a 65 mph zone.

- Odor of alcohol: There was a strong smell of alcohol emanating from the vehicle.

- Bloodshot eyes: Mr. Thompson's eyes were red and glossy.

- Slurred speech: Mr. Thompson's speech was incoherent and mumbled.

- Lack of coordination: He fumbled while retrieving his driver's license and registration.

- Failed field sobriety tests: Mr. Thompson could not successfully complete any of the sobriety tests administered.

- Unsteady on feet: He was swaying and had difficulty balancing during the One-Leg Stand test.

- Admission of drinking: Mr. Thompson admitted to consuming alcohol when questioned.

- Positive breathalyzer result: Preliminary breath test indicated a BAC of 0.10.

- Erratic behavior: Mr. Thompson showed signs of agitation and was argumentative during the interaction.

These observations formed the basis for the arrest and subsequent charges filed against Mr. Thompson for Driving Under the Influence of Alcohol.

End of Report.

Driving Without Privileges

Criminal Elements

These elements must be proven beyond a reasonable doubt in court:[1]

☐ **State the approximate date (and time if known) when the offense occurred.**

- ‣ This confirms the offense occurred within the statute of limitations.

☐ **Specify where the offense occurred.**

- ‣ This establishes the court's jurisdiction over the offense.

☐ **Explain how the suspect drove or was in actual physical control of a motor vehicle:**

- ‣ Keys in ignition;

- ‣ Engine running;

- ‣ Seen driving;

- ‣ Seat belted in;

- ‣ Seat position appropriate for the driver's size and weight;

- ‣ Personal possessions within arm's reach.

☐ **Specify what highway, street or bridge or upon what public or private property open to the public the incident occurred.**

☐ **Articulate how you confirmed the suspect's driver's license, driving privileges, or permit to drive was revoked, disqualified, or suspended in any state or jurisdiction.**

☐ **Finally, explain why you think the suspect had knowledge of such revocation, disqualification or suspension:**

- ‣ Admissions;

- ‣ Privileges have been revoked past the typical renewal period;

- ‣ No license in possession;

- ‣ License is marked in a manner consistent with notice that it's only valid for ID, not driving (ID has hole in it);

- ‣ Prior license violations;

---

[1] For a common statutory example, see I.C. § 18–8001

- Lives at same address on license and should have received formal notice from DMV.

Sample Report

Note: An actual police report would typically contain additional detailed information. This sample is designed to emphasize the specific elements related to this particular crime and does not encompass other procedural aspects such as evidence collection, adherence to Miranda rights, and additional investigative measures.

At approximately 9:15 PM on November 3, 2023, I, Deputy Sarah Collins, while on routine patrol, observed a blue sedan (California license plate: 4JTY678) swerving erratically on Sunset Boulevard near Vine Street. I initiated a traffic stop, and the vehicle pulled over to the side of the road.

I approached the vehicle and made contact with the driver, identified as Mr. Johnathan Doe. I asked Mr. Doe for his driver's license, registration, and proof of insurance, to which he responded that he did not have his driver's license with him. He provided his name and date of birth, allowing me to run a check through the DMV database.

The DMV check revealed that Mr. Doe's driving privileges were revoked on July 8, 2023, and he was not eligible for reinstatement until further review due to prior DUI offenses. The address listed on the revoked license was 2517 Sunset Boulevard, Hollywood, Los Angeles, California, which Mr. Doe confirmed was his current residence.

Evidence of Knowledge of Revocation:

Upon further questioning, Mr. Doe admitted that he was aware his license had been revoked and that he had received multiple notices from the DMV, all sent to his current address, which matched the address on his driver's license. He stated he chose to drive despite knowing his lack of legal driving privileges.

Charges and Actions Taken:

Mr. Doe was arrested for driving without privileges, a violation of California Vehicle Code 14601. The vehicle was towed from the scene, and Mr. Doe was transported to the Hollywood Station for processing. He was fingerprinted, photographed, and held for a bail hearing. Copies of the DMV revocation notices, along with a recording of Mr. Doe's admission, have been attached to this report as evidence.

Conclusion:

Given Mr. Doe's admission, his receipt of formal notices, and the discovery of the DMV document in his vehicle, there is substantial evidence to believe that Mr. Doe knowingly operated a motor vehicle after his driving privileges had been revoked. This report and all relevant evidence will be forwarded to the Los Angeles County District Attorney's office for review and prosecution.

Reckless Driving

Criminal Elements

These elements must be proven beyond a reasonable doubt in court:[1]

☐ **State the approximate date (and time if known) when the offense occurred.**

- ‣ This confirms the offense occurred within the statute of limitations.

☐ **Specify where the offense occurred.**

- ‣ This establishes the court's jurisdiction over the offense.

☐ **Explain how the suspect drove or was in actual physical control of a motor vehicle:**

- ‣ Keys in ignition;

- ‣ Engine running;

- ‣ Seen driving;

- ‣ Seat belted in;

- ‣ Seat position appropriate for the driver's size and weight;

- ‣ Personal possessions within arm's reach.

☐ **Specify what highway, street or bridge or upon what public or private property open to the public the incident occurred.**

☐ **Explain how he suspect drove the vehicle:**

- ‣ Carelessly;

- ‣ Without due caution and at a speed or in a manner so as to endanger or be likely to endanger any person or property; or

- ‣ The suspect passed when there was passing restriction;

- ‣ Other factors.

Sample Report

Note: An actual police report would typically contain additional detailed information. This sample is designed to emphasize the specific elements related to this particular crime and does not encompass other procedural aspects such as evidence collection, adherence to Miranda rights, and additional investigative measures.

---

[1] For a common statutory example, see I.C. § 49-1401(1)

At approximately 2:30 PM on November 3, 2023, our dispatch unit received multiple calls regarding a vehicle driving erratically along Main Street, swerving across lanes, and nearly causing collisions. Witnesses described the vehicle as a red sports car with the license plate GTR456. I was dispatched to the scene and arrived at approximately 2:40 PM.

Upon arrival, I observed a red sports car matching the description parked haphazardly on the sidewalk near the intersection of Main and Elm Street. The vehicle's engine was still running, and the driver's door was open. A male individual, later identified as Michael Richardson, was standing outside the car, appearing agitated and pacing.

Witness Statements:

Three eyewitnesses provided statements at the scene:

Sarah Jennings, a pedestrian, stated she saw the vehicle run through a red light and nearly hit a cyclist. She confirmed the driver was Mr. Richardson, whom she saw exiting the vehicle.

David Fletcher, a driver from another vehicle, reported that Mr. Richardson's car had overtaken him at a high speed, cutting him off, and causing him to swerve and hit the curb to avoid a collision.

Lisa Montgomery, operating a nearby food truck, described seeing the vehicle driving at a high speed down Main Street, ignoring pedestrian right-of-way and causing public endangerment.

Evidence at the Scene:

The vehicle's engine was running upon my arrival, with the keys in the ignition.

Mr. Richardson's wallet and mobile phone were observed on the passenger seat, within easy reach.

The driver's seat was adjusted for someone of Mr. Richardson's height and build, and the seatbelt was still extended, indicating recent use.

Skid marks indicative of harsh braking were visible on the road near where the car was parked.

Suspect's Behavior and Statements:

Mr. Richardson was questioned at the scene. He admitted to driving the car, stating he was "just having a bit of fun." He smelled strongly of alcohol, his speech was slurred, and he was unsteady on his feet. Field sobriety tests were administered, which Mr. Richardson failed.

Charges and Actions Taken:

Given the danger posed to public safety, the eyewitness accounts, and Mr. Richardson's condition, he was arrested for reckless driving under the state's vehicle code. The vehicle was impounded, and Mr. Richardson was transported to the county jail for processing. He was informed of his Miranda rights and agreed to provide a statement without an attorney present, further admitting to "driving like a race car driver" as he thought the roads were "pretty empty."

Conclusion:

The combination of eyewitness statements, Mr. Richardson's admissions, and the physical evidence at the scene establish the reckless nature of his driving. All evidence will be forwarded to the District Attorney's office for further action. The witnesses were thanked, and their contact information has been recorded for follow-up statements or court appearances if necessary.

End of Report.

Inattentive Driving

Criminal Elements

These elements must be proven beyond a reasonable doubt in court:[1]

☐ **State the approximate date (and time if known) when the offense occurred.**

- This confirms the offense occurred within the statute of limitations.

☐ **Specify where the offense occurred.**

- This establishes the court's jurisdiction over the offense.

☐ **Explain how the suspect drove or was in actual physical control of a motor vehicle:**

- Keys in ignition;

- Engine running;

- Seen driving;

- Seat belted in;

- Seat position appropriate for the driver's size and weight;

- Personal possessions within arm's reach.

☐ **Specify what highway, street or bridge or upon what public or private property open to the public the incident occurred.**

☐ **Explain how the suspect drove the vehicle:**

- In an inattentive, careless or imprudent manner, in light of the circumstances then existing;

- Drove in a manner where the danger to persons or property from the suspect's conduct was slight (otherwise it would be reckless).

Sample Report

Note: An actual police report would typically contain additional detailed information. This sample is designed to emphasize the specific elements related to this particular crime and does not encompass other procedural aspects such as evidence collection, adherence to Miranda rights, and additional investigative measures.

At around 4:15 PM on November 3, 2023, while on routine patrol, I observed a blue sedan swerving slightly within its lane and reducing speed erratically on

---

[1] For a common statutory example, see I.C. § 49-1401(3).

Hawthorne Boulevard. The vehicle then drifted close to the neighboring lane, nearly side-swiping an adjacent car. I initiated a traffic stop, suspecting the driver might be impaired or experiencing a medical issue.

Upon approach, I identified the driver as one Jonathan Bell. Mr. Bell appeared flustered and was quick to put away his smartphone, which I observed on his lap.

Evidence at the Scene:

Mr. Bell's smartphone was within easy reach, displaying an open text conversation.

I observed no signs of alcohol or drug impairment during our interaction.

Suspect's Behavior and Statements:

When questioned about his erratic driving, Mr. Bell admitted to responding to texts while driving, stating it was a "quick reply" and he thought it "wouldn't be a big deal." He acknowledged that he might have drifted from his lane but believed the road was relatively clear.

Charges and Actions Taken:

Given Mr. Bell's admission, the observed behavior, and the potential risk posed to other road users, I issued a citation for inattentive driving under the relevant municipal code. Mr. Bell was informed of his court date and released at the scene.

Conclusion:

Mr. Bell was cited for inattentive driving, primarily due to texting, created a potential hazard on the road.

End of Report.

Felony Eluding

Criminal Elements

These elements must be proven beyond a reasonable doubt in court:[1]

☐ **State the approximate date (and time if known) when the offense occurred.**

- ‣ This confirms the offense occurred within the statute of limitations.

☐ **Specify where the offense occurred.**

- ‣ This establishes the court's jurisdiction over the offense.

☐ **Explain why you knew the suspect was driving a motor vehicle:**

- ‣ You saw him driving;

- ‣ He was pulled from the driver's seat upon termination of the pursuit, etc.

☐ **Describe how the suspect intentionally fled or attempted to elude:**

- ‣ A pursuing police vehicle;

- ‣ The officer gave a visual and/or audible signal to stop

- ‣ The suspect traveled 30 MPH above the posted speed limit, or cause property damage or injury to another.

☐ **Finally, describe how the driver did one or more of the following:**

- ‣ Traveled 30 MPH above the posted speed limit.

- ‣ Caused property damage or bodily injury to another;

- ‣ Drove the vehicle in a manner so as to endanger or be likely to endanger another person or another person's property;

Sample Report

Note: An actual police report would typically contain additional detailed information. This sample is designed to emphasize the specific elements related to this particular crime and does not encompass other procedural aspects such as evidence collection, adherence to Miranda rights, and additional investigative measures.

On the night of November 4, 2023, at approximately 9:30 PM, while patrolling the area near Main Street and Elm Avenue, I observed a red sports coupe fail to stop at a red light. The vehicle made a high-speed right turn,

---

[1] For a common statutory example, see I.C. § 49-1404(2)\

almost colliding with another vehicle. I activated my patrol car's lights and siren to initiate a traffic stop.

Instead of complying, the driver, later identified as Michael Thompson, accelerated, entering Interstate 45. I relayed the situation via radio, requesting backup and informing dispatch of the pursuit.

Evidence and Observations During Pursuit:

- The suspect's vehicle was clocked at speeds exceeding 90 MPH in a 60 MPH zone.
- Mr. Thompson executed several risky maneuvers, including tight overtaking and abrupt lane changes without signaling.
- The pursuit continued for approximately 15 minutes, during which Mr. Thompson's vehicle sideswiped a sedan, causing noticeable damage to both cars. The driver of the sedan appeared shaken but unharmed.
- The chase ended when the suspect's vehicle was cornered by responding units at a service station off Exit 22.

Suspect Apprehension:

Mr. Thompson was ordered out of the vehicle and was taken into custody without further incident. He was pulled from the driver's seat, confirming he was operating the vehicle. No passengers were in the car.

Charges and Actions Taken:

Given the blatant disregard for traffic laws, public safety, and the direct command to stop, Mr. Thompson was arrested for felony eluding. Additional charges include reckless driving and property damage due to the collision with the sedan.

Conclusion:

The suspect's actions posed a significant danger to public safety, evidenced by excessive speeding, property damage, and the potential for causing bodily harm. The pursuit and subsequent apprehension of Mr. Thompson were conducted following protocol, with high emphasis on public safety. Mr. Thompson was transported to the county jail, and his vehicle was seized as evidence pending further investigation.

End of Report.

Leaving the Scene with Injuries

Criminal Elements

These elements must be proven beyond a reasonable doubt in court:[1]

☐ **State the approximate date (and time if known) when the offense occurred.**

▸ This confirms the offense occurred within the statute of limitations.

☐ **Specify where the offense occurred.**

▸ This establishes the court's jurisdiction over the offense.

☐ **Explain why you believe the suspect was driving the motor vehicle involved in the accident:**

▸ Admissions;

▸ Eye witness;

▸ Damage on vehicle consistent with accident;

▸ Paint transfer;

▸ Based on routine travel plans suspect would have been in the area, etc.

☐ **Specify what highway, street or bridge or upon what public or private property open to the public the incident occurred.**

☐ **Describe how the victim was injured.**

☐ **Explain why the suspect knew or had reason to know that the accident had resulted in an injury to the other person:**

▸ Significant damage to both vehicles;

▸ Suspect got out, saw victim, and left;

▸ Suspect also sustained injuries;

▸ Witness told suspect someone was injured;

▸ Admissions by suspect, etc.

☐ **Finally, the suspect failed to do any of the following:**

▸ Render reasonable medical assistance to injured people (e.g. call 911, transport to hospital, etc.)

---

[1] For a common statutory example, see I.C. § 18-8007

- Provide the victim with name, address, registration, or insurance information;
- Show the victim his driver's license.

Sample Report

Note: An actual police report would typically contain additional detailed information. This sample is designed to emphasize the specific elements related to this particular crime and does not encompass other procedural aspects such as evidence collection, adherence to Miranda rights, and additional investigative measures.

On November 5, 2023, at approximately 7:45 PM, our department received multiple 911 calls reporting a hit-and-run incident involving two vehicles at the intersection of 5th Street and Parker Avenue. Upon arrival at the scene, I observed a blue sedan with significant front-end damage stationary in the roadway. The vehicle's driver, Ms. Emily Harris, was experiencing noticeable distress and pain, holding her arm, which appeared to be fractured.

Witness Statements and Evidence Collected:

Multiple witnesses stated that a black pickup truck had collided with the sedan and that the driver of the truck (male, approximately 5'10", dark hair) had exited his vehicle, approached the sedan, observed the injured driver, and then hurriedly departed the scene without offering assistance or exchanging information.

One witness, Mr. George Stanton, captured a photo of the truck's license plate, which was run through our database, identifying the owner as one Mr. Johnathan Smith.

Paint transfer on Ms. Harris's car was consistent with the witnesses' description of the truck.

Investigation and Suspect Apprehension:

Officers proceeded to Mr. Smith's address listed on the vehicle registration. The black truck was found in the driveway with damage consistent with the collision, including blue paint scuffs that matched Ms. Harris's vehicle.

Mr. Smith answered the door with visible abrasions on his forehead, consistent with injuries from a recent collision. He initially denied involvement but later admitted to "panicking" after seeing Ms. Harris's condition and fleeing the scene.

Charges and Actions Taken:

Mr. Smith was placed under arrest for leaving the scene of an accident involving injuries. He failed to provide aid, neglected to share his personal and insurance information with the victim, and did not report the incident to law enforcement.

Conclusion:

The evidence, including witness statements, physical evidence at the scene, and Mr. Smith's admissions, established his involvement in the accident. His disregard for the victim's well-being and legal obligations constitutes a serious offense. Ms. Harris was transported to Hometown General Hospital for her injuries, and a detailed statement was taken. Mr. Smith was processed at the local station, and his vehicle was impounded for further examination. The case will be forwarded to the District Attorney's office for prosecution.

End of Report.

Leaving the Scene - Unattended Vehicle

Criminal Elements

These elements must be proven beyond a reasonable doubt in court:[1]

☐ **State the approximate date (and time if known) when the offense occurred.**

   ‣ This confirms the offense occurred within the statute of limitations.

☐ **Specify where the offense occurred.**

   ‣ This establishes the court's jurisdiction over the offense.

☐ **Explain why you believe the suspect was driving the motor vehicle involved in the accident:**

   ‣ Admissions;

   ‣ Eye witness;

   ‣ Damage on vehicle consistent with accident;

   ‣ Paint transfer;

   ‣ Based on routine travel plans suspect would have been in the area, etc.

☐ **Specify what highway, street or bridge or upon what public or private property open to the public the incident occurred.**

☐ **Explain why the suspect knew or had reason to know that he was involved in an accident with an unoccupied vehicle:**

   ‣ Eye witness;

   ‣ Admissions;

   ‣ Got out and looked at damage;

   ‣ Significant damage to both vehicles, etc.

☐ **Finally, the suspect failed to do any of the following:**

   ‣ Locate the operator or owner of the unattended vehicle and notify him or her of the suspect's name and address and of the name and address of the owner of the vehicle the suspect was driving, or

---

[1] For a common statutory example, see I.C. § 49-1303

- Leave in a conspicuous place in the unattended vehicle a written notice giving the suspect's name and address, the name and address of the owner of the vehicle the suspect was driving, and a statement of the circumstances.

Sample Report

Note: An actual police report would typically contain additional detailed information. This sample is designed to emphasize the specific elements related to this particular crime and does not encompass other procedural aspects such as evidence collection, adherence to Miranda rights, and additional investigative measures.

On November 4, 2023, at approximately 2:30 PM, the Las Vegas Police Department was notified of a hit-and-run incident that occurred in the parking lot of the Fresh Market Grocery store located at 1500 Sunset Boulevard. The report stated that a silver compact car struck a parked, unattended black SUV and then left the scene without following proper procedures.

Witness Statements and Evidence Collected:

- Ms. Linda Torres, a shopper at the grocery store, reported she witnessed the silver car hit the SUV. She noted the driver (male, around 30 years old, blond hair) got out of his vehicle, inspected the damage, appeared agitated, and then quickly drove away.

- Ms. Torres managed to take several photos with her phone, capturing the silver car's license plate and the damage to both vehicles.

- The owner of the black SUV, Mr. Jason Kim, was notified and returned to his vehicle, confirming he had not been aware of the incident until notified.

Investigation and Suspect Apprehension:

Using the license plate information, the vehicle was registered to one Mr. Robert Dalton. Officers proceeded to the registered address and identified a silver compact car matching the description, with corresponding damage and black paint transfers in the parking area.

Mr. Dalton was questioned and initially denied the incident but eventually confessed to hitting the SUV and leaving in a panic, as he was in a rush to an urgent appointment.

Charges and Actions Taken:

Mr. Dalton was placed under arrest for leaving the scene of an accident involving an unattended vehicle. He failed to locate the owner or leave any contact information or explanation of the incident for the owner of the SUV, as required by law.

Conclusion:

The evidence, including the witness's account, photos, and the suspect's admission, confirms Mr. Dalton's involvement in the accident. His failure to perform his legal obligations after the collision constitutes a violation of the law. Mr. Kim was advised to contact his insurance company with the details provided, including the witness's statement and photos. Mr. Dalton was processed at the local station, and the case will be referred to the Traffic Violations Bureau for further action.

End of Report.

Leaving the Scene - Stationary Objects

Criminal Elements

These elements must be proven beyond a reasonable doubt in court:[1]

☐ **State the approximate date (and time if known) when the offense occurred.**

- ‣ This confirms the offense occurred within the statute of limitations.

☐ **Specify where the offense occurred.**

- ‣ This establishes the court's jurisdiction over the offense.

☐ **Explain why you believe the suspect was driving the motor vehicle involved in the accident:**

- ‣ Admissions;

- ‣ Eye witness;

- ‣ Damage on vehicle consistent with accident;

- ‣ Paint transfer;

- ‣ Based on routine travel plans suspect would have been in the area, etc.

☐ **Specify what highway, street or bridge or upon what public or private property open to the public the incident occurred.**

☐ **Explain why the suspect knew or had reason to know that he was involved in an accident with a stationary object near the roadway:**

☐ **Finally, the suspect failed to do any of the following:**

- ‣ Take reasonable steps to locate the owner or person in charge of the property;

- ‣ Notify such person of the accident, the suspect's name and address, the name of the suspect's insurance agent or company if the suspect had automobile liability insurance, and the motor vehicle registration number of the vehicle the suspect was driving; and

- ‣ Exhibit his driver's license, if it was available and the suspect was requested to exhibit it.

---

[1] For a common statutory example, see I.C. § 49-1304

Sample Report

Note: An actual police report would typically contain additional detailed information. This sample is designed to emphasize the specific elements related to this particular crime and does not encompass other procedural aspects such as evidence collection, adherence to Miranda rights, and additional investigative measures.

On November 5, 2023, at approximately 11:30 PM, the Henderson Police Department received a report of a hit-and-run incident involving a blue sedan and the Hawthorne Bridge on River Road. The caller, a pedestrian named Eric Walton, reported hearing a loud crash and then observing the vehicle in question speeding away from the bridge.

Witness Statements and Evidence Collected:

Mr. Walton provided a partial license plate number and described the vehicle as a blue sedan with noticeable front-end damage. He stated that the driver (male, medium build) did not exit the vehicle or attempt to inspect the damage to the bridge.

Concerned, Mr. Walton decided to follow the vehicle at a safe distance, observing it pull into "The Rusty Anchor," a local bar, approximately two miles from the scene of the accident.

Upon arrival at the scene, officers noted fresh damage to the bridge's railing, including blue paint chips and vehicle debris consistent with a recent collision.

Investigation and Suspect Apprehension:

Officers proceeded to "The Rusty Anchor," where they located the blue sedan in the parking lot, with front-end damage matching the description provided by Mr. Walton.

Inside the bar, officers identified the suspect as Mr. Johnathan Grimes, who matched the witness's description of the driver. Mr. Grimes appeared to be consuming alcohol and was in a visibly agitated state.

Upon questioning, Mr. Grimes admitted he had hit the bridge after swerving to avoid an animal on the road. He confirmed that he panicked and decided to drive to the bar instead of reporting the accident.

Charges and Actions Taken:

Mr. Grimes was placed under arrest for leaving the scene of an accident involving a stationary object. He failed to take reasonable steps to notify any person in charge of the property, provide his personal and insurance information, or exhibit his driver's license.

Conclusion:

The evidence, including the witness's account, the vehicle's damage, and Mr. Grimes's admission, confirms his involvement in the accident. His failure to perform his legal obligations after the collision constitutes a violation of the law. The Department of Transportation has been informed of the damage to the bridge for assessment and repair. Mr. Grimes was processed at the local station, and the case has been referred to the Traffic Violations Bureau for further action. Additionally, the bar's surveillance footage was secured to corroborate the timeline of events as part of the evidence.

Fictitious Display

Criminal Elements

These elements must be proven beyond a reasonable doubt in court:[1]

☐ **State the approximate date (and time if known) when the offense occurred.**

   ‣ This confirms the offense occurred within the statute of limitations.

☐ **Specify where the offense occurred.**

   ‣ This establishes the court's jurisdiction over the offense.

☐ **Describe how the suspect was responsible for displaying a fictitious license plate, temp tag, or vehicle registration.**

☐ **Explain why you think the suspect knew it was fictitious:**

   ‣ Admissions;

   ‣ Criminal history for fraud or theft;

   ‣ Unemployed;

   ‣ Vehicle belongs to suspect;

   ‣ Suspect admits he is the sole driver;

   ‣ Suspect has possessed the car for a long time, especially longer than renewal period (year or more); etc.

Sample Report

Note: An actual police report would typically contain additional detailed information. This sample is designed to emphasize the specific elements related to this particular crime and does not encompass other procedural aspects such as evidence collection, adherence to Miranda rights, and additional investigative measures.

On November 7, 2023, at approximately 3:45 PM, I was on routine patrol traveling eastbound on Westridge Lane. I observed a red 2019 Ford Mustang traveling at a high rate of speed in a 35-mph zone. Utilizing my patrol vehicle's radar system, I recorded the Mustang's speed at 52 mph. I initiated a traffic stop for the speeding violation.

Observations and Evidence Collected:

---

[1] For a common statutory example, see I.C. § 49-456(2)

The vehicle pulled over to the side of the road, and I approached the driver's side. The driver was identified as Mr. Michael Thompson through his California driver's license.

I noticed that the license plate displayed on the vehicle appeared newer, yet the registration sticker showed a date inconsistent with current records, indicating expiration in 2022.

Mr. Thompson appeared nervous during the interaction and was unable to provide a satisfactory explanation for the discrepancy in the registration date.

A quick check through the DMV database revealed that the actual registration for the plate number XYZ123 belonged to a 2017 Toyota Camry. The database showed no records for the Ford Mustang under Mr. Thompson's name or the fictitious plate.

Investigation and Suspect Statements:

When questioned about the vehicle's ownership, Mr. Thompson initially claimed that the car was recently purchased and he had not yet updated the registration. However, he later admitted, after being presented with the DMV discrepancies, that he found the plate in a junkyard and placed it on his vehicle. He confessed that he did so to avoid registration fees and potential police attention due to a suspended driver's license.

Further investigation into Mr. Thompson's background revealed a history of minor fraud-related offenses and recent unemployment, which he acknowledged might have influenced his decision to use a fictitious plate.

Charges and Actions Taken:

Mr. Thompson was placed under arrest for the fictitious display of a license plate and vehicle registration, a violation under California Vehicle Code 4463 VC. He was also issued a citation for speeding. His vehicle was impounded pending further investigation.

Conclusion:

The evidence, including the fictitious license plate, the suspect's admission, and his background, suggests a clear intent to deceive law enforcement and avoid legal obligations associated with vehicle ownership and operation. Mr. Thompson was processed at the Riverside Police Station, and the case will be forwarded to the County District Attorney's office for prosecution. Further investigation will be conducted to determine if there are any additional legal infractions related to Mr. Thompson's actions.

End of Report.

Crimes Against Persons

Assault

Criminal Elements

These elements must be proven beyond a reasonable doubt in court:[1]

- ☐ **State the approximate date (and time if known) when the offense occurred.**

  ‣ This confirms the offense occurred within the statute of limitations.

- ☐ **Specify where the offense occurred.**

  ‣ This establishes the court's jurisdiction over the offense.

- ☐ **Describe what the suspect did or said which would place a reasonable person in fear of imminent harm.**

Sample Report

Note: An actual police report would typically contain additional detailed information. This sample is designed to emphasize the specific elements related to this particular crime and does not encompass other procedural aspects such as evidence collection, adherence to Miranda rights, and additional investigative measures.

On November 15, 2023, at approximately 11:15 PM, our patrol unit was dispatched to "The Night Owl" Bar and Lounge following a report of a potential assault. Upon arrival, I, Officer Samantha Reid, encountered a group of patrons outside the establishment, creating an atmosphere of heightened tension.

Scene Assessment:

I was led by bar staff to the main area inside the establishment, where I observed one individual, later identified as Mr. Bryan Wallace, who appeared visibly shaken and distressed. Another individual, identified as Mr. Derek Stewart, was being held back by several patrons and bar security personnel.

Preliminary Investigation:

Initial statements collected from witnesses, including the bartender, Ms. Jenny Harrows, indicated that Mr. Stewart had threatened Mr. Wallace. According to these accounts, Mr. Stewart, in an apparently intoxicated state, approached Mr. Wallace and began issuing verbal threats, aggressively invading his personal space and raising a clenched fist as if to strike him. Witnesses confirmed that no physical contact had occurred before I arrived on the scene.

---

[1] For a common statutory example, see I.C. § 18–901

Victim Statement:

Mr. Wallace stated that he feared for his safety during the confrontation, believing that Mr. Stewart was about to physically attack him. He confirmed that Mr. Stewart used threatening language and made menacing gestures but did not actually strike him.

Suspect Apprehension:

Given the circumstances and after reading Mr. Stewart his Miranda rights, I detained him for assault, intending to cause fear of imminent physical harm in Mr. Wallace. Mr. Stewart was transported to the local station for processing. Throughout, he exhibited hostile behavior and was verbally abusive.

Victim Assistance:

Although unharmed, Mr. Wallace was offered assistance, and details for victim support services were provided to ensure his psychological well-being following the traumatic event.

Charges and Processing:

Mr. Stewart has been charged with assault. His actions, including the threatening behavior and intent to instill fear in Mr. Wallace, substantiate this charge. He is being held pending further legal proceedings, as per the district attorney's guidance.

Conclusion:

This report, all witness statements, and any available security footage from "The Night Owl" Bar and Lounge have been forwarded to the district attorney's office for further review and action. The incident involving Mr. Wallace, characterized by the threat of physical harm, meets the criteria for an assault charge.

End of Report.

Battery

Criminal Elements

These elements must be proven beyond a reasonable doubt in court:[1]

☐ **State the approximate date (and time if known) when the offense occurred.**

  ‣ This confirms the offense occurred within the statute of limitations.

☐ **Specify where the offense occurred.**

  ‣ This establishes the court's jurisdiction over the offense.

☐ **Describe what the suspect did which caused an injury or an unlawful touching of another person.**

Sample Report

Note: An actual police report would typically contain additional detailed information. This sample is designed to emphasize the specific elements related to this particular crime and does not encompass other procedural aspects such as evidence collection, adherence to Miranda rights, and additional investigative measures.

On November 15, 2023, at approximately 11:15 PM, our patrol unit was dispatched to "The Night Owl" Bar and Lounge in response to a reported battery. Upon arrival, I, Officer Samantha Reid, observed a crowd of patrons outside the establishment, and the situation appeared tense.

Scene Assessment:

The bar staff quickly ushered me to the main area inside the establishment, where I noticed one individual, later identified as Mr. Bryan Wallace, seated with a bloodied nose and a rapidly swelling eye. Opposite him, and being restrained by several patrons, was another individual, identified as Mr. Derek Stewart.

Preliminary Investigation:

Initial statements collected from witnesses, including the bartender, Ms. Jenny Harrows, indicated that Mr. Stewart, without provocation, launched a sudden physical attack on Mr. Wallace. Witnesses stated that Mr. Stewart's body language was aggressive, and he used his fists to strike Mr. Wallace in the face, causing the visible injuries.

---

[1] For a common statutory example, see I.C. § 18–903

Mr. Stewart's unprovoked attack and the resulting physical harm to Mr. Wallace led to the situation being brought under control by the bar staff and concerned patrons until my arrival.

Victim Statement:

Mr. Wallace claimed that he had never met Mr. Stewart before and that the attack was completely unprovoked. He confirmed that Mr. Stewart approached him and, without warning, began to strike him in the face, causing him to fall off his stool and sustain injuries.

Suspect Apprehension:

Given the circumstances and after reading Mr. Stewart his Miranda rights, I placed him under arrest for battery. He was transported to the local station for processing. Mr. Stewart was relatively un-cooperative, continuing to exhibit aggressive behavior.

Medical Attention:

Paramedics were called to the scene to tend to Mr. Wallace's injuries. They recommended he visit the emergency room for further assessment due to the swelling around his eye, which could indicate more severe trauma.

Charges and Processing:

Mr. Stewart has been charged with battery. The unprovoked attack, physical contact, and resulting harm substantiate the charge. He is being held pending further proceedings, as per the district attorney's guidance.

Conclusion:

This report and all statements, along with security footage from "The Night Owl" Bar and Lounge, have been submitted to the district attorney's office for further review and action. The battery on Mr. Wallace was unprovoked and caused physical harm, fulfilling the criteria for a battery charge.

End of Report.

Aggravated Assault

Criminal Elements

These elements must be proven beyond a reasonable doubt in court:[1]

☐ **State the approximate date (and time if known) when the offense occurred.**

   ‣ This confirms the offense occurred within the statute of limitations.

☐ **Specify where the offense occurred.**

   ‣ This establishes the court's jurisdiction over the offense.

☐ **Describe what the suspect did or said which would place a reasonable person in fear of imminent harm.**

☐ **Explain what weapon or other object the suspect possessed capable of producing great bodily harm:**

   ‣ Deadly weapon;

   ‣ Corrosive acid;

   ‣ Baseball bat; etc.

Sample Report

Note: An actual police report would typically contain additional detailed information. This sample is designed to emphasize the specific elements related to this particular crime and does not encompass other procedural aspects such as evidence collection, adherence to Miranda rights, and additional investigative measures.

On November 15, 2023, at approximately 11:15 PM, I, Officer Samantha Reid, responded to a distress call from "The Night Owl" Bar and Lounge. Upon arrival, I was met with a scene of disarray as patrons were gathered outside the establishment, exhibiting signs of distress.

Scene Assessment:

I was directed by onlookers toward the adjacent parking area where I discovered the victim, Mr. Bryan Wallace, on the ground, semi-conscious, and with evident head trauma. Nearby, a blood-stained baseball bat was observed on the pavement.

Preliminary Investigation:

---

[1] For a common statutory example, see I.C. § 18–905

Initial statements collected from witnesses, including Ms. Jenny Harrows (bartender) and several bystanders, indicated that the suspect, Mr. Derek Stewart, became enraged following a brief interaction between Mr. Wallace and Mr. Stewart's girlfriend inside the bar. According to witness accounts, Mr. Stewart perceived this interaction as offensive.

Lead-up to the Assault:

Witnesses recounted that a visibly agitated Mr. Stewart engaged in a heated confrontation with Mr. Wallace inside the establishment. The argument then spilled into the parking lot, where it escalated. Mr. Stewart, seemingly in a fit of rage, proceeded to his vehicle, retrieved a baseball bat, and assaulted Mr. Wallace.

Victim Statement:

While awaiting the arrival of medical services, I gathered preliminary information from Mr. Wallace amidst his evident distress and pain. He confirmed the assault and alluded to the altercation inside the bar, sparked by a casual conversation he had with Mr. Stewart's girlfriend.

Suspect Apprehension:

I identified and detained Mr. Stewart at the scene without incident. He was verbally non-compliant and visibly upset, repeatedly stating that he "lost it" when Mr. Wallace "disrespected" him by talking to his girlfriend. He was informed of his Miranda rights and taken into custody. No additional weapons were found upon him.

Medical Assessment:

Paramedics arrived by approximately 11:30 PM, attending to Mr. Wallace's injuries. They suspected severe trauma, including a possible concussion and skull fracture, necessitating immediate hospitalization.

Charges and Processing:

Considering the intentional retrieval and use of a deadly weapon, resulting in serious bodily harm, Mr. Stewart was charged with aggravated assault. The motive appeared to be a sudden, intense emotional reaction to the victim's interaction with his girlfriend.

Evidence Collection:

The baseball bat, suspected of being the assault weapon, was seized as evidence, following standard evidence collection protocols. CCTV footage from the bar, particularly covering the parking area, has been requisitioned for further investigation.

Conclusion:

The case, inclusive of witness testimonies, the suspect's statements, and collected evidence, has been forwarded to the district attorney's office for further action. The assault, underlined by the suspect's impulsive, emotionally charged reaction, fulfills the criteria for an aggravated assault charge due to the use of a deadly weapon and the infliction of serious injury.

End of Report.

Felonious Administration of Drugs

Criminal Elements

These elements must be proven beyond a reasonable doubt in court:[1]

☐ **State the approximate date (and time if known) when the offense occurred.**

- ‣ This confirms the offense occurred within the statute of limitations.

☐ **Specify where the offense occurred.**

- ‣ This establishes the court's jurisdiction over the offense.

☐ **Describe how the suspect administered or aided in administering any:**

- ‣ Chloroform;
- ‣ Ether;
- ‣ Narcotic;
- ‣ Anesthetic;
- ‣ Intoxicating agent, and so forth.

☐ **State that the victim gave no valid consent.**

☐ **Finally, explain why the administration of the drugs was with intent to enable or assist the suspect or any other person to commit a felony (e.g. rape).**

Sample Report

Note: An actual police report would typically contain additional detailed information. This sample is designed to emphasize the specific elements related to this particular crime and does not encompass other procedural aspects such as evidence collection, adherence to Miranda rights, and additional investigative measures.

On November 20, 2023, at approximately 9:50 PM, our department received a call from "Jolly's Bar & Grill" regarding a potential drug-related offense. I, Officer Alex Mercer, arrived at the scene at approximately 10:00 PM.

Scene Assessment:

Upon arrival, the atmosphere in the bar was tense, with several patrons appearing agitated. The bar staff had cordoned off a section where the

---

[1] For a common statutory example, see I.C. § 18–913

incident reportedly occurred. I was quickly approached by the bartender, Ms. Lana Reed, who identified herself as the caller.

Witness Statements:

Ms. Reed urgently directed my attention to a male suspect, later identified as Mr. Jason Kline, who was being confronted by several patrons. According to Ms. Reed and corroborated by witnesses, Mr. Kline was observed slipping a substance into a woman's drink while she was away from her table. The woman, later identified as Ms. Sarah Jennings, was notified by the witnesses before she consumed the beverage.

Suspect Apprehension:

I approached Mr. Kline for questioning, and he appeared nervous and defensive. Due to the severity of the allegations and the number of eyewitness accounts, Mr. Kline was detained for further questioning. He was informed of his rights per standard procedure.

Victim Interaction:

I spoke with Ms. Jennings, who appeared visibly shaken but was unharmed. She confirmed she had not consumed the drink and was unaware of Mr. Kline's actions until informed by other patrons. She specified that she had no prior relationship with Mr. Kline and had not given him permission to interact with her drink.

Evidence Collection:

The drink suspected to be contaminated was secured as evidence, and a sample was taken for immediate preliminary field testing. The initial test indicated the presence of a sedative agent commonly associated with date rape drugs. The remaining substance was sealed for detailed laboratory analysis.

Charges and Processing:

Mr. Kline was arrested on charges of felonious administration of drugs. The eyewitness accounts, coupled with the preliminary field test results, established a basis for his intent to incapacitate Ms. Jennings potentially to facilitate a further felony, such as sexual assault.

Further Investigation:

CCTV footage from the establishment has been secured, which reportedly captured the incident. The video material will be integral to the ongoing investigation. Additionally, statements from all cooperative eyewitnesses were recorded at the scene.

Conclusion:

The case has been referred to the criminal investigation department for further analysis of the collected samples and review of the CCTV footage. The prompt response of the bar patrons and staff significantly aided in the prevention of potential harm to Ms. Jennings. The incident stands as a severe violation of law and public safety, warranting thorough investigation and legal action.

End of Report.

Attempted Strangulation

Criminal Elements

These elements must be proven beyond a reasonable doubt in court:[1]

☐ **State the approximate date (and time if known) when the offense occurred.**

  ‣ This confirms the offense occurred within the statute of limitations.

☐ **Specify where the offense occurred.**

  ‣ This establishes the court's jurisdiction over the offense.

☐ **Describe how the suspect intentionally choked or attempted to strangle the victim.**

  ‣ There is no requirement that the officer prove the suspect intended to kill the victim. The only intent required is to show an intent to choke or strangle.

☐ **Describe the suspect and victim's relationship at the time of the act:**

  ‣ Household member;

  ‣ Child-in-common;

  ‣ Prior dating relationship, etc.

Sample Report

Note: An actual police report would typically contain additional detailed information. This sample is designed to emphasize the specific elements related to this particular crime and does not encompass other procedural aspects such as evidence collection, adherence to Miranda rights, and additional investigative measures.

On November 15, 2023, at approximately 7:40 PM, Dispatch directed me to 4571 Oakwood Lane following a 911 call reporting a domestic disturbance possibly involving physical assault. I, Officer Samantha Pryce, along with Officer Liam Dale, arrived at the specified location at approximately 7:45 PM.

Scene Assessment:

Upon arrival, we encountered a visibly distressed female, later identified as Ms. Rebecca Torres, who was clutching her neck and hyperventilating. We immediately called for medical support to address her condition. Inside the

---

[1] For a common statutory example, see I.C. § 18–923; I.C. §§ 18-918, 39-6303

residence, we found a male, Mr. Daniel Peterson, who appeared agitated and was pacing back and forth in the living room.

Victim's Statement:

Ms. Torres, after receiving initial care from the responding paramedics, reported that Mr. Peterson, her live-in boyfriend, had accused her of infidelity and, during the heated argument, had lunged at her and attempted to strangle her. She managed to free herself from his grasp and called 911. Ms. Torres did not report losing consciousness but was experiencing pain around her throat and difficulty swallowing.

Suspect's Statement:

Mr. Peterson was brought in for questioning. He was highly defensive, initially denying the accusation. However, upon further interrogation, he admitted to "losing control" but insisted he hadn't intended to cause serious harm. He acknowledged that he had used force around Ms. Torres' neck.

Physical Evidence:

Ms. Torres presented redness and abrasions around her neck, consistent with her account of the event. Photographs of her injuries were taken for evidence. The living room area where the altercation occurred was disheveled, with various items, including furniture, showing signs of a struggle.

Witnesses:

There were no other witnesses present in the home at the time of the incident. Neighbors reported hearing loud voices and thuds but did not witness the event.

Charges and Processing:

Given the physical evidence, the victim's statement, and Mr. Peterson's partial admission, he was arrested for attempted strangulation. The nature of the relationship between Ms. Torres and Mr. Peterson, established as intimate partners living together, further substantiated the domestic context of the crime.

Further Investigation:

Ms. Torres was advised to seek a more thorough medical evaluation, and arrangements were made for her to stay with a family member for safety. A restraining order process was initiated per her request. The case has been flagged for follow-up support and resources for Ms. Torres, considering the domestic nature of the violence.

Conclusion:

The case is now pending further investigation, with Mr. Peterson in custody.

End of Report.

Hazing

Criminal Elements

These elements must be proven beyond a reasonable doubt in court:[1]

☐ **State the approximate date (and time if known) when the offense occurred.**

‣ This confirms the offense occurred within the statute of limitations.

☐ **Specify where the offense occurred.**

‣ This establishes the court's jurisdiction over the offense.

☐ **Identify the suspect and his membership status in:**

‣ Fraternity;

‣ Sorority; or

‣ Member of living or social organization organized or operating on or near a college or university campus for purposes of participating in student activity.

☐ **Describe how the suspect hazed or conspired to haze the victim with the intent to:**

‣ Pledge the person as a member of the organization;

‣ Activity constituting hazing was a condition or precondition of attaining membership, status, or any office in the organization.

☐ **Finally, specify that the hazing did not take place as part of the curricular activities or athletic team activities of the college or university.**

Sample Report

Note: An actual police report would typically contain additional detailed information. This sample is designed to emphasize the specific elements related to this particular crime and does not encompass other procedural aspects such as evidence collection, adherence to Miranda rights, and additional investigative measures.

On September 14, 2023, at approximately 9:30 PM, the department received an anonymous tip regarding a suspected hazing incident at the Delta Gamma Phi Fraternity House on the campus of Stanford University. I, Officer Alex

---

[1] For a common statutory example, see I.C. § 18–917

Hartman, along with Officer Jenna Rowley, responded to the scene to investigate the allegations.

Scene Assessment:

Upon arrival at the Delta Gamma Phi house, we encountered a group of individuals, noticeably distressed, standing outside the fraternity house. We identified ourselves as campus police and initiated an inquiry into the reported activities.

Victim's Statement:

A freshman student, Tyler Reed, visibly shaken, reported undergoing what he described as a "hazing ritual" as part of his initiation into Delta Gamma Phi. Mr. Reed detailed an event where he and other pledges were forced to stand naked in a line while fraternity members, including senior students, shouted derogatory remarks and insults at them. He emphasized that this humiliating act was not associated with any university curriculum or athletic program but was a requirement for fraternity membership.

Suspect's Statement:

Upon questioning, the fraternity president, Lucas Bennett, attempted to classify the activities as "traditional rites of passage." However, under further questioning, he conceded that the pledges were subjected to these degrading acts specifically for fraternity induction. He acknowledged his involvement in organizing and facilitating these events.

Physical Evidence:

The area where the pledges stood was cordoned off for evidence collection. We recovered several items used during the hazing, including clothes belonging to the victims and smartphones, potentially containing recordings or photographs of the incident. These items were cataloged and secured for further analysis.

Witnesses:

Other pledges supported Mr. Reed's account, stating they felt compelled to participate, fearing ostracization or retaliation if they refused. Their statements were documented, and confidentiality was assured.

Charges and Processing:

Given the evidence, witness testimonies, and Mr. Bennett's admission, he was arrested under charges of hazing, a violation of both Stanford University's policies and state law. His direct involvement as the orchestrator of these events established the grounds for his arrest.

Further Investigation:

Stanford University's administration was informed of the incident, prompting an immediate internal review, parallel to our criminal investigation. We are also examining the potential complicity of other fraternity members present during the incident. Psychological support and counseling services were extended to Mr. Reed and the other victims.

Conclusion:

The investigation is ongoing, with the possibility of additional charges as more information comes to light. This case underscores the urgent need to address the culture of hazing on campuses and enforce a zero-tolerance policy to safeguard students' dignity and well-being.

End of Report.

Mayhem

Criminal Elements

These elements must be proven beyond a reasonable doubt in court:[1]

☐ **State the approximate date (and time if known) when the offense occurred.**

- ‣ This confirms the offense occurred within the statute of limitations.

☐ **Specify where the offense occurred.**

- ‣ This establishes the court's jurisdiction over the offense.

☐ **Describe how the suspect maliciously injured the victim by engaging in any of the following conduct:**

- ‣ Removes a piece of the victims body;

- ‣ Disables, disfigures or renders a part of the body useless;

- ‣ Cuts out or disables the tongue, puts out an eye, slits the nose, ear or lip.

Sample Report

Note: An actual police report would typically contain additional detailed information. This sample is designed to emphasize the specific elements related to this particular crime and does not encompass other procedural aspects such as evidence collection, adherence to Miranda rights, and additional investigative measures.

On the night of October 21, 2023, at approximately 9:15 PM, I, Officer Jane Patterson, responded to a distress call received by the Hemsford Police Department. The caller, a passerby, reported a violent altercation in the downtown alley near the 1500 Block of Harrison Street.

Upon arrival at the scene, I observed two individuals in the alley, one of whom was lying on the ground with significant facial injuries, identified as Victor Martinez. The other individual, later identified as Andrew Sullivan, was standing a few feet away, with what appeared to be blood on his hands and clothing.

I immediately called for medical assistance for Mr. Martinez and secured the scene. Mr. Martinez was conscious but in extreme pain, holding the side of his face, where it became apparent that a portion of his ear was missing.

---

[1] For a common statutory example, see I.C. § 18–5001

Mr. Sullivan was detained for questioning. Preliminary inquiries at the scene led to the understanding that an argument had escalated, during which Mr. Sullivan had attacked Mr. Martinez. According to witness statements and security footage from a nearby establishment, Mr. Sullivan had maliciously and deliberately bitten off a part of Mr. Martinez's ear, consistent with the injuries observed.

Evidence Collected:

- Security footage from nearby cameras.

- Witness statements.

- Medical report from emergency responders detailing the extent of Mr. Martinez's injuries.

- Photographs of the scene and the injuries sustained by Mr. Martinez.

- Blood-stained clothing from Mr. Sullivan.

Initial Action:

Mr. Sullivan was arrested under the suspicion of committing mayhem, as defined under the jurisdiction's penal code, which involves causing disfiguring injuries, including the removal of a body part. He was informed of his rights and transported to the Hemsford Police Department for further processing. Mr. Martinez was taken to Hemsford General Hospital, where he received medical treatment for his injuries.

Charges Filed:

Andrew Sullivan is being charged with mayhem, given the deliberate nature of the attack and the resulting permanent disfigurement of Victor Martinez. The specific actions that led to these charges include:

Maliciously causing an injury that led to the removal of a part of the victim's body (part of the ear).

The act of disabling, disfiguring, and rendering a part of the body useless.

Conclusion:

This report is a preliminary document, and the investigation remains ongoing. Further actions will include a more in-depth interrogation of the suspect, additional witness testimonies, and a thorough review of the medical reports following the treatment of Mr. Martinez's injuries. The District Attorney's office will be consulted to proceed with the case.

End of report.

Kidnapping

Criminal Elements

These elements must be proven beyond a reasonable doubt in court:[1]

☐ **State the approximate date (and time if known) when the offense occurred.**

  ‣ This confirms the offense occurred within the statute of limitations.

☐ **Specify where the offense occurred.**

  ‣ This establishes the court's jurisdiction over the offense.

☐ **Describe how the suspect seized, confined, enticed, or kidnapped the victim.**

☐ **Describe how the suspect concealed or imprisoned the victim and transported them (however slightly) without consent or authority of law.**

☐ **Explain whether the suspect had any intent to extort money or property to secure the victim's release.**

Sample Report

Note: An actual police report would typically contain additional detailed information. This sample is designed to emphasize the specific elements related to this particular crime and does not encompass other procedural aspects such as evidence collection, adherence to Miranda rights, and additional investigative measures.

On November 2, 2023, at around 8:20 PM, our unit responded to a 911 call concerning a potential kidnapping incident that occurred near the intersection of 47th Street and 9th Avenue. The caller, a bystander, reported seeing a woman being forced into a black sedan by a man wielding a handgun.

Upon arrival, witnesses provided a description of the suspect and the vehicle, including the license plate number. An immediate APB was issued, and the vehicle was spotted and intercepted within 30 minutes by patrolling units near 65th Street.

The victim, identified as Emily Thompson, was found in the back seat, visibly distressed and with her wrists bound with zip ties. The suspect, identified as Jonathan Harris, was immediately apprehended and a handgun was recovered from the vehicle. Preliminary investigation revealed that Ms. Thompson is Mr. Harris's ex-girlfriend.

---

[1] For a common statutory example, see I.C. § 18–4501

Ms. Thompson reported that Mr. Harris had unexpectedly approached her as she was leaving her workplace, threatened her with a gun, and forced her into his car. He then drove away from the location while she was confined in the back seat. She stated that Mr. Harris was irrationally accusing her of betraying him and was demanding that she return to him, making several threatening remarks in the process.

Evidence Collected:

- Witness statements.

- Security footage from street cameras and nearby businesses.

- The handgun found in Mr. Harris's possession.

- The vehicle used in the kidnapping.

- Photographs of the scene and the vehicle.

- Victim's statement.

Initial Action:

Mr. Harris was arrested on charges of kidnapping, and illegal possession of a firearm. He was informed of his rights and transported to the local precinct for further processing. Ms. Thompson was assisted on the scene by emergency medical services and provided with resources for psychological support due to the traumatic experience.

Charges Filed:

Jonathan Harris is being charged with kidnapping, as his actions directly align with the criminal elements of seizing, confining, and transporting a victim without their consent and with the use of a deadly weapon. The specific actions leading to these charges include:

- Forcibly seizing and confining Ms. Thompson.

- Using a handgun to threaten and control the victim.

- Illegally detaining and transporting the victim in a vehicle without her consent.

Conclusion:

This report serves as a preliminary summary of the incident, and the investigation is ongoing. Further actions include a detailed interrogation of the suspect, forensic analysis of the recovered handgun, examination of the vehicle, and a comprehensive review of the collected video footage.

End of report.

False Imprisonment

Criminal Elements

These elements must be proven beyond a reasonable doubt in court:[1]

☐ **State the approximate date (and time if known) when the offense occurred.**

  ‣ This confirms the offense occurred within the statute of limitations.

☐ **Specify where the offense occurred.**

  ‣ This establishes the court's jurisdiction over the offense.

☐ **Describe how the suspect unlawfully prohibited the victim from coming and going to a place the victim had a lawful right to be.**

Sample Report

Note: An actual police report would typically contain additional detailed information. This sample is designed to emphasize the specific elements related to this particular crime and does not encompass other procedural aspects such as evidence collection, adherence to Miranda rights, and additional investigative measures.

On the evening of November 2, 2023, our unit responded to a distress call received from Emily Thompson, who claimed that she was being held against her will at her ex-boyfriend, Jonathan Harris's residence. The call was received at approximately 8:00 PM, and units were immediately dispatched to the location.

Upon arrival at the specified address, officers heard muffled shouting from inside the residence. After announcing our presence, Mr. Harris opened the door. He was agitated and un-cooperative. We asked to enter the premises to ensure the safety of all parties, to which he reluctantly agreed.

Inside, we found Ms. Thompson in the living room, visibly upset and scared. She reported that after a brief encounter outside her workplace, Mr. Harris insisted she accompany him to his house to discuss "something urgent." Once there, he refused to let her leave, physically blocking her path and taking her phone to prevent her from calling for help. She managed to retrieve her phone when Mr. Harris was distracted and called 911.

Evidence Collected:

• Victim's statement.

---

[1] For a common statutory example, see I.C. § 18–2901

- Suspect's statement (recorded post-Miranda warning).

- Testimonies from neighbors who reported hearing disturbances.

- Physical evidence from the scene, including the victim's cellphone.

Initial Action:

Mr. Harris was taken into custody under the suspicion of false imprisonment. He was read his rights and transported to the precinct for further questioning. Ms. Thompson was given immediate care to ensure her physical and emotional state was stable, and she was asked if she wished to press charges, to which she responded affirmatively.

Charges Filed:

Jonathan Harris is being charged with false imprisonment. His actions directly violated the victim's personal liberty, which includes:

Forcibly detaining the victim within his residence.

Depriving the victim of her mobile phone, hindering her ability to seek help.

Physically restricting the victim's freedom of movement without legal authority.

Conclusion:

This report is a preliminary document, and the investigation is ongoing. The next steps include a more in-depth interrogation of Mr. Harris, a full statement from Ms. Thompson, and inquiries with potential witnesses from the surrounding area. We are also in the process of obtaining any security footage that may be available from Ms. Thompson's workplace to document the initial encounter. Further updates to this case will follow as additional information becomes available.

End of report.

Child Custody Interference

Criminal Elements

These elements must be proven beyond a reasonable doubt in court:[1]

☐ **State the approximate date (and time if known) when the offense occurred.**

› This confirms the offense occurred within the statute of limitations.

☐ **Specify where the offense occurred.**

› This establishes the court's jurisdiction over the offense.

☐ **Describe how the suspect intentionally, and without legal authority, took or withheld a child from the child's legal custodian who had a present right to custody.**

› The "right to custody" includes custody, joint custody, visitation, or other parental rights, whether such rights arise from a temporary or permanent custody order or from the equal custodial rights of each parent in the absence of a custody order.

› It may not be unlawful to take and withhold a child if such action is taken to protect the child from imminent physical harm.

› Some states allow up to 24 hours for the child to be returned after authorized visitation before there is a presumption for custodial interference.

Sample Report

Note: An actual police report would typically contain additional detailed information. This sample is designed to emphasize the specific elements related to this particular crime and does not encompass other procedural aspects such as evidence collection, adherence to Miranda rights, and additional investigative measures.

On November 4, 2023, at approximately 4:15 PM, I responded to a distress call from Sarah Johnson, who reported a case of child custody interference. Ms. Johnson informed that her ex-husband, Michael Anderson, had not returned their child following a scheduled visitation, which was a direct violation of their court-ordered custody agreement.

Ms. Johnson provided a copy of the custody agreement, which indicated clear custody terms. Mr. Anderson was granted visitation rights from Friday afternoon through Sunday evening, and the child was to be under Ms.

---

[1] For a common statutory example, see I.C. § 18–4506

Johnson's care for the remainder of the week. Mr. Anderson had failed to return the child by Sunday evening and had ceased all forms of communication with Ms. Johnson, who was visibly distressed and concerned for her child's wellbeing.

Evidence Collected:

- A copy of the court-ordered custody agreement.
- Call and message records from Ms. Johnson's phone, showing her unsuccessful attempts to reach Mr. Anderson.

Investigative Action:

An immediate investigation was initiated given the serious nature of the allegations. Attempts to contact Mr. Anderson on November 4th were unsuccessful. On November 6th, with no word from Mr. Anderson and in cooperation with local authorities, we conducted a welfare check at his residence. The child was found in the home, appearing physically unharmed but distressed. Mr. Anderson was taken into custody without incident.

Charges Filed:

Mr. Anderson was arrested and charged with child custody interference under the state laws governing such offenses. He was transported to the local precinct for processing. The child was safely returned to Ms. Johnson, who was advised to take the child for a medical evaluation to ensure their wellbeing.

Conclusion:

This report is a comprehensive record of the child custody interference incident that transpired starting November 4, 2023. The situation was handled with the utmost urgency, ensuring the safe return of the minor to the custodial parent. Mr. Anderson is currently being held pending a court hearing, and Child Protective Services have been notified to provide additional support and assessment in the wake of these events.

End of report.

Child Endangerment or Injury

Criminal Elements

These elements must be proven beyond a reasonable doubt in court:[1]

☐ **State the approximate date (and time if known) when the offense occurred.**

- ‣ This confirms the offense occurred within the statute of limitations.

☐ **Specify where the offense occurred.**

- ‣ This establishes the court's jurisdiction over the offense.

☐ **Describe how the suspect intentionally caused or permitted a child to suffer, or intentionally inflicted unjustifiable physical pain or mental suffering, including:**

- ‣ The suspect allowed the child to be harmed despite having the ability to prevent it;
- ‣ The child was inside a vehicle while the driver was intoxicated

☐ **Explain how the suspect had care and custody of the child.**

Sample Report

Note: An actual police report would typically contain additional detailed information. This sample is designed to emphasize the specific elements related to this particular crime and does not encompass other procedural aspects such as evidence collection, adherence to Miranda rights, and additional investigative measures.

On November 6, 2023, at approximately 9:30 PM, I, along with Officer Daniels, responded to a call from a concerned citizen who reported a potentially intoxicated driver in a public parking lot. The caller expressed concern as they had seen a young child in the back seat of the vehicle.

Upon arrival at the scene, we identified the vehicle in question and approached it to find a female driver, later identified as Linda Bates, and a young child in the back seat. Ms. Bates exhibited signs of intoxication, including slurred speech, bloodshot eyes, and a strong odor of alcohol emanating from her person.

Evidence Collected:

• Testimony from the concerned citizen, recorded at the scene.

---

[1] For a common statutory example, see I.C. §§ 18–1501& 32–101

- Dashcam footage capturing the state of the suspect's vehicle and her erratic behavior.
- Results from a field sobriety test administered to Ms. Bates.

Investigative Action:

Ms. Bates was asked to step out of the vehicle and perform a standard field sobriety test, which she failed. A child safety officer was called to the scene to take custody of the young child, ensuring her immediate safety. The child was visibly upset and mentioned being scared while Ms. Bates was driving.

Ms. Bates was taken into custody, and during questioning at the station, she admitted to consuming alcohol at a friend's house before deciding to drive her daughter back home. She acknowledged her understanding of the risks but stated she thought she was "okay to drive."

Charges Filed:

Ms. Bates was arrested and charged with child endangerment and driving under the influence with a minor in the vehicle, under the relevant state laws. The child was temporarily placed under protective custody while family services were contacted for a safety assessment and to determine the next steps for the child's welfare.

Conclusion:

This report serves as a complete account of the incident pertaining to the injury to a child that occurred on November 6, 2023. Immediate action was taken to secure the child's safety, and the suspect was detained without further incident. Ms. Bates is awaiting a court hearing, and further investigation will be conducted to assess the living conditions and safety of the child involved.

End of report.

Desertion of a Child

Criminal Elements

These elements must be proven beyond a reasonable doubt in court:[1]

- [ ] **State the approximate date (and time if known) when the offense occurred.**
  - ‣ This confirms the offense occurred within the statute of limitations.
- [ ] **Specify where the offense occurred.**
  - ‣ This establishes the court's jurisdiction over the offense.
- [ ] **Describe how the suspect deserted a child who was dependent on the suspect for care, education, or support.**
- [ ] **Explain why you think this desertion was intentional.**

Sample Report

Note: An actual police report would typically contain additional detailed information. This sample is designed to emphasize the specific elements related to this particular crime and does not encompass other procedural aspects such as evidence collection, adherence to Miranda rights, and additional investigative measures.

On November 12, 2023, at approximately 3:15 PM, I responded to a call from Elmwood Park Mall security, reporting a young child found alone near the food court. Upon arrival, I encountered a distressed male child, approximately four years old, who had been alone for an extended period. Mall security footage revealed the child had been unaccompanied for over two hours.

The child was able to provide his name and mentioned that his father told him to "stay put" while he was going away. Efforts to locate the father within the mall premises were unsuccessful.

Evidence Collected:

- Security footage from Elmwood Park Mall showing Mr. Walsh leaving the child alone near the food court.

- Testimony from mall security officers and witnesses.

- Recorded statement from the child.

Investigative Action:

---

[1] For a common statutory example, see I.C. § 18–401(1)

The child was taken into protective custody while efforts were made to contact any relatives. Upon reaching the child's mother, it was discovered that Mr. Walsh was supposed to have the child for the weekend per a custody agreement. The mother confirmed that this was not the first time Mr. Walsh had neglected his son, but it was the first incident of this severity.

At approximately 8:00 PM, Mr. Walsh returned to the mall and was apprehended by officers. He appeared disoriented and initially claimed not to remember where he had left his son. Upon further questioning, Mr. Walsh admitted that he met a friend and left the mall to visit a nearby bar, losing track of time. He confirmed he told his son to stay put and thought the child would be safe.

Charges Filed:

Mr. Walsh was arrested and charged with desertion of a child under the relevant state laws. The child was released into the mother's custody, and Child Protective Services were notified to conduct a welfare check and further investigation.

Conclusion:

This report is a comprehensive account of the incident pertaining to the desertion of a child on November 12, 2023. Immediate action was taken to ensure the child's safety, and the suspect was detained without further incident. Mr. Walsh's actions were deemed intentional, given his acknowledgment of leaving his son unattended for personal leisure, disregarding his son's safety and well-being. He is awaiting a court hearing, and further investigation will be conducted to assess the living conditions and safety of the child involved.

End of report.

Obstructing an Officer

Criminal Elements

These elements must be proven beyond a reasonable doubt in court:[1]

☐ **State the approximate date (and time if known) when the offense occurred.**

- ‣ This confirms the offense occurred within the statute of limitations.

☐ **Specify where the offense occurred.**

- ‣ This establishes the court's jurisdiction over the offense.

☐ **Describe how the suspect intentionally resisted, delayed, or obstructed a public officer in the discharge of official duties.**

- ‣ Remember, exercising First Amendment rights alone is not a valid obstruction charge.

Sample Report

Note: An actual police report would typically contain additional detailed information. This sample is designed to emphasize the specific elements related to this particular crime and does not encompass other procedural aspects such as evidence collection, adherence to Miranda rights, and additional investigative measures.

On November 17, 2023, at around 9:30 PM, I, along with Officer Jenna Rowlands, responded to a noise complaint at an apartment on the 1200 block of Bellwood Street. Upon arrival, we encountered loud music emanating from the apartment 3B. We knocked on the door, and it was answered by Mr. Michael Thompson, who appeared agitated by our presence.

When informed of the reason for our visit, Mr. Thompson became verbally abusive and refused to lower the volume, stating he was within his rights to play his music. We advised Mr. Thompson of the local noise ordinances and asked for his cooperation to avoid any further legal action.

Mr. Thompson responded by attempting to slam the door on us. I placed my foot in the doorway to prevent the door from closing, reiterating the need to comply with the law. Mr. Thompson then proceeded to push me backward, initiating a physical altercation. Officer Rowlands intervened, and Mr. Thompson continued to resist, delaying our ability to resolve the noise complaint and causing a disturbance in the apartment complex.

Evidence Collected:

---

[1] For a common statutory example, see I.C. § 18–705

- Bodycam footage from both responding officers showing the altercation and Mr. Thompson's resistance.

- Statements from witnesses in neighboring apartments.

Investigative Action:

After a brief struggle, Mr. Thompson was handcuffed and informed of his rights. He was arrested for obstructing a public officer in the discharge of official duties. The noise level in the apartment was measured with a decibel meter, confirming it exceeded the legal limits set by the city ordinance.

Charges Filed:

Mr. Thompson was transported to the Harrison Police Department, where he was booked and charged with obstruction of a public officer and violation of **local noise** ordinances. He was held for arraignment.

Conclusion:

The suspect's actions, including physical resistance and refusal to comply with lawful orders, directly obstructed public officers in the performance of their duties. The situation required an escalated response to restore order and ensure public safety.

End of report.

False Report

Criminal Elements

These elements must be proven beyond a reasonable doubt in court:[1]

☐ **State the approximate date (and time if known) when the offense occurred.**

▸ This confirms the offense occurred within the statute of limitations.

☐ **Specify where the offense occurred.**

▸ This establishes the court's jurisdiction over the offense.

☐ **Describe how the suspect knowingly gave a false report to a person the suspect knew was a peace officer.**

▸ Note: A false report connotes a statement, written or oral, made upon the initiative of the suspect to a peace officer for the specific purpose of having some action taken with respect thereto and not a false statement in response to a question asked by an officer.

Sample Report

Note: An actual police report would typically contain additional detailed information. This sample is designed to emphasize the specific elements related to this particular crime and does not encompass other procedural aspects such as evidence collection, adherence to Miranda rights, and additional investigative measures.

On November 15, 2023, at approximately 2:00 PM, I was approached by Mr. Jonathan Walsh near the main entrance of Central Park. Mr. Walsh appeared frantic and reported an alleged robbery. He claimed that while he was walking through the park, an individual, described as a male in a red hoodie and black jeans, forcibly stole his backpack containing a laptop, a smartphone, and personal documents.

Given the seriousness of the allegation, immediate action was taken. Additional units, including K-9 support, were dispatched for a thorough search, and the nearby CCTV footage was promptly reviewed.

However, inconsistencies in Mr. Walsh's narrative became apparent when:

- He became evasive and contradictory in his responses upon detailed questioning.

---

[1] For a common statutory example, see I.C. § 18–705

- No individuals matching the description were spotted in the vicinity around the reported time, as per witnesses and CCTV footage.

- A check-in with park security personnel confirmed no such incident was reported by park-goers or observed.

Evidence Collected:

- CCTV footage around the time of the alleged incident.

- Recorded statement of Mr. Walsh detailing the alleged robbery.

- Statements from potential witnesses and park security personnel.

Investigative Action:

Confronted with these inconsistencies, Mr. Walsh eventually admitted he fabricated the entire story. He claimed the reason was to file a false insurance claim on the "stolen" items, which he needed due to financial hardships.

Charges Filed:

Mr. Walsh was arrested under the charge of providing a false report to a peace officer. He was transported to the Crescent City Police Department for processing and was held for arraignment.

Conclusion:

This report is a comprehensive account of the incident involving Mr. Jonathan Walsh on November 15, 2023. The investigation concluded that Mr. Walsh's report was knowingly false, made with the intent to deceive law enforcement, and caused an unnecessary allocation of police resources. The case is now pending further judicial proceedings.

End of report.

Intimidating a Witness

Criminal Elements

These elements must be proven beyond a reasonable doubt in court:[1]

☐ **State the approximate date (and time if known) when the offense occurred.**

- ‣ This confirms the offense occurred within the statute of limitations.

☐ **Specify where the offense occurred.**

- ‣ This establishes the court's jurisdiction over the offense.

☐ **Explain how the the suspect, directly or indirectly, did one or more of the following to the witness with intent to prevent the witness from testifying freely, fully, and truthfully in any judicial proceeding:**

- ‣ Intimidated;

- ‣ Influenced;

- ‣ Impeded;

- ‣ Deterred;

- ‣ Threatened;

- ‣ Harassed; or

- ‣ Obstructed the witness.

Sample Report

Note: An actual police report would typically contain additional detailed information. This sample is designed to emphasize the specific elements related to this particular crime and does not encompass other procedural aspects such as evidence collection, adherence to Miranda rights, and additional investigative measures.

On November 14, 2023, at approximately 4:30 PM, I, along with Officer Daniels, were on routine patrol when we noticed an individual, later identified as Michael Thompson, standing on the sidewalk opposite a residence on Hillside Avenue. Mr. Thompson is known to the department as the primary suspect in a recent high-profile burglary case. We approached him for a consensual encounter to inquire about his presence in the area.

During our conversation, Mr. Thompson appeared nervous and provided inconsistent explanations about his reasons for being there. His behavior,

---

[1] For a common statutory example, see I.C. § 18-2604

coupled with his known involvement in the pending legal case, prompted further investigation.

We identified the residence as belonging to Ms. Rebecca Lewis, a key witness in the burglary case against Mr. Thompson. We contacted Ms. Lewis, who confirmed she was home and expressed immediate concern when informed of Mr. Thompson's presence outside her property. She interpreted this as a direct attempt to intimidate or influence her upcoming testimony.

Evidence Collected:

- Documentation of the interaction with Mr. Thompson, including his inconsistent statements.

- CCTV footage from security cameras around Ms. Lewis's residence, showing Mr. Thompson's prolonged presence opposite the property.

- A written statement from Ms. Lewis, detailing her fear and interpretation of Mr. Thompson's presence as intimidation.

Investigative Action:

Given the severity of the situation and the potential for witness tampering, we detained Mr. Thompson for further questioning at the Harrison City Police Department. During the interrogation, Mr. Thompson became agitated and implied that his presence was to "send a message" to Ms. Lewis, though he denied any intention of physical harm.

Charges Filed:

After consulting with the District Attorney's office and considering Mr. Thompson's intent, his current charges in the burglary case, and the potential impact on the witness, we filed additional charges against him for witness intimidation. He was remanded into custody without bail, considering the risk posed to the integrity of the judicial process.

Conclusion:

This incident highlights the importance of vigilance in protecting witnesses, particularly in high-profile cases. The department has taken steps to ensure Ms. Lewis's safety and is coordinating with the prosecution team to address any further attempts at witness intimidation or tampering.

End of report.

Riot

Criminal Elements

These elements must be proven beyond a reasonable doubt in court:[1]

☐ **State the approximate date (and time if known) when the offense occurred.**

- ‣ This confirms the offense occurred within the statute of limitations.

☐ **Specify where the offense occurred.**

- ‣ This establishes the court's jurisdiction over the offense.

☐ **Describe how the suspect, acting together with others, engaged in any action, or used force or violence with the purpose of breaching the peace.**

☐ **Describe how the suspect(s) had the immediate power to carry out their actions or violence.**

☐ **Finally, describe what injuries, property damage, or breaches of the peace occurred as a result.**

Sample Report

Note: An actual police report would typically contain additional detailed information. This sample is designed to emphasize the specific elements related to this particular crime and does not encompass other procedural aspects such as evidence collection, adherence to Miranda rights, and additional investigative measures.

On November 15, 2023, at around 8:00 PM, Riverdale Police Department units were dispatched to the Downtown Plaza area in response to multiple reports of a large group causing a disturbance. Upon arrival, officers observed approximately 30 individuals, many wearing masks and carrying various objects, who were actively participating in destructive behavior. The group was seen throwing stones, overturning trash bins, and vandalizing properties.

I identified one individual, later known as Jonathan Pryce, who was particularly aggressive, throwing a large rock through the window of 'Downtown Electronics,' a local business. Mr. Pryce was rallying several participants, clearly orchestrating the escalation of violence, and had the immediate power to carry out violent actions, evidenced by his direct participation in property destruction.

Evidence Collected:

---

[1] For a common statutory example, see I.C. § 18–6401

- CCTV footage from street cameras and 'Downtown Electronics,' showing the suspect's active participation in the riot.

- Photographs of the damaged property and the surrounding area.

- Witness statements from bystanders and Mr. Harold Finch, owner of the vandalized property.

- A large rock used to break the window, recovered from the scene.

Investigative Action:

Officers, including myself, approached the rioters and ordered them to disperse. Most complied, but Mr. Pryce and a few others refused, responding with verbal aggression. With the assistance of backup units, we were able to detain Mr. Pryce and several other instigators.

During the detention, Mr. Pryce was found to have a backpack. Given the ongoing violent and chaotic situation, and in accordance with the law regarding searches during lawful arrests, officers conducted a search of the backpack for weapons and items that could pose a danger to officers or the public. The search revealed spray paint cans, a crowbar, and other items typically used for vandalism.

Charges Filed:

After a thorough review of the collected evidence and consultation with the District Attorney's office, Mr. Pryce was charged with inciting a riot, property damage, and other related charges. The severity of his actions, coupled with the clear intent and the resulting chaos and property damage, warranted these charges.

Conclusion:

The quick response of the Riverdale Police Department units helped in de-escalating the situation and preventing further damage or potential physical harm to citizens. The lawful search of Mr. Pryce's backpack was instrumental in substantiating his active role in the riot and his preparation for criminal activity. This incident has prompted a review of strategies to handle similar situations in the future, ensuring the safety and security of the community.

End of report.

Stalking

Criminal Elements

These elements must be proven beyond a reasonable doubt in court:[1]

☐ **State the approximate date (and time if known) when the offense occurred.**

▸ This confirms the offense occurred within the statute of limitations.

☐ **Specify where the offense occurred.**

▸ This establishes the court's jurisdiction over the offense.

☐ **Describe how the suspect knowingly and maliciously engaged in conduct that:**

▸ Seriously alarmed, annoyed, or harassed the victim; and

▸ Would also cause a reasonable person (not just the victim) substantial emotional distress.

Sample Report

Note: An actual police report would typically contain additional detailed information. This sample is designed to emphasize the specific elements related to this particular crime and does not encompass other procedural aspects such as evidence collection, adherence to Miranda rights, and additional investigative measures.

On November 14, 2023, I responded to a call from Ms. Emily Harris, who reported a case of stalking. Ms. Harris stated that over the past month, she had noticed the suspect, identified as Scott Green, following her on multiple occasions. She reported instances of Mr. Green showing up uninvited near her workplace, outside her gym, and, most recently, while she was walking in Huntington Park.

List of Stalking Incidents:

Ms. Harris provided a detailed account of the stalking incidents, which are as follows:

• October 3, 2023: Scott Green was seen loitering outside Ms. Harris's workplace around lunchtime.

• October 7, 2023: Scott Green followed Ms. Harris to a coffee shop near her office and attempted to initiate conversation.

---

[1] For a common statutory example, see I.C. § 18–7905 and § 18-7906

- October 11, 2023: Scott Green was spotted outside Ms. Harris's gym, watching her through the window.
- October 15, 2023: Scott Green showed up at the grocery store where Ms. Harris was shopping and followed her to her car.
- October 19, 2023: Scott Green was seen sitting on a bench across from Ms. Harris's residence for several hours.
- October 23, 2023: Scott Green followed Ms. Harris during her evening jog in Huntington Park.
- October 27, 2023: Scott Green sent flowers to Ms. Harris's workplace with a note asking her to meet him.
- October 31, 2023: Scott Green was spotted by neighbors near Ms. Harris's house late at night.
- November 5, 2023: Scott Green approached Ms. Harris's friends asking about her whereabouts.
- November 14, 2023: Scott Green attempted to approach Ms. Harris in Huntington Park, leading to her call to the police.

Evidence Collected:

- Photographic evidence from Ms. Harris's phone, showing Mr. Green at various locations.
- A written log maintained by Ms. Harris, detailing the dates, times, and nature of each encounter.
- CCTV footage from locations near Ms. Harris's workplace and gym, corroborating her accounts.

Investigative Action:

Based on the information provided by Ms. Harris, a background check on Mr. Green was conducted, revealing a prior restraining order against him from a different individual, further substantiating Ms. Harris's claims.

I visited Mr. Green at his residence, where he was informed of the investigation. He initially denied the allegations but became defensive when presented with evidence. He insisted his presence at all those locations was coincidental.

Given the serious nature of the allegations, the consistency in Ms. Harris's documented encounters, and Mr. Green's previous history, he was taken into custody for further questioning.

Charges Filed:

After consulting with the District Attorney's office and considering the psychological impact on Ms. Harris, charges of stalking were filed against Mr.

Green. His actions clearly indicate a pattern of behavior that significantly alarmed and caused substantial emotional distress to Ms. Harris, fulfilling the criteria for stalking under state law.

Conclusion:

This report and subsequent charges rely on the compelling evidence provided by the victim, the corroboration of this evidence through an independent investigation, and the suspect's history. The Huntington Police Department takes such cases very seriously, recognizing the profound impact on the victims' mental well-being and overall quality of life.

End of report.

Domestic Battery

Criminal Elements

These elements must be proven beyond a reasonable doubt in court:[1]

☐ **State the approximate date (and time if known) when the offense occurred.**

  ‣ This confirms the offense occurred within the statute of limitations.

☐ **Specify where the offense occurred.**

  ‣ This establishes the court's jurisdiction over the offense.

☐ **Describe how the suspect battered the victim.**

☐ **Specify what relation the suspect had with the victim in order to qualify for domestic assault:**

  ‣ Current or former spouse;

  ‣ Co-habitant;

  ‣ Child-in-common, and so forth.

Sample Report

Note: An actual police report would typically contain additional detailed information. This sample is designed to emphasize the specific elements related to this particular crime and does not encompass other procedural aspects such as evidence collection, adherence to Miranda rights, and additional investigative measures.

On the evening of November 19, 2023, I responded to a report of a domestic disturbance at 4512 Willow Lane. Upon arrival at approximately 8:30 PM, I encountered a visibly shaken and injured Laura Bennett. Mrs. Bennett reported that during an escalated argument, her husband, Michael Bennett, had physically assaulted her.

Evidence of Domestic Battery:

- Visible Injury: Laura Bennett had a noticeable bruise on her left cheek and a cut on her lower lip.

- Witness Testimony: The couple's 10-year-old son, Jacob Bennett, provided a statement that he heard shouting and witnessed his father strike his mother.

---

[1] For a common statutory example, see I.C. §§ 18-903 & 18-918(1)&(3)

- Suspect's Admission: During questioning, Michael Bennett admitted to "losing control" during the argument, though he did not explicitly state he intended to harm Laura.
- Physical Evidence: A broken vase and overturned furniture in the living room, suggesting a struggle or physical altercation.
- Medical Report: Emergency medical services were called to the scene, and the responding EMTs provided a preliminary report confirming Mrs. Bennett's injuries were consistent with a physical assault.

Relation to Victim:

Michael Bennett is currently married to Laura Bennett, and they reside together at the aforementioned address. They share custody of their minor child, establishing the domestic context required under the relevant statute.

Investigative Action:

After ensuring Laura Bennett received appropriate medical attention, I proceeded with the arrest of Michael Bennett based on the physical evidence, witness testimony, and his partial admission. He was transported to the station for further processing. Child Protective Services was notified regarding the incident witnessed by the minor.

Charges Filed:

Michael Bennett was charged with domestic assault under the state law, considering the substantial evidence pointing to an intentional act of violence against a household member.

Conclusion:

This incident has been thoroughly documented and will be handed over to the prosecuting authority for further action. The Rochester Police Department has also initiated support services for Laura Bennett and her son, ensuring they receive necessary assistance following this traumatic incident.

End of report.

Violation of Civil Protection Order

Criminal Elements

These elements must be proven beyond a reasonable doubt in court:[1]

☐ **State the approximate date (and time if known) when the offense occurred.**

  ‣ This confirms the offense occurred within the statute of limitations.

☐ **Specify where the offense occurred.**

  ‣ This establishes the court's jurisdiction over the offense.

☐ **Describe how the suspect violated the provisions of a protection order issued by a court.**

☐ **Explain how the suspect had notice of the order before the violation.**

Sample Report

Note: An actual police report would typically contain additional detailed information. This sample is designed to emphasize the specific elements related to this particular crime and does not encompass other procedural aspects such as evidence collection, adherence to Miranda rights, and additional investigative measures.

On December 4, 2023, at around 7:20 PM, I responded to a distress call at Parkside Mall regarding a potential violation of a civil protection order. Upon arrival, I encountered a visibly shaken Jessica Reed, who reported that her ex-boyfriend, Brian Clark, had not only followed her as she moved through various stores in the mall but also confronted her, thereby violating the protection order she had against him.

Evidence of Protection Order Violation:

• Protection Order Details: Jessica provided a copy of the protection order, issued on October 8, 2023, by the Harrison County Court. The order explicitly states that Mr. Clark is prohibited from making any form of contact or coming within 200 yards of Ms. Reed.

• Witness Statements: I interviewed several witnesses, including two mall patrons, Sarah Fuller and Greg Watkins, and a store clerk. All witnesses provided statements that they saw Brian Clark following Jessica Reed from store to store before finally approaching and confronting her.

---

[1] For a common statutory example, see I.C. § 39-6312(1)

- Mall Security Footage: Security footage retrieved from Parkside Mall clearly shows Mr. Clark trailing Ms. Reed through several stores. The video later shows a confrontation between the two, confirming Ms. Reed's statement and the witness accounts.

- Suspect's Acknowledgment: Mr. Clark was questioned at the scene, where he became defensive, insisting the encounter was a "coincidence." However, the evidence, including the video footage and multiple witness statements, suggests otherwise.

Notice of Order:

The file for the protection order includes a form signed by Brian Clark, acknowledging his understanding of the order's conditions. This acknowledgment was dated October 9, 2023, confirming his awareness of the order's stipulations before this incident.

Investigative Action:

Based on the evidence and the serious nature of the violation, Brian Clark was arrested and transported to the station for further processing. Ms. Reed was encouraged to press charges for the violation, to which she consented.

Charges Filed:

Brian Clark was formally charged with violating a civil protection order. All collected evidence, including the mall's security footage, witness statements, and the protection order acknowledgment form, have been attached to this report for the district attorney's office.

Conclusion:

This incident is a clear violation of the terms stipulated in the civil protection order held by Ms. Reed against Mr. Clark. The case, along with all pertinent evidence, is hereby submitted for further legal proceedings. The Harrison Police Department will continue to provide necessary assistance and support to Ms. Reed during this process.

End of report.

Telephone Harassment

Criminal Elements

These elements must be proven beyond a reasonable doubt in court:[1]

☐ **State the approximate date (and time if known) when the offense occurred.**

- ‣ This confirms the offense occurred within the statute of limitations.

☐ **Specify where the offense occurred.**

- ‣ This establishes the court's jurisdiction over the offense.

☐ **Describe why the suspect had the intent to annoy, terrify, threaten, intimidate, harass, or offend the victim.**

☐ **Describe what the suspect said to the victim over the telephone. For example, the suspect was:**

- ‣ Obscene;
- ‣ Lewd;
- ‣ Profane;
- ‣ Made sexual, indecent, or lewd proposals;
- ‣ Made threats to commit physical harm or property damage.

☐ **Describe whether the suspect made repeated anonymous calls.**

☐ **Finally, describe whether the suspect attempted to disturb the victim's peace and quiet by calling the home in the middle of the night, or called the victim's work repeatedly.**

Sample Report

Note: An actual police report would typically contain additional detailed information. This sample is designed to emphasize the specific elements related to this particular crime and does not encompass other procedural aspects such as evidence collection, adherence to Miranda rights, and additional investigative measures.

Between November 30, 2023, and December 5, 2023, Laura Simmons received multiple harassing phone calls at her residence from an unidentified individual. The calls were predominantly late at night, disturbing her peace and causing substantial emotional distress.

---

[1] For a common statutory example, see I.C. § 18-6710

Detailed List of Harassing Calls:

- November 30, 11:45 PM: Obscene language and unsolicited descriptions of lewd acts.

- December 1, 12:30 AM: Threat of physical harm, including a description of following the victim home.

- December 1, 3:15 AM: Repeated ringing, hanging up upon answer, four times in succession.

- December 2, 1:10 AM: Descriptions of violence against the victim's property; threat to break into the house.

- December 2, 9:20 PM: Call made to the victim's workplace, causing embarrassment; lewd suggestions made openly.

- December 3, 2:00 AM: Silent call, heavy breathing heard, followed by a soft, threatening whisper before hanging up.

- December 3, 11:50 PM: Explicit threats to the victim's family members.

- December 4, 4:25 AM: Series of text messages following a call, detailing victim's recent public movements.

- December 4, 10:15 PM: Harassing call received by a family member at their residence, extending threats.

- December 5, 12:01 AM: Final call before report, reiterating previous threats with increased aggression.

Evidence Collected:

- Call Records and Text Messages: Provided by Ms. Simmons, highlighting the received calls and messages.

- Voice Mail Recordings: Obscene and threatening messages saved and documented.

- Witness Statements: Collaborated by colleagues and family members who received or witnessed the calls.

Suspect Identification:

Through the cooperation with the telecommunications company and pursuant to a warrant, we were able to obtain detailed call logs and successfully trace the origin of the calls. The phone number was linked to the suspect, whose identity has been confirmed but is redacted in this report for privacy reasons pending formal charges. Further, voice analysis of the recorded calls matched the suspect's known voice patterns from previous records.

Investigative Action:

Detailed call logs obtained through a warrant served on the telecommunications company.

Voice analysis conducted comparing the threatening messages with existing records of the suspect's voice.

The suspect was brought in for questioning and, upon presentation of the gathered evidence, confessed to making the calls.

Charges Pending:

The suspect has been detained and is facing charges for telephone harassment, with the possibility of additional charges based on the comprehensive review of all documented threats and the psychological impact on the victim.

Conclusion:

The investigation has reached a critical point with the suspect's identification and confession. The case will be forwarded to the district attorney's office for official charging procedures, and support measures have been arranged for the victim.

End of report.

Disturbing the Peace

Criminal Elements

These elements must be proven beyond a reasonable doubt in court:[1]

☐ **State the approximate date (and time if known) when the offense occurred.**

  ‣ This confirms the offense occurred within the statute of limitations.

☐ **Specify where the offense occurred.**

  ‣ This establishes the court's jurisdiction over the offense.

☐ **Describe how the suspect maliciously and intentionally disturbed the peace or quiet of a neighborhood, family, or person by:**

  ‣ Loud or unusual noise;

  ‣ Tumultuous or offensive conduct;

  ‣ Threatening, quarreling, or challenging (to a fight) conduct.

Sample Report

Note: An actual police report would typically contain additional detailed information. This sample is designed to emphasize the specific elements related to this particular crime and does not encompass other procedural aspects such as evidence collection, adherence to Miranda rights, and additional investigative measures.

On the night of October 13, 2023, at approximately 10:00 PM, our department received multiple complaints from residents of Westwind Drive regarding loud, disruptive noises and aggressive behavior emanating from the street. The complaints specifically referenced loud music, shouting, and car engines revving.

Upon arrival at the scene, I observed the suspect, later identified as Brandon Walsh, engaged in what appeared to be a heated argument with another unidentified individual. They were surrounded by a group of onlookers. The suspect was visibly agitated, shouting obscenities, and challenging the other person to a fight. Additionally, a car stereo was playing music at a volume that could be heard several houses away.

Disturbances Noted:

- Loud Music: The suspect's vehicle was identified as the source of the loud music disturbing the neighborhood's peace.

---

[1] For a common statutory example, see I.C. § 18-6409

- Verbal Altercation: Mr. Walsh's aggressive and loud interaction with the other individual was causing a significant disturbance, as noted by the gathered crowd's reactions and the complainants' statements.

- Challenge to Physical Altercation: The suspect was observed in a fighting stance, yelling, and encouraging a physical fight, further contributing to the chaotic scene.

- Engine Revving: The suspect, along with others, was revving car engines, which significantly contributed to the noise level reported by the complainants.

Evidence Collected:

- Witness Statements: Multiple written statements were collected from the residents who filed the complaints, detailing the disturbance caused by the suspect's actions.

- Audio/Video Recordings: Bodycam footage from the responding officers captured the scene, including the loud music, the suspect's aggressive behavior, and the revving engines.

Investigative Action:

Upon my approach, Mr. Walsh was advised to turn down the music and was informed about the complaints. Initially defiant, Mr. Walsh complied after he was informed of the potential legal repercussions of his actions. The crowd was dispersed without further incident, and Mr. Walsh was taken into custody based on the severity of the disturbance and the risk of escalation if left unaddressed.

Charges Pending:

Mr. Walsh is being charged with disturbing the peace, pursuant to the local statutes governing such offenses. The case will be forwarded to the local district attorney's office for review and potential additional charges based on witness statements and collected evidence.

Conclusion:

This incident was resolved with the suspect's detention without further escalation. The residents were advised to contact the department should any further disturbances occur. Counseling and community mediation resources were offered to Mr. Walsh to prevent future incidents.

End of report.

Abuse or Neglect of Vulnerable Adult

Criminal Elements

These elements must be proven beyond a reasonable doubt in court:[1]

☐ **State the approximate date (and time if known) when the offense occurred.**

- ‣ This confirms the offense occurred within the statute of limitations.

☐ **Specify where the offense occurred.**

- ‣ This establishes the court's jurisdiction over the offense.

☐ **Describe how the suspect abused or neglected the victim:**

- ‣ "Abuse" means the intentional or negligent infliction of physical pain, injury or mental injury. This establishes the court's jurisdiction over the offense.

- ‣ "Neglect" means failure of a caretaker to provide food, clothing, shelter or medical care to a vulnerable adult, in such a manner as to jeopardize the life, health and safety of the vulnerable adult.

☐ **Explain why at the time the victim was a vulnerable adult:**

- ‣ "Vulnerable adult" means a person 18 years of age or older who is unable to protect himself or herself from abuse, neglect or exploitation due to physical or mental impairment which affects the person's judgment or behavior to the extent he or she lacks sufficient understanding or capacity to make or communicate or implement decisions regarding his or her person, property, or finances.

☐ **Finally, if applicable, explain why the circumstances would likely produce great bodily harm or death (for felony charges).**

Sample Report

Note: An actual police report would typically contain additional detailed information. This sample is designed to emphasize the specific elements related to this particular crime and does not encompass other procedural aspects such as evidence collection, adherence to Miranda rights, and additional investigative measures.

On November 3, 2023, Springfield Police Department received a call from a concerned neighbor regarding potential neglect of an elderly resident, Mrs. Margaret Thompson, living at 4775 Oakwood Avenue. The caller expressed

---

[1] For a common statutory example, see I.C. § 18–1505

concern as Mrs. Thompson, known to have severe arthritis and early-stage dementia, had not been seen for several days.

Upon arrival at the specified location, I, along with Officer James Peterson, conducted a welfare check. We were met by Ms. Elaine Cummings, who identified herself as Mrs. Thompson's live-in caregiver. Ms. Cummings was initially resistant to allow entry into the home, citing Mrs. Thompson's resting period. However, given the nature of the welfare check, we insisted on visual confirmation of Mrs. Thompson's well-being.

Findings at the Scene:

- Physical State of the Victim: Mrs. Thompson was found in an extremely unkempt state, with visible signs of poor hygiene and malnourishment. She was seated in a worn-out armchair, appearing disoriented and in distress.

- Living Conditions: The living conditions were deplorable, with spoiled food, a strong odor of waste, and clutter that posed tripping hazards. The temperature in the residence was notably chilly, with no active heat source identified, despite the cold weather outside.

- Medical Neglect: Mrs. Thompson's prescription medication appeared untouched, with pills remaining in containers well past the prescribed usage date, indicating a lack of proper medical care and medication management.

- Lack of Basic Necessities: There was a scarcity of fresh food or water accessible to Mrs. Thompson in her vicinity. The refrigerator contained minimal, mostly spoiled food.

Evidence Collected:

- Photographic Evidence: Photos were taken of the living conditions, the victim's physical state, and neglected medication.

- Witness Statement: The initial statement from the concerned neighbor, along with observations from other neighbors, was collected, noting the infrequent sightings of Mrs. Thompson and rare grocery trips made by Ms. Cummings.

- Medical Evaluation: An immediate health assessment was conducted by arriving medical personnel, confirming the neglected state of health and the urgent need for medical intervention.

Investigative Action:

Ms. Cummings was taken into custody for further questioning following the discovery of the neglectful conditions under which Mrs. Thompson was living. Mrs. Thompson was transported to Springfield General Hospital for immediate medical care and evaluation. Adult Protective Services were notified to ensure the long-term well-being and care of Mrs. Thompson.

Charges Pending:

Ms. Cummings is facing charges for the abuse and neglect of a vulnerable adult, as her intentional negligence directly jeopardized Mrs. Thompson's life, health, and safety. The case is under review by the district attorney's office for additional charges based on the collected evidence and medical reports.

Conclusion:

The swift intervention was crucial in safeguarding Mrs. Thompson's health and initiating legal proceedings against Ms. Cummings for failing in her duty of care. Follow-ups with Adult Protective Services and Mrs. Thompson's healthcare team are scheduled to ensure her future welfare.

End of report.

Exploitation of a Vulnerable Adult

Criminal Elements

These elements must be proven beyond a reasonable doubt in court:[1]

☐ **State the approximate date (and time if known) when the offense occurred.**

▸ This confirms the offense occurred within the statute of limitations.

☐ **Specify where the offense occurred.**

▸ This establishes the court's jurisdiction over the offense.

☐ **Describe how the suspect exploited the victim:**

▸ "Exploit" means an action which may include, but is not limited to, the unjust or improper use of a vulnerable adult's financial power of attorney, funds, property or resources by another person for profit or advantage.

☐ **Explain why at the time the victim was a vulnerable adult:**

▸ "Vulnerable adult" means a person 18 years of age or older who is unable to protect himself or herself from abuse, neglect or exploitation due to physical or mental impairment which affects the person's judgment or behavior to the extent he or she lacks sufficient understanding or capacity to make or communicate or implement decisions regarding his or her person, property, or finances.

☐ **Finally, if applicable, explain why the exploitation was over a certain amount (for felony charges).**

Sample Report

Note: An actual police report would typically contain additional detailed information. This sample is designed to emphasize the specific elements related to this particular crime and does not encompass other procedural aspects such as evidence collection, adherence to Miranda rights, and additional investigative measures.

On November 3, 2023, the Harrisonburg Police Department was contacted by Mr. Harold Finch's bank manager, who expressed concerns over several large and unusual transactions from Mr. Finch's accounts over the past three months. The bank manager also mentioned that Mr. Finch, an elderly individual with diagnosed cognitive impairment, had recently granted financial power of attorney to his nephew, Mr. Jonathan Gilbert.

---

[1] For a common statutory example, see I.C. § 18–1505

Findings at the Scene:

Upon visiting Mr. Finch at his residence, I observed that he appeared confused and unaware of the financial activities in his accounts. Mr. Finch confirmed that he had granted his nephew control over his finances but was under the impression that the money was being used for his own care and daily expenses.

Evidence of Exploitation:

- Financial Statements: Bank statements and financial documents indicated numerous large withdrawals and transfers to accounts unrelated to Mr. Finch's expenses. Several purchases were clearly for luxury items that Mr. Finch had no knowledge of.

- Legal Documents: A copy of the power of attorney document showed that Mr. Finch had indeed granted comprehensive financial control to Mr. Gilbert.

- Medical Records: Medical evaluations from Mr. Finch's physician outlined his diminished cognitive capacity, classifying him as a vulnerable adult.

- Witness Testimonies: Statements from close friends and other family members of Mr. Finch indicated that Mr. Gilbert had recently acquired expensive items, and they had seen no improvements or investments in Mr. Finch's care.

Investigative Action:

Mr. Jonathan Gilbert was brought in for questioning on November 4, 2023. Initially, he claimed all transactions were for Mr. Finch's benefit. However, when confronted with specific luxury purchases, Mr. Gilbert became evasive and inconsistent with his explanations.

Charges Pending:

Mr. Gilbert is facing charges for the exploitation of a vulnerable adult. The total sum of questionable transactions from Mr. Finch's accounts exceeds $50,000, meeting the threshold for felony charges under state law.

Conclusion:

The investigation is ongoing, with a detailed forensic financial analysis pending. Protective measures are being arranged for Mr. Finch to prevent further exploitation. The case has been referred to the district attorney's office for prosecution, and a court date is being scheduled.

End of report.

Firearms Offenses

Possession by a Felon

Criminal Elements

These elements must be proven beyond a reasonable doubt in court:[1]

☐ **State the approximate date (and time if known) when the offense occurred.**

> ‣ This confirms the offense occurred within the statute of limitations.

☐ **Specify where the offense occurred.**

> ‣ This establishes the court's jurisdiction over the offense.

☐ **Describe why the suspect knowingly owned, purchased, or possessed a firearm:**

> ‣ Actual possession is easy (e.g. was in his hand or pocket).
>
> ‣ For constructive possession, articulate the following:
>
>> 1. **Location**: Explain why you think the suspect knew the contraband was at the location/container found;
>>
>> 2. **Ability**: Explain how the suspect had the ability to control the contraband; and
>>
>> 3. **Intention**: Explain why you think the suspect had the intent to possess the contraband in the past, present, or future.

☐ **Specify what felony conviction the suspect had.**

Sample Report

Note: An actual police report would typically contain additional detailed information. This sample is designed to emphasize the specific elements related to this particular crime and does not encompass other procedural aspects such as evidence collection, adherence to Miranda rights, and additional investigative measures.

On November 7, 2023, at approximately 9:30 PM, while on routine patrol, I observed a blue sedan commit a traffic violation by running a stop sign on Main St. I initiated a traffic stop, and the vehicle complied, pulling over near the intersection of Main St and 7th Avenue.

Observations and Evidence Collected:

---

[1] For a common statutory example, see I.C. s 18-3316

I approached the vehicle and identified the driver and the passenger. The passenger was recognized as Mr. Johnathan Smith, known to have a criminal background.

While speaking to the occupants, I noticed Mr. Smith appeared extremely nervous and was sweating profusely, despite the cool evening temperature.

Given Mr. Smith's known history and the suspicious behavior exhibited, I called for backup and asked both individuals to step out of the vehicle to conduct a search, as per protocol.

Under the back seat of the vehicle, I discovered a .38 caliber handgun. Neither the driver nor Mr. Smith claimed ownership of the firearm.

Investigation and Suspect Statements:

A quick background check confirmed that Mr. Smith had a prior felony conviction for armed robbery, making it illegal for him to own, purchase, or come into possession of a firearm.

When questioned separately, Mr. Smith became defensive, denying knowledge of the gun. However, his continued nervous demeanor, the proximity of the weapon to his seat, and his known criminal history led me to believe he was aware of the gun's presence and had the ability and intention to control it.

The driver, when questioned, expressed shock and mentioned that Mr. Smith had been the only passenger in the back seat. He also stated that he was giving Mr. Smith a ride from a mutual friend's house and had no knowledge of the firearm.

Charges and Actions Taken:

Mr. Smith was arrested for being a felon in possession of a firearm, a violation of [Relevant Section] of the California Penal Code. The driver was released after questioning, with a warning issued for the traffic violation. The firearm was tagged, and the vehicle was towed to the police impound lot for further investigation.

Conclusion:

Based on Mr. Smith's prior felony conviction, his behavior, the statements from the driver, and the location and accessibility of the firearm, there is reasonable cause to believe that Mr. Smith constructively possessed the gun. The case will be referred to the District Attorney's office for further action, and Mr. Smith was booked into the county jail. Further investigation, including potential forensic testing on the firearm, will be conducted to solidify the case for prosecution.

End of Report.

Unlawful Discharge

Criminal Elements

These elements must be proven beyond a reasonable doubt in court:[1]

☐ **State the approximate date (and time if known) when the offense occurred.**

- ‣ This confirms the offense occurred within the statute of limitations.

☐ **Specify where the offense occurred.**

- ‣ This establishes the court's jurisdiction over the offense.

☐ **Describe how the suspect intentionally discharged a firearm at a house, camper, building, or occupied motor vehicle.**

☐ **Explain whether the structure was occupied at the time of the shooting.**

- ‣ If the structure of vehicle was unoccupied explain why the structure was currently being used for human occupancy, but was physically unoccupied at the time of the shooting.

Sample Report

Note: An actual police report would typically contain additional detailed information. This sample is designed to emphasize the specific elements related to this particular crime and does not encompass other procedural aspects such as evidence collection, adherence to Miranda rights, and additional investigative measures.

On November 7, 2023, at approximately 10:15 PM, our dispatch unit received multiple calls reporting gunshots in the 4500 block of Pine Street. I was dispatched and arrived on the scene at approximately 10:25 PM.

Observations and Evidence Collected:

Upon arrival, I observed clear signs of disturbance at a residential property, including broken windows and multiple shell casings visible on the street.

Witnesses at the scene were in a state of distress and reported seeing an individual, later identified as Mr. Michael Johnson, firing a handgun multiple times toward a nearby house before fleeing on foot.

I secured the scene and conducted a preliminary investigation, collecting seven shell casings and documenting damage to the property, including a front door riddled with bullet marks and shattered windows.

---

[1] For a common statutory example, see I.C. s 18-3317

It was determined that the house was unoccupied at the time of the shooting. However, neighbors confirmed that the property was currently used for human occupancy, and the residents were away for the evening.

Investigation and Suspect Statements:

Immediate area search was conducted, and Mr. Johnson was located and detained near the vicinity at approximately 11:00 PM. He was found in possession of a 9mm handgun, which was seized for evidence.

Mr. Johnson was read his Miranda rights, after which he agreed to speak with me. He appeared to be under the influence of alcohol and was highly agitated. He admitted to discharging the firearm but claimed he was "just letting off steam" and didn't intend to hurt anyone.

A background check revealed Mr. Johnson had multiple prior disturbances reported, including disorderly conduct and public intoxication.

Charges and Actions Taken:

Mr. Johnson was arrested for the unlawful discharge of a firearm into an occupied structure, a violation of Nebraska Penal Code. He was transported to the county jail and booked accordingly.

Conclusion:

Based on witness statements, evidence collected at the scene, Mr. Johnson's admission, and the known occupancy status of the house, there is substantial cause to charge Mr. Johnson with the unlawful discharge of a firearm. The case will be referred to the District Attorney's office for further action. Additional statements from neighbors and potential security camera footage from the area will be collected and reviewed during the follow-up investigation.

End of Report.

Carrying Concealed on School Property

Criminal Elements

These elements must be proven beyond a reasonable doubt in court:[1]

- ☐ **State the approximate date (and time if known) when the offense occurred.**
  - ‣ This confirms the offense occurred within the statute of limitations.
- ☐ **Specify where the offense occurred.**
  - ‣ This establishes the court's jurisdiction over the offense.
- ☐ **Explain where the suspect was carrying on school property or school bus:**
  - ‣ If the incident occurred after hours describe what school-sponsored event was taking place.
- ☐ **Describe the weapon carried, such as pistol, dirk, bowie knife, metal knuckles, or other dangerous weapon.**
- ☐ **Describe how the weapon was concealed on the suspect's person, and**
- ☐ **The suspect was at that time under 21 years of age.**

Sample Report

Note: An actual police report would typically contain additional detailed information. This sample is designed to emphasize the specific elements related to this particular crime and does not encompass other procedural aspects such as evidence collection, adherence to Miranda rights, and additional investigative measures.

On November 7, 2023, at approximately 7:30 PM, I responded to a call from Harrison High School regarding a potential weapon on school premises. The call was made by the school's security officer, Mr. Greg Harper, during a school-sponsored basketball game.

Observations and Evidence Collected:

Upon arrival, I met with Mr. Harper, who had detained the suspect, later identified as Dylan Rivers, an 18-year-old student at the school. Mr. Harper reported that other students had seen a bulge in Mr. Rivers' waistband and believed it to be a weapon.

---

[1] For a common statutory example, see I.C. 18-3302D

With Mr. Harper present, I conducted a search of Mr. Rivers and found a loaded 9mm pistol concealed in his waistband. The weapon was secured immediately.

Mr. Rivers did not resist the search and appeared to be cooperative yet nervous during the interaction.

Investigation and Suspect Statements:

Mr. Rivers was read his Miranda rights, after which he agreed to speak with me. He stated that he had been carrying the weapon for "protection" due to issues unrelated to school activities but did not realize the severity of bringing it onto school property.

A background check on Mr. Rivers revealed no prior criminal history. However, he is under the legal age limit of 21 for legally carrying a concealed weapon.

Charges and Actions Taken:

Mr. Rivers was arrested for carrying a concealed weapon on school property, a violation of Section 12590(a) of the Montoria Penal Code. He was transported to the local precinct for further processing. The school administration was informed of the incident, and they will be conducting their internal investigation and response.

Conclusion:

Based on the evidence collected, witness statements, and Mr. Rivers' admission, there is substantial cause to charge him with carrying a concealed weapon on school property, especially given his age and the location's sensitive nature. The case will be referred to the Montoria District Attorney's office for prosecution. Further investigation will be conducted to understand Mr. Rivers' motive and ensure there are no broader safety concerns related to this incident.

End of Report.

Carrying a Concealed Weapon

Criminal Elements

These elements must be proven beyond a reasonable doubt in court:[1]

☐ **State the approximate date (and time if known) when the offense occurred.**

> ‣ This confirms the offense occurred within the statute of limitations.

☐ **Specify where the offense occurred and why this is a prohibited place to carry concealed.**

> ‣ This establishes the court's jurisdiction over the offense.

☐ **Describe the weapon carried, such as pistol, dirk, bowie knife, metal knuckles, or other dangerous weapon.**

☐ **Describe how the weapon was concealed on the suspect's person.**

☐ **Explain what you did to confirm the suspect does not have a valid concealed carry permit.**

☐ **The suspect did not have a license to carry a concealed weapon (if applicable).**

Sample Report

Note: An actual police report would typically contain additional detailed information. This sample is designed to emphasize the specific elements related to this particular crime and does not encompass other procedural aspects such as evidence collection, adherence to Miranda rights, and additional investigative measures.

On November 7, 2023, at approximately 10:15 PM, while on routine patrol, I noticed an individual, later identified as Michael Thompson, conspicuously adjusting an object in his waistband while standing outside a nightclub on Lexington Avenue.

Observations and Preliminary Interaction:

Upon observing Mr. Thompson's behavior, I approached him for a casual inquiry, considering the location's sensitivity, which was crowded with patrons at the time.

I identified myself as an NYPD officer and inquired if Mr. Thompson was carrying anything he shouldn't be. He appeared nervous, prompting me to ask

---

[1] For a common statutory example, see I.C. s 18-3302

directly if he had a weapon on his person and, if so, whether he possessed a valid permit for such.

Mr. Thompson hesitated before admitting he had a "pistol" in his waistband but claimed he did not have a permit for it. Given the admission and the potential threat to public safety, I informed him that I would need to conduct a patdown for officer and public safety.

Evidence Collected and Suspect Statements:

The patdown search led to the discovery of a loaded .38 caliber revolver concealed in his waistband. The weapon was seized, ensuring it was safe, and Mr. Thompson was handcuffed without incident.

After being read his Miranda rights, Mr. Thompson agreed to speak. He reiterated that he carried the gun for self-defense, unaware of the legal requirements for carrying a firearm in public spaces, especially within the sensitive area he was found.

A subsequent database search confirmed Mr. Thompson's lack of a valid New York State concealed carry permit. His possession of the concealed weapon without a permit constituted a violation under New York Penal Law Section 265.01(1).

Charges and Actions Taken:

Mr. Thompson was arrested for carrying a concealed weapon without a permit. He was transported to the local precinct for processing, and the weapon was submitted to the evidence room following standard protocols.

Despite his lack of awareness of the law, Mr. Thompson's cooperation after the initial apprehension was noted.

Conclusion:

This incident underscores the importance of public awareness of firearm laws, particularly concerning concealed carry in sensitive areas. Mr. Thompson's immediate admission and subsequent cooperation simplified the on-site investigation. However, the violation is clear, given the legal stipulations regarding firearm possession in public spaces. The case is now in the hands of the District Attorney's office for further legal proceedings.

End of Report.

ABOUT THE AUTHOR

Anthony Bandiero, JD, ALM

Anthony is an attorney and retired law enforcement officer with experience as both a municipal police officer and sergeant with a state police agency. Anthony has studied constitutional law for over twenty years and has trained countless police officers in advanced search and seizure.

View his bio at BlueToGold.com/about

Made in the USA
Las Vegas, NV
09 October 2024

96568297R00176